New Jersey

A History

Thomas Fleming

**With a Historical Guide
prepared by the editors of
the American Association for
State and Local History**

W. W. Norton & Company
New York · London

American Association for State and Local History
Nashville

Author and publishers make grateful acknowledgment to New Directions Publishing Corporation for permission to quote from *Paterson,* Book 4. II, by William Carlos Williams. Copyright © 1951 by William Carlos Williams. Reprinted by permission of New Directions Publishing Corporation.

Library of Congress Cataloging in Publication Data

Fleming, Thomas J.
  New Jersey: a history.

  (The States and the Nation series)
  Bibliography: p.
  Includes index.
  1. New Jersey—History. I. Title. II. Series.
F134.F54   974.9   77–22005
ISBN 0-393-30180-X

Published and distributed by W.W. Norton & Company, Inc.
500 Fifth Avenue
New York, New York 10110

Printed in the United States of America
2 3 4 5 6 7 8 9 0

Contents

Historical Guide

TO NEW JERSEY

prepared by the editors of the
American Association for State and Local History

Introduction

The following pages offer the reader a guide to places in this state through which its history still lives.

This section lists and describes museums with collections of valuable artifacts, historic houses where prominent people once lived, and historic sites where events of importance took place. In addition, we have singled out for detailed description a few places that illustrate especially well major developments in this state's history or major themes running through it, as identified in the text that follows. The reader can visit these places to experience what life was like in earlier times and learn more about the state's rich and exciting heritage.

James B. Gardner and Timothy C. Jacobson, professional historians on the staff of the American Association for State and Local History, prepared this supplementary material, and the association's editors take sole responsibility for the selection of sites and their descriptions. Nonetheless, thanks are owed to many individuals and historical organizations, including those listed, for graciously providing information and advice. Our thanks also go to the National Endowment for the Humanities, which granted support for the writing and editing of this supplement, as it did for the main text itself.   —*The Editors*

Morristown National Park

Morristown

★ For New Jerseyans, the American Revolution became a virtual civil war between loyalists to the British Crown and patriotic supporters of colonial independence. Bitter conflict led to violent excesses on both sides, and Governor William Livingston

Ford House

faced the nearly impossible tasks of quelling continued loyalist activity, organizing rebel manpower and material, and establishing a new state government. Indeed, the state might very well have fallen to the British if it were not for George Washington's occupation of Morristown and the consequent consolidation of rebel control. The Morristown National Historical Park commemorates both the activities of Washington and his Continental Army in the Morristown region and New Jersey's larger role in the American Revolution.

When the Revolution began, the village of Morristown consisted of about two hundred fifty residents and fifty or sixty buildings. Around the town green stood the Morris County courthouse and jail, Jacob Arnold's Tavern, and the Presbyterian and Baptist churches. Henry Wick and other area residents farmed the surrounding countryside, growing vegetables, fruit, wheat, corn, rye, and other grains. Lumbering activity supported other residents, while Jacob Ford, Jr., and his family operated iron mines and furnaces in the mountains to the northwest. What attracted George Washington and the Continental Army to the region, however, was the strategic location of the town. The Watchung Mountains to the northeast provided an easily defensible barrier and hence made it possible for the rebels to set up winter camp relatively close to British posts at New York City and along the Jersey coast. From this base, the Continental Army could safely monitor British activities and consolidate patriot control over men and resources in the badly divided state.

Washington arrived at Morristown on January 6, 1777, fresh from victories at Trenton and Princeton that spoiled British hopes of making New Jersey the first colony to return to the loyalist fold. Although the success of the Jersey campaign buoyed rebel hopes, prospects for the Continental Army were not good. Washington's troops numbered five thousand in early January, but the expiration of enlistments soon reduced the total to three thousand. Smallpox threatened to shrink the army further, but Washington wisely ordered inoculations, a bold decision in that day. The Continental Congress promised additional men to fill the ranks, but for several months the Commander-in-Chief had to depend on undisciplined recruits and militia. A chronic shortage of food and clothing and cramped housing in local residences, public buildings, and barns further aggravated the situation. Working from his headquarters at Arnold's Tavern on the Morristown green, Washington tried to make the best of the situation. He sent out details of men to secure provisions and block British access to supplies, engaged in recurrent skirmishes with the enemy, and generally reasserted rebel control over New Jersey.

In the spring, the long-promised reinforcements arrived, raising the army to over eight thousand by May. When the British began moving out of their winter quarters that same month, Washington prepared to evacuate Morristown. Rather than simply abandoning the village and the supply base he had established, Washington ordered the construction of an earthen fortification on the crest of Mount Kemble. The trenches and embankments were completed just before the army broke camp in late May to pursue the British. Originally known as the "Hill," or "Kinney's Hill," the earthwork was later dubbed "Fort Nonsense" by skeptics who questioned Washington's motive in erecting a fortification that was never used.

General Washington did not return to Morristown for another two and a half years. Although the war was far from over, the rebels had secured a stronger position in the north by the time the Commander-in-Chief arrived at the New Jersey village on December 1, 1779. Work began immediately on organizing the campgrounds and erecting housing for the ten to twelve thousand troops assembled there. Washington, his wife Martha, and his aides took up residence in the home of Mrs. Theodosia Ford, while senior officers moved into other private homes. Junior officers joined the soldiers in crude log huts erected in nearby Jockey Hollow. Some six hundred acres of timber were used in the construction of over a thousand huts by mid-February of 1780. These log structures were carefully grouped by brigades in assigned areas that included space for parade grounds, streets, and separate housing for officers and enlisted men. The Jockey Hollow encampment included as well a hospital, a guard house, an orderly room, and a Grand Parade for training, orders, and ceremonies.

Washington faced many of the same problems that winter which had plagued the encampment in 1777. The mounting financial problems of the young republic made it even more difficult to keep the army adequately clothed and provisioned, and discontent mounted within the ranks over short supplies and worthless pay. To top it all off, the Morristown encampment experienced the worst winter of the century. Twenty-eight snowfalls blocked supply lines and exacerbated an already critical problem. For loyalists in nearby New York, conditions seemed perfect for a counter-revolution in New Jersey.

Loyalists led by former New Jersey governor William Franklin convinced the British to launch an attack on June 6, 1780. The British hoped to move swiftly into New Jersey and overcome the Continental Army at Morristown, but on June 7 the New Jersey Brigade of the Continental Army and the local militia combined forces to stop the British at Connecticut Farms. The British and German troops then regrouped and waited for reinforcements led by General Sir Henry Clinton. On June 23 the Royal Army, led by loyalist regiments, advanced to Springfield but could not penetrate the Watchung Mountains. The British retreat ended the last royal invasion of New Jersey. As the enemy pulled back to Staten Island, Washington ordered his army to evacuate Morristown, ending the town's nearly seven-month reign as the military capital of the American Revolution.

In 1933 the United States Congress designated Washington's Morristown campsite as the nation's first historical park owned and maintained by the federal government. The Morristown National Historical Park comprises over one thousand acres divided into three units: Fort Nonsense, erected in 1777; the Ford House, Washington's headquarters in 1779–80; and Jockey Hollow, which includes the Wick House (circa 1750) and reconstructions of the Continental Army's log huts. All three are administered by the National Park Service, which provides markers, tours, exhibits, and other programs on the history of Revolutionary New Jersey.

Conflict and division have played a significant role in New Jersey history, and at no point was this more evident than during the Revolutionary War era. Numerous historic sites remain in the state from that pivotal period, but Morristown clearly occupied the center stage. The Morristown National Historical Park brings to life those critical years of the birth of the new republic.

Great Falls Historic District

Paterson

★ New Jersey has thrived on political conflict throughout its long history, but the Federalist-Jeffersonian rivalry of the 1790s had particular long-term significance. The Federalists' brief hegemony made it possible for Alexander Hamilton and his associates to secure state support of a plan to establish a manufacturing city at the falls of the Passaic River. Jeffersonians decried this modern encroachment on rural New Jersey and staunchly defended agrarian virtues, but the die was cast by the time they forced their opponents out of office. The extraordinary privileges granted to the city's developers by the Federalists in 1791 gave rise to the nation's first planned industrial center, the city of Paterson. The Great Falls of the Passaic/Society for Useful Manufactures Historic District preserves the remnants of this "Cradle of American Industry" and commemorates New Jersey's pivotal role in the shaping of modern America.

Thomas Rogers Building

Energy, entrepreneurs, and immigrants provided the keys to Paterson's success. The source of energy was the Great Falls of the Passaic River, the second largest falls in the eastern United States. Hamilton first viewed the falls in 1778, while serving as an aide to George Washington in the Revolutionary War. He immediately recognized the site's potential and had it in mind years later when he advocated that the government establish a ''national manufactory'' to stimulate industrial development in the new republic. Rebuffed by Congress, he took his proposal to the Federalist New Jersey legislature, which promptly gave the project the official support of the State of New Jersey.

Hamilton and his fellow Federalist entrepreneurs incorporated in 1791 as the Society for the Establishment of Useful Manufactures. The New Jersey legislature recognized the group as the sole governing body of the Great Falls project and granted the entrepreneurs exclusive water-power rights, tax exemption, and other special privileges to insure the venture's success. Despite such initial advantages, the SUM project seemed doomed by 1795 because of financial mismanagement, and the original investors soon abandoned the failing enterprise.

The eventual success of Paterson reflected the tenacity of Peter Colt, who had been hired by the SUM in 1793 to govern the new industrial development. He stayed on despite the project's apparent failure, bought up corporate shares, and took over the SUM. Paterson's time finally came when the War of 1812 cut off access to British manufactured goods and stimulated domestic production. The new manufacturing city boomed in the decades that followed, and Colt became one of the nation's first industrial giants. Although retaining tight control over power development and real estate, the SUM eventually abandoned actual manufacturing activity, thereby clearing the way for a new generation of entrepreneurial leaders who made Paterson an industrial showcase of innovation and invention. This new generation included John Colt, who stimulated textile production by introducing the cotton duck sail in 1821; John Ryle and George Murray, the fathers of the American silk industry; John Clark, the first in a distinguished roster of trained mechanics; Samuel Colt, the inventor of the Colt revolver; Thomas Rogers, the nation's leading locomotive manufacturer; and John P. Holland, the inventor of the submarine. These and many other entrepreneurs and inventors made Paterson the ''Cradle of American Industry.''

But of course there would have been no factories without workers. Successive waves of German, Irish, Italian, East European, and other immigrant groups in the nineteenth century provided the bulk of Paterson's labor force, working long hours in dangerous and unhealthy workplaces in return for meager pay. Armed with special powers granted by the state legislature, the city's industrial aristocrats attempted to exercise absolute control over the men, women, and children who labored in their factories. Conflict was inevitable. Between 1881 and 1900, Paterson workers staged 137 strikes. Each failed, contributing to increased worker frustration and giving rise to frequent vandalism and rioting. The most famous job action came in 1913, when silk workers went on strike for maintenance of the two-loom system. Despite the supportive activities of the Industrial Workers of the World and noted radical leaders like William D. "Big Bill" Haywood and Carlo Tresca, the workers eventually capitulated. But as before, the strike's failure did not curb labor militancy, and Paterson's workers continued in the next decades to seek redress against the arrogance and indifference of the industrial aristocracy.

The Society for Useful Manufactures continued to operate until 1945, when the city of Paterson purchased its property, assets, charter rights, power plant, and raceway system. In the decades that followed, industrial activity declined because of a range of economic problems, and by the 1960s highway construction threatened the manufacturing district. A citizens' group stopped the proposed demolition and in 1971 established the Great Falls Development Corporation to preserve the old mill structures and promote reuse. Designated a National Historic Landmark in 1976, the Great Falls of the Passaic/SUM Historic District effectively demonstrates the valuable role multi-use development can play in the preservation of our nation's architectural heritage.

Visitors to Paterson can still view the reason for the city's development—the Great Falls of the Passaic River—and the three-tiered raceway system completed in 1846 to harness the water for mill sites located along the banks. Numerous mill structures also still stand in the district, including the Phoenix Mill Complex, erected between 1816 and 1870 and the oldest surviving mill in the district, and the Colt Gun Mill, a portion of the four-story structure used by Samuel Colt for the production of the first commercially successful revolver and then by John Ryle and George Murray for manufacturing silk in the

1840s. Apart from the textile industry, Paterson's leading business was the manufacture of locomotives; several structures remain from the Rogers Locomotive Works, the industry leader. Visitors can also see where some of Paterson's nineteenth-century residents lived, ranging from the John Ryle House on Mill Street to the Irish working-class community of Dublin, just outside the historic district.

The structures that make up the Great Falls of the Passaic/SUM Historical District now house a variety of different businesses, restaurants, and lofts, but the fabric of the nineteenth-century industrial city remains intact. The Great Falls Tour Office provides walking tours and slide lectures on this historic district, and visitors can tour exhibits on the city's industrial past at the Paterson Museum in the Thomas Rogers Building. The programs and activities of the Great Falls Development Corporation insure the continued preservation and development of this unique historical resource.

Historic Cape May

Cape May

★ New Jersey's long history of social, political, and economic conflict should not obscure the prominence and fame of its seashore resorts. In the late nineteenth and early twentieth centuries, any city-dweller in the mid-Atlantic states who could afford it temporarily escaped the trials and tribulations of urban life by a visit to the Jersey shore. Foremost among the seaside havens were Cape May, Long Beach, and Atlantic City, each renowned for its grand hotels, fine beaches, and varied amusements. Few historic structures remain at either Long Beach or Atlantic City, but the Cape May National Historic Landmark District preserves over six hundred hotels, cottages, and other structures from the resort era.

Emlen Physick House

The district provides a showcase of Victorian architecture and brings to life this colorful era in New Jersey history.

A Dutch explorer first laid claim to the area around present-day Cape May in 1616, but the cape bears the name of another Dutchman, Cornelius Jacobsen Mey, a representative of the Dutch West Indies Company in the New Netherlands colony in the 1620s. The Dutch surrendered control of the region to the English in 1664, and a decade later New Jersey became a proprietary colony. The leading proprietor in West Jersey was Dr. Daniel Coxe, a Quaker speculator who owned a large tract of land that included Cape Island, as it was then known. Through Coxe's influence, local government was organized in 1687, but settlement and development of the cape did not actually commence until the early eighteenth century. The first residents were farmers, fishermen, and sea pilots, totaling over six hundred fifty by 1726.

The first paying guests at Cape May were probably pirates and their crews, who took up temporary residence there in the late seventeenth and early eighteenth centuries. It is not clear, however, just when the cape began developing as a resort. By 1801 the tourist trade was such that Ellis Hughes advertised his hotel in a Philadelphia newspaper. Hughes' establishment was probably the first real hotel, although large houses had undoubtedly provided guest accommodations for several decades. By that time, regular stagecoach service from Philadelphia and Camden augmented coastwise travel by sloop and improved accessibility to the cape. But the resort business did not really begin to flourish until after the War of 1812 and the establishment of regular steamboat service between Cape Island and Philadelphia.

Thomas Hughes, the son of early entrepreneur Ellis Hughes, was the first to take full advantage of the cape's natural attractions and newly developed accessibility. In 1816 he began construction of an enormous hotel that he hoped to fill with wealthy visitors from Philadelphia, Baltimore, Delaware, and Virginia, Locals at first dubbed the structure "Tommy's Folly," but Hughes' strategy worked. His hotel, later named Congress Hall, became the basis of a fashionable resort community.

Development of resort facilities on the cape accelerated in succeeding decades. The community had only three hotels and numerous boarding houses in the 1820s, but by the 1850s Cape May, as it had become known, accommodated nearly three thousand visitors a day. Most stayed in large beach-side hotels like Congress Hall, but after the Civil War prominent Philadelphia families began building their own summer cottages. Construction of the West Jersey Railroad also improved accessibility to the cape.

Clearly, the heyday for Cape May came in the decades between 1850 and 1900, when the resort reigned as one of the most popular and fashionable vacation spots on the Atlantic. Distinguished guests included Presidents Franklin Pierce, James Buchanan, Ulysses S. Grant, Chester A. Arthur, and Benjamin Harrison as well as such notable political and social figures as Horace Greeley and John Wanamaker. During this same period, several fires unfortunately damaged many of the older hotels and houses but also made it possible for entrepreneurs and summer residents to erect an exceptional array of Victorian structures that testify to the tastes and fashions of the American gentry in the last decades of the nineteenth century. Although Cape May declined in popularity as a resort in the early twentieth century, its fine old hotels, businesses, and residences survived surprisingly unaltered, and the city now boasts perhaps the greatest concentration of Victorian architecture in America.

Along Beach Drive, opposite the promenade and the beach, Cape May entrepreneurs erected grand hotels that catered to the needs of the community's wealthy visitors. Thomas Hughes' Congress Hall was the first of these structures, and a successor still bears that historic name. Erected in 1879 at Beach and Congress, the present Congress Hall was constructed of brick in the Second Empire style. It has a striking three-story columned veranda surmounted by a mansard roof with dormer windows. More typical of Cape May was the frame construction of the Windsor Hotel, erected on Beach Avenue at Windsor in 1879 according to plans by Stephen Decatur Button, perhaps the most prolific architect on the cape. Even more striking is the Colonial Hotel, a four-and-a-half-story Second Empire structure erected at Beach and Ocean by the Church brothers in 1894–1895. All the hotels were not built along the coast, however, and two particularly fine examples are the Chalfonte Hotel, erected in 1876 at Sewell Avenue and Howard Street, and Carroll Villa, erected in 1882 at 19 Jackson Street. These two have the fretwork details and bracketed eaves typical of American Bracketed Villa, an American architectural style that gives Cape May much of its distinctive flavor.

Visitors to Cape May expected to be amused, and local entrepreneurs endeavored to meet their needs. There were, of course, bathhouses along the beach, special events like automobile races, and, for a time, a race track on nearby Diamond Beach. But nothing rivaled the popularity of gambling houses. At North and Windsor streets on the lawn of Congress Hall, gambler Henry Cleveland erected in 1845 an establishment that became famous as the Blue Pit. A rival gambling house was Jackson's Clubhouse, built in 1872 at 635 Columbia Avenue. Button also designed this structure in the popular American Bracketed Villa style.

Inland from the beachfront hotels stood the summer homes of Cape May's wealthier patrons. Some were designed by distinguished architects like Button, Frank Furness, and Samuel Sloan, but others reflected the talents of individual carpenter-builders, who turned to pattern books, textbooks, and trade journals for inspiration. While many of these structures are hybrids of various styles and are more appropriately categorized as vernacular, Cape May also boasts many fine examples of the prevailing architectural styles of the period.

For example, the J. Stratton Ware House at 655 Hughes Street was erected in 1868 in the Gothic Revival style, as was the Eldridge Johnson House (the Pink House), erected in 1882 at 33 Perry Street. The popularity of American Bracketed Villa is evident in the George Allen House at 720 Washington, erected in 1863 according to a design by Samuel Sloan, and in the Neafie-Levy House, constructed in 1866 at 28–30 Congress Street. A fine example of Second Empire style is the George Hildreth House (1882) at 17 Jackson Street. One of the most important residences in the city and an exceptional example of the Stick style is the Emlen Physick House, a sixteen-room structure erected between 1887 and 1889 at 1050 Washington Street. The Mid-Atlantic Center for the Arts now operates the structure as an historic-house museum. A final example is the Dr. Henry F. Hunt House at 209 Congress Place, an elaborate Queen Anne house that dates from 1881. These are but a few from among Cape May's hundreds of fine examples of American Victorian architecture.

The best starting point for a tour of historic Cape May is the Mid-Atlantic Center for the Arts at the Emlen Physick House. Whether by foot, automobile, or trolley, a tour of the city's unique architectural heritage enriches the visitor's appreciation of the Victorian lifestyle.

From its grand beachfront hotels to its gingerbread cottages, Cape May typifies the famous Jersey Coast resorts that provided both New Jerseyans and out-of-state visitors with temporary refuge from the accelerating pace of industrializing America.

Other Places of Interest

*The following suggest other places of
historical interest to visit. We recommend that
you check hours of operation in advance.*

ALLAIRE VILLAGE, *Allaire State Park, state 524, Allaire.* Preserved 1830 village with Howell Iron Works and Monmouth Furnace.

ATSION VILLAGE, *U.S. 206, Atsion.* Deserted industrial community with foundations of gristmill and several houses from the 1700s, some restored houses and buildings; with a museum.

BATSTO, *state 542 ten miles east of Hammonton.* Restored eighteenth-century village with ironworks and 1800s glassworks and other buildings; visitor center.

CLINTON HISTORICAL MUSEUM VILLAGE, *Main Street, Clinton.* Mill, schoolhouse, lime kilns, and other structures showing rural and industrial life from the eighteenth to the twentieth century.

DEY MANSION, *199 Totowa Road, Wayne.* House built in 1740 that was headquarters for George Washington in 1780; contains a museum.

EDISON NATIONAL HISTORIC SITE, *Main Street at Lakeside Avenue, West Orange.* Laboratories where Thomas A. Edison made the first motion pictures and other inventions; with tours of both laboratories and Edison's home, Glenmont.

FERRY MUSEUM, *Washington Crossing State Park, near Titusville.* Tavern where Washington rested briefly after crossing the Delaware on Christmas night, 1776.

GROVER CLEVELAND BIRTHPLACE, *207 Bloomfield Avenue, Caldwell.* Manse of the Presbyterian church where the future president's father was pastor; with Cleveland possessions from childhood to presidency.

HANCOCK HOUSE, *Hancock's Bridge.* Where patriots were ambushed by Loyalists in 1778 during the American Revolution.

HERMITAGE, *335 N. Franklin Turnpike, Ho-Ho-Kus.* Early Gothic Revival house, rebuilt in 1845; site of visits by Burr, Benedict Arnold, Lafayette, and Washington; with a museum.

HISTORIC GARDNER'S BASIN, *N. New Hampshire Avenue and the Bay, Atlantic City.* Maritime village predating Atlantic City, with twenty-five vessels and maritime artifacts, including whaling gear, exhibits on lobster-men, and exhibits of clammer and sail loft.

INDIAN KING TAVERN, *233 King's Highway East, Haddonfield.* Built in 1750; where the first New Jersey legislature met in 1777.

LONGSTREET FARM, *Holmdel Park, Holmdel.* A living history farm de-picting agriculture in the 1890s.

MILLER-CORY HOUSE, *614 Mountain Avenue, Westfield.* A 1740 house with antique furniture and farm implements; demonstrations of open-hearth cooking and colonial crafts September–May.

MONMOUTH COUNTY HISTORICAL ASSOCIATION, *70 Court Street, Freehold.* Library and museum with records of North American Phalanx, communal society of the 1800s near Red Bank; a number of historic build-ings nearby.

MORVEN, *55 Stockton Street, Princeton.* Built in the early 1750s by Richard Stockton, signer of the Declaration of Independence; headquarters for Corn-wallis in 1777 and New Jersey executive mansion 1954–1981; with period rooms and exhibits.

NASSAU HALL, *Princeton.* Completed in 1756 to house the College of New Jersey; occupied by both British and American troops during the Revolu-tion, and the meetingplace for the Continental Congress in 1783.

NEWARK MUSEUM, *43–49 Washington Street, Newark.* Art and natural history collections; includes the Newark Fire Museum, a schoolhouse from the 1700s, and restored Ballantine House of 1885.

NEW JERSEY HISTORICAL SOCIETY MUSEUM, *230 Broadway, New-ark.* Extensive collections and displays of American and New Jersey his-tory, including maritime, transportation, industrial, and domestic items.

NEW JERSEY STATE MUSEUM, *205 W. State Street, Trenton.* General museum with fine arts, natural history, decorative arts, and other history.

OLD BARRACKS, *South Willow Street at Mahlon Stacy Park, Trenton.* Building dating from the French and Indian War, now a museum.

OLD DUTCH PARSONAGE, *65 Washington Place, Somerville.* Dutch fur-nishings in a 1751 house where Rutgers University began.

PRINCETON HISTORICAL SOCIETY, *158 Nassau Street, Princeton.* Pe-riod rooms and changing exhibits in a house built about 1766; where the commander of "Old Ironsides" (U.S.S. *Constitution*), William Bainbridge, was born.

SPEEDWELL VILLAGE, *333 Speedwell Avenue (U.S. 202), Morristown.* Where Alfred Vail and Samuel F. B. Morse developed the electric telegraph and gave the first public demonstration in 1838; with an iron foundry and nine historic buildings.

TRENT HOUSE, *539 S. Warren Street, Trenton*. Oldest private house in Trenton, built 1719.

TWIN LIGHTS MUSEUM, *Atlantic Highlands*. Where the Navesink lighthouse was built in 1828 and replaced in 1862; with a nautical museum.

VON STEUBEN HOUSE, *Main Street, River Edge*. Built about 1695, occupied during American Revolution, and given to General Von Steuben for his services; with a museum.

WALT WHITMAN HOUSE, *330 Mickle Street, Camden*. Where the poet lived 1884–1892; with his furnishings and mementos.

WATERLOO VILLAGE, *Waterloo Road, Stanhope*. Restoration of nineteenth-century businesses and homes on site of Andover Forge and Morris Canal.

WHEATON VILLAGE, *Millville*. Restored glassmaking community of the 1880s, with museum and glassmaking demonstrations.

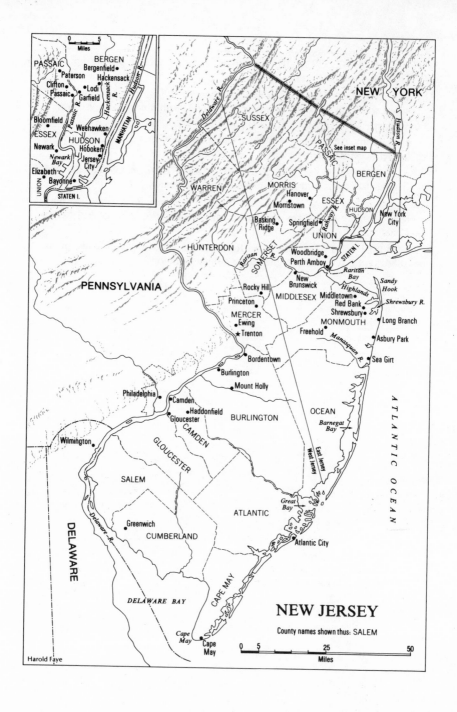

NEW JERSEY

County names shown thus: SALEM

Harold Faye

Invitation to the Reader

IN 1807, former President John Adams argued that a complete history of the American Revolution could not be written until the history of change in each state was known, because the principles of the Revolution were as various as the states that went through it. Two hundred years after the Declaration of Independence, the American nation has spread over a continent and beyond. The states have grown in number from thirteen to fifty. And democratic principles have been interpreted differently in every one of them.

We therefore invite you to consider that the history of your state may have more to do with the bicentennial review of the American Revolution than does the story of Bunker Hill or Valley Forge. The Revolution has continued as Americans extended liberty and democracy over a vast territory. John Adams was right: the states are part of that story, and the story is incomplete without an account of their diversity.

The Declaration of Independence stressed life, liberty, and the pursuit of happiness; accordingly, it shattered the notion of holding new territories in the subordinate status of colonies. The Northwest Ordinance of 1787 set forth a procedure for new states to enter the Union on an equal footing with the old. The Federal Constitution shortly confirmed this novel means of building a nation out of equal states. The step-by-step process through which territories have achieved self-government and national representation is among the most important of the Founding Fathers' legacies.

The method of state-making reconciled the ancient conflict between liberty and empire, resulting in what Thomas Jefferson called an empire for liberty. The system has worked and remains unaltered, despite enormous changes that have taken place in the nation. The country's extent and variety now surpass anything the patriots of '76 could likely have imagined. The United States has changed from an agrarian republic into a highly industrial and urban democracy, from a fledgling nation into a major world power. As Oliver Wendell Holmes remarked in 1920, the creators of the nation could not have seen completely how it and its constitution and its states would develop. Any meaningful review in the bicentennial era must consider what the country has become, as well as what it was.

The new nation of equal states took as its motto *E Pluribus Unum*—"out of many, one." But just as many peoples have become Americans without complete loss of ethnic and cultural identities, so have the states retained differences of character. Some have been superficial, expressed in stereotyped images—big, boastful Texas, "sophisticated" New York, "hillbilly" Arkansas. Other differences have been more real, sometimes instructively, sometimes amusingly; democracy has embraced Huey Long's Louisiana, bilingual New Mexico, unicameral Nebraska, and a Texas that once taxed fortunetellers and spawned politicians called "Woodpecker Republicans" and "Skunk Democrats." Some differences have been profound, as when South Carolina secessionists led other states out of the Union in opposition to abolitionists in Massachusetts and Ohio. The result was a bitter Civil War.

The Revolution's first shots may have sounded in Lexington and Concord; but fights over what democracy should mean and who should have independence have erupted from Pennsylvania's Gettysburg to the "Bleeding Kansas" of John Brown, from the Alamo in Texas to the Indian battles at Montana's Little Bighorn. Utah Mormons have known the strain of isolation; Hawaiians at Pearl Harbor, the terror of attack; Georgians during Sherman's march, the sadness of defeat and devastation. Each state's experience differs instructively; each adds understanding to the whole.

The purpose of this series of books is to make that kind of understanding accessible, in a way that will last in value far beyond the bicentennial fireworks. The series offers a volume on every state, plus the District of Columbia—fifty-one, in all.

Each book contains, besides the text, a view of the state through eyes other than the author's—a "photographer's essay," in which a skilled photographer presents his own personal perceptions of the state's contemporary flavor.

We have asked authors not for comprehensive chronicles, nor for research monographs or new data for scholars. Bibliographies and footnotes are minimal. We have asked each author for a summing up—interpretive, sensitive, thoughtful, individual, even personal—of what seems significant about his or her state's history. What distinguishes it? What has mattered about it, to its own people and to the rest of the nation? What has it come to now?

To interpret the states in all their variety, we have sought a variety of backgrounds in authors themselves and have encouraged variety in the approaches they take. They have in common only these things: historical knowledge, writing skill, and strong personal feelings about a particular state. Each has wide latitude for the use of the short space. And if each succeeds, it will be by offering you, in your capacity as a *citizen* of a state *and* of a nation, stimulating insights to test against your own.

James Morton Smith
General Editor

New Jersey
A History

Dissonance
(If you are interested)
Leads to discovery.

William Carlos Williams
Paterson

Introduction

AS I began writing this book, the New Jersey legislature was locked in furious combat with Gov. Brendan Byrne over a bill for a state income tax. The governor insisted on the measure. The legislature resisted it. Both sides issued declarations of defiance and prophecies of chaos. A visiting Chinese might have thought anarchy or revolution was imminent. But for Jerseyans it was business as usual. Their legislators have been quarreling ferociously with governors—and with each other—since 1668, when the colonial assembly informed Gov. Philip Carteret that he had better abandon his expectations "that things must go according to your opinions."

New Jersey's motto might well be: "Divided we stand." Conflict has been a standard ingredient in her life for three centuries. There is no reason for Jerseyans to hang their heads in shame over this interesting fact. Every state has had its internal feuds and broils. A weary Thomas Jefferson once remarked, "An association of men who will not quarrel with one another is a thing which never yet existed, from the greatest confederacy of nations down to a town meeting or a vestry."

But most states have focussed their quarrels around a single difference—usually a dispute based on geography. Thus in the eighteenth century, rural western Massachusetts bickered with the merchant-dominated East, the grandees of the Tidewater looked askance on the less-genteel Virginians from the Blue

Ridge, the wealthy low-country planters treated the upcountry Carolinians with undisguised contempt. New Jersey has suffered from a similar geographical split between a Philadelphia-hipped south and a New York-tilted north. But Jerseyans have added all other imaginable divisions—religious, ethnic, racial, economic—and these have often erupted into conflicts at the same time. Few states have equalled the multiplicity and duration of New Jersey's internal quarrels.

Such a perspective enables us to clarify that murky concept, New Jersey's identity, which is not a fixed thing, but a process, something that is still evolving. Watching New Jersey deal with her divisions is also instructive, for it demonstrates on a small scale how Americans have dealt with alarming social conflicts.

In New Jersey as in the nation, this approach inevitably leads to an emphasis on politics. For most of her 300 years, politics has been the arena in which New Jersey displayed her furious feuds and explosive frictions. In this use of politics, as in so many other things, New Jersey has been a microcosm of the larger American experiment.

The violent conflicts and revolutionary rhetoric of the Vietnam era jolted historians and other Americans out of the consensus view of the nation's past. We have begun looking anew at the painful conflicts from which a consensus slowly emerged. We have become more aware of our present reality—our interest-group democracy within which bruising conflict continues between cities and suburbs, unions and corporations, races and ethnic minorities.

New Jersey's experience conveys a surprising message of hope that such conflicts can be contained within the comparatively bloodless arena of politics, that the American struggle for power and profit can be restricted to wars of words instead of bullets. But these political struggles have exacted their own special toll. They have left moral and spiritual wounds.

In *Paterson,* New Jersey's great poet, William Carlos Williams, personifies that city as a man in search of his soul, his meaning. The search forced him to discover his past, the repository of his hopes and ideals. Perhaps the same necessity applies to the state of New Jersey.

As the soul seeks to order the unruly, instinctual body, often without success, Jerseyans have attempted in their politics to order their fractured and often fractious commonwealth. Theirs has been a search, not for the dead order of power, but for the life-giving order of freedom and justice, for the "more equal liberty" the American Revolution sought to establish. In this perspective, New Jersey, like America, has discovered, lost, and then rediscovered her soul again and again. For three hundred years she has struggled to cope with the harsh realities of human greed and the corruptions of power and repeatedly failed. But she has just as repeatedly found the strength to try again, with new men and new measures. This stubborn faith is not unique to New Jersey. It flows from wellsprings of the greater American experiment, from its faith in the ability of free men to govern themselves. The author hopes that this book, which does not blink at the harsh realities, will contribute to that faith.

1

Power to the Proprietors

*O*N March 12, 1664, King Charles II of England granted to his "dearest brother James," the duke of York, a princely chunk of North America—all the land between the Connecticut and Delaware rivers. This grant included major portions of present Connecticut, New York, and New Jersey. But none of these names were on the Dutch-drawn map used by the king and his brother. In fact, most of the duke's chunk of the continent was claimed and ostensibly controlled by the Dutch, who had founded the colony of New Netherlands on the tip of Manhattan Island, with outlying farms across the Hudson River at places called Bergen, Communipaw, Pavonia, and Hobocan.

Early in May 1664, James, who doubled as the king's lord high admiral, sent a fleet of four ships commanded by one Richard Nicolls to inform the Dutch that they were now part of the British Empire. Without firing a shot, New Netherlands surrendered and its name was changed to New York. The Dutch across the river were included in the capitulation. With them came a small colony of Swedes and Finns on the Delaware, a settlement the English subdued with a few rounds of artillery.

This aggressive behavior was part of a conscious effort to show England that the king and his aristocrats could lead the nation to new prosperity and power. It was also an attempt to find more of the commodity that aristocrats—especially kings—always needed: money. The aristocrats' ability to rule turbulent, divided England was still very much in doubt. Twenty years earlier, the nobility had lost a bitter civil war that was triggered by their religious and economic intransigence.

It is worth taking a glance at the causes of this civil war, because the controversies reappeared, with local variations, in New Jersey. The aristocrats had refused to recognize the triumph of the Protestant idea in England. They had leaned toward the Roman Catholic side of the religious compromise known as the Anglican church, in which bishops appointed by the king still decided on beliefs. Money was also part of the argument, with the aristocrats insisting on the king's divine right to an independent income and Parliament grimly maintaining that the people who supplied the cash had a right to decide how it was spent.

When the arguments exploded into gunfire in 1642, strong man Oliver Cromwell emerged from the chaos to rout the aristocrats and behead King Charles I. Cromwell ruled England as a dictator for a dolorous decade. After his death in 1658, a majority of Englishmen reacted against religious fanaticism and economic recession and restored the aristocrats to power. Charles II, son of the beheaded king, was invited to assume the throne. His first order of business was to make the overseas colonies a cohesive empire. The Navigation Acts banned foreign ships from colonial ports and forced colonial ships to trade only with England. The capture of New Netherlands was followed by the settlement of the Carolinas, making the North American coast a solidly English show. The Lords of Trade, a committee drawn from the king's Privy Council, was created to oversee colonial affairs.

On Manhattan Island, Richard Nicolls, the king's loyal and vigorous servant, wasted no time incorporating New Netherlands into the empire. He changed its name to New York and began surveying the realm he was to govern. Nicolls decided that the rich soil and empty acres west of the Hudson looked particularly promising. He named the region "Albania," after the dukedom of Albany, the Scottish title of the duke of York, and offered generous terms to prospective settlers. Within six months, Nicolls had confirmed grants to two groups.

The first grant comprised the land between the Raritan and the Passaic rivers, mostly present Essex County. The second extended from Sandy Hook to Barnegat Bay and twenty-five miles up the Raritan River—present Ocean and Monmouth counties. Some of these first comers were Quaker and Baptist refugees from England; most were emigrants from New England, who were looking for better soil than they could find on sandy eastern Long Island. Nicolls guaranteed all of them the right to hold town meetings and practice their religions in freedom in "Albania." At Nicolls's insistence, the settlers in turn negotiated the purchase of the land from New Jersey's easygoing Indians, the Lenni-Lenape.

As the settlers moved onto their tracts, Governor Nicolls received dismaying news from England. The duke of York, exhibiting a carelessness that was later to cost him a kingdom, had given Albania to two close friends, Lord John Berkeley and Sir George Carteret. Both were veterans of the civil war who had stuck with the duke and his royal brother throughout the years of exile in France. Rewarding their loyalty at last, the duke drew a line on his Dutch map from a branch of the upper Delaware at 41°40' N latitude to the Hudson River, grandly handing Berkeley and Carteret the 7,500 square miles, or 4.8 million acres, south of the line. Because a nonexistent river ran along the line on the map, the duke decided the gift was an island, and named it New Jersey, after Sir George Carteret's native island of Jersey.

Governor Nicolls was so annoyed by this unexpected move that he resigned. Nicolls was convinced that the weather of northern New York was too severe to attract colonists. He told the duke that he had given away the best part of his property. The duke's response was another blunder. He took Staten Island away from New Jersey, to whom it obviously belonged, and gave it to New York. Otherwise, he let Berkeley and Carteret keep their province, and they went to work on turning it into a profitable business.

The two proprietors sent twenty-six-year-old Philip Carteret, a distant cousin of Sir George, to serve as their governor. To attract settlers, they armed him with a statement of "concessions and agreements," which guaranteed a general assembly, freedom of trade, and liberty of conscience. Extremely important, both in 1665 and in the future, was the promise that the governor and council were "not to impose, nor suffer to be imposed, any tax, custom, subsidy or any other duty whatsoever upon any colour or pretense upon the said province and inhabitants thereof, other than what shall be imposed by the authority and consent of the general assembly." [1]

Some men are born to rule. Philip Carteret was not one of them. An unstable mixture of aristocratic arrogance and indecision, he had charm but no personal force. Late in July 1665, he arrived in New Jersey with an entourage of thirty French-speaking servants from the island of Jersey. The governor was nonplussed to discover that his colony was already a going concern. He must have been even more dismayed by the colonists. Most of them were descendants of men and women who had left England before the Civil War to escape aristocratic persecution for their refusal to worship in the Anglican church. The aristocrats had contemptuously called them "puritans" for their insistence on expunging all traces of Catholicism from the state religion. Now Governor Carteret found himself 3,000 miles away from the support of the Royal Army and Navy, the unexpected ruler of this contentious breed of Englishmen. Instinctively he must have fingered his throat and wondered how long his head would remain on his shoulders.

The colonists at Elizabethtown (present Elizabeth), which Governor Carteret named after Sir George's wife, were even less pleased with him. A proprietary government was not a popular idea among Puritans, who had a fierce, instinctive contempt for aristocratic privileges. Proprietors were relics of another era. In the fourteenth century, the English crown had given certain nobles "proprietary" powers of government along its northern borders to encourage resistance to marauding Scots. Earlier proprietors in America, like Lord Baltimore in Maryland, had at least paid the expenses of founding the colony. As the settlers

1. Samuel Smith, *The History of the Colony of Nova Caesarea or New Jersey* (Burlington, N.J.: Printed and sold by James Parker, 1765), p. 517.

saw it, Lord John Berkeley and Sir George Carteret had done nothing to earn their right to govern New Jersey but cozy up to the duke of York and his royal brother.

The settlers had little enthusiasm for taking an oath of loyalty to these court favorites. They had no enthusiasm whatsoever for paying them quitrents—another leftover from the feudal era. A quitrent was a small sum a landowner paid annually in lieu of services the local nobleman might otherwise require. This confrontation between the aristocrats and the average man, between the holders of power and the powerless, began a theme that was to be repeated with innumerable variations throughout New Jersey's history.

Both sides proceeded cautiously. Carteret bought out one of the purchasers of Elizabethtown's 400,000-acre grant and agreed to confirm the ownership of the other buyers if they took an oath of loyalty to the proprietors. He followed a similar policy with the Quakers and Baptists who had bought the Monmouth tract. Both groups took the oath. But when Carteret convened an assembly in 1668, resentments boiled to the surface. The Monmouth people announced they had the right to hold their own assembly and disowned the Carteret assembly for several reasons: it had accepted the proprietors' "obscure" claims to New Jersey, passed a tax of five pounds per town, and given Berkeley and Carteret the power to charge any quitrent they chose. Nicolls had granted a grace period before quitrents were to be paid and had not specified a price. When the grace period expired in 1670, and Governor Carteret tried to collect the money, his unpopularity increased ominously. Quitrent payments were few and slow.

The conflict acquired revolutionary overtones when Capt. James Carteret, the proprietor's ne'er-do-well son, made an unexpected appearance in 1672. James was the weak-willed product of a short-tempered father. Sir George Carteret was famous for his verbal explosions. The diarist, Samuel Pepys, who worked for him, called him "the most passionate man in the world." James was supposed to be en route to South Carolina, where he was to share in another proprietary colony run by royal favorites. But once he got beyond the range of his father's sharp tongue, James revealed he had delusions of grandeur. He saw the stuff of greatness when he looked in the mirror; and permitted the dissidents to convene an assembly and elect him "President of the province."

Here was a moment for the legal governor, Philip Carteret, to show some backbone. He should have declared martial law, called out the militia, and had a showdown with cousin James and the dissidents. Instead, like a frightened schoolboy running home to his parents, he boarded the first available ship and retreated to England to ask the proprietors to reconfirm his powers.

Philip Carteret got what he wanted and more. The proprietors persuaded an angry duke of York to declare the Nicolls land grant titles null and void. Anyone who did not have a title from the proprietors forfeited his land. Anyone who refused to pay quitrents could have his cattle, grain, furniture, or other movable goods seized by a constable to settle the debt. Only freemen could vote, and only the governor and his council could decide who was a freeman. No one but the governor could charter towns, establish courts, appoint officials, or sell unpurchased land. James Carteret was blasted from his dreams of glory by an order to depart forthwith for Carolina. New Jersey's first and only president shuddered—he could practically hear Sir George thundering the command—and hastily obeyed. The comedy was over.

For a few years Gov. Philip Carteret rode high. But he got bad news from England in 1676. The vagaries of the aristocratic style of life had halved his domain. Desperate for cash after building an expensive London mansion, Lord John Berkeley had sold his half of New Jersey to two Quakers, Maj. John Fenwick and Edward Byllynge, for a paltry thousand pounds. In 1676, the new owners and Sir George Carteret decided they were strange bedfellows and partitioned the province into West Jersey and East Jersey. The canny Quakers drove a sharp bargain with the seventy-six-year-old courtier, getting 1,500 square miles more land in their western half. The dividing line ran from Little Egg Harbor, just north of present Atlantic City, to latitude 41° 40′ on the upper Delaware. No one consulted the people of New Jersey on this division, which was to have fundamental effects on the colony and state for the next three hundred years.

Reduced to being governor of East Jersey, Philip Carteret at first tried to reconcile his contentious subjects. He offered amnesty for all those who participated in the revolution of 1672 and apparently approved an assembly recommendation that the past "be buried in oblivion." But the arbitrary powers handed Carteret by the declarations of 1672 soon began causing new troubles. Especially resented were the "prerogative courts" that the governor created to enforce his will. The delegates to the assembly were soon declaring that "the inhabitants are not obliged to conform themselves" to the declarations of 1672. They said the duke of York's edicts had subverted their liberties as Englishmen.

By 1681, the governor and his assembly were quarreling in the following fashion:

> It is the opinion of this House that wee are now about ours and the countreys businesse. everything is beautiful in his season. this House expects those Acts already before you should be passed and returned back to this House.

The governor and his council replied in equally condescending style.

> True wisdome would teach you better manners than to Stile Yourselves the Generall Assembly. Doubtlesse there was no wont of Ignorance and Disloyalty where this Bratt had its educac'on. Insomuch as that the generall assembly consists of the Governor, Counsells, and Deputies, ergo the Deputies no generall assembly. . . . Everything being beautiful in its season and soe we bid you farewell.

The governor's unpopularity exposed him to a misfortune that foreshadowed another perennial New Jersey dilemma: New York's arrogant pursuit of power at her small neighbor's expense. A tough, aggressive soldier named Sir Edmund Andros had become governor of New York in 1674. Like his predecessor Nicolls, Andros regarded the duke of York's giveaway as a mistake that had left New York "cooped up" between New England and New Jersey. The duke's colony was not making a profit commensurate with his royal wants, and Andros decided to squeeze some extra cash out of New Jersey. He made a distinction between the "right of soil," which he could hardly deny the duke had given to the New Jersey proprietors, and the "right of government," which he claimed still resided in New York.

Andros sent ships and soldiers to West Jersey where the Quakers meekly permitted him to collect customs on the Delaware. Philip Carteret declared that the ports of East Jersey would never pay such duties. Andros issued a proclamation warning Carteret to cease his "distinct government." Carteret replied that he and his people were ready to defend themselves to the point of shedding blood, if necessary. He was soon forced to eat those brave words. Although there were by this time (1679) 5,000 settlers in East Jersey, no one lifted a finger when Governor Andros dispatched eighty soldiers to Elizabethtown. Governor Carteret was dragged out of bed at midnight, beaten and kicked unmercifully, and hauled back to New York wearing little but his nightshirt.

Governor Andros tried to convict Governor Carteret of the crime of "persistently, riotously, and routously endeavouring to govern within the Duke of York's dominions without legal authority." To Andros's chagrin the jury acquitted Carteret and advised him to go back to New Jersey and be a nongovernor until the king decided the quarrel. In England, the duke of York took Quaker William Penn's advice and submitted the dispute to an arbitrator, a distinguished attorney who ruled against Andros and New York. Andros was recalled, and New Jersey temporarily staggered from New York's grasp. Philip Carteret never recovered from the beating and the ordeal of the trial. He died in 1682 at the age of forty-four.

In West Jersey the Quakers flourished so well that when Sir George Carteret died in 1680, twelve of the wealthiest Friends bought East Jersey from his widow. They soon saw there was no hope of turning this into a New Jerusalem—their original purpose in buying West Jersey—by limiting it to Quaker settlers. Too many Congregationalist, Baptist, Anglican, and Dutch Reformed churchgoers had already settled in East Jersey. So the Quakers went into the real estate business, selling off "twenty-fourths" to twelve other speculators, mostly Scotsmen. The new owners organized themselves into the East Jersey Board of Proprietors and began trying to attract immigrants and sell them land. They voted themselves generous dividends, as much as 17,600 acres per proprietor in a single year. They also tried to collect quitrents from the Nicolls settlers, leading to titantic legal battles and dubious court verdicts that neither side accepted. The buyers of the original Monmouth and Essex tracts insisted that even if the duke of York had voided their original purchases from Nicolls, they had still bought the land from the Indians, the real owners. The proprietors considered this revolutionary doctrine. Most of the proprietors stayed in London, which made them an external, practically foreign enemy, easier to hate.

Between 1677 and 1686 West Jersey had different problems that created the same result, social instability. Edward Byllynge, the chief proprietor, insisted on being elected governor on the strength of his property rights, but he never bothered to leave London to govern. He sent a deputy, London-born Samuel Jenings, to run things for him. Jenings sided with the locals so often they defiantly elected him governor one year, by way of thumbing their noses at Byllynge. Dr. Daniel Coxe, court physician and land speculator extraordinary, replaced Byllynge as the local ogre. Coxe bought up so many proprietary shares that the residents formed a West Jersey Council of Proprietors, consisting of forty or fifty owners of partial shares, to resist him. Jenings, a forceful politician as well as a decent man, became a controlling voice on this council, a position that assured him of a long career in the legislature. Coxe, busy with colonizing schemes from Maine to the Gulf of Mexico, never visited New Jersey either, although he too insisted on becoming governor. He finally sold his more than one million acres to the West Jersey Society, an association of London merchants who formally abandoned the policy of limiting settlement to Quakers. But the Friends remained a strong influence in West

Jersey. They permitted every adult male to vote and wrote a code of laws that displayed a remarkable concern for human rights. For instance, if an Indian were tried for a crime, six Indians had to sit on the jury with six white men.

In England, the duke of York became King James II on the death of his brother in February 1685. His colonial advisers, among them Sir Edmund Andros, advised him to get a better grip on his contentious northern colonies by consolidating them into one powerful government. In August 1688, Andros arrived in New York to announce that the "Dominion of New England" included New York and New Jersey with Boston as the capital. New Yorkers were horrified because they felt their shipping trade would be ruined by their puritan competitors. Jerseyans welcomed Andros as a deliverer from the proprietors, who meekly agreed to surrender their right of government to the king.

In April 1689, more startling news arrived from England. The man who had created New Jersey, James II, had been deposed in a bloodless revolution, dubbed "glorious" by the winners. The king's obtuse insistence on flaunting his Catholicism had alienated the aristocrats, who invited William of Orange, ruler of Holland, to invade England and restore the Protestant ascendancy. Bostonians reacted by arresting Governor Andros. New Yorkers revolted under the leadership of a demagogue named Jacob Leisler. New Jersey remained calm. Her citizens were not as pleased by the fall of James, because it meant the return of the proprietors.

In the next twelve years, tension between the proprietors and the people mounted in both East and West Jersey. The East Jersey proprietors tried to keep their foes out of the political process by denying them the vote. The proprietors maintained that only someone who had a land title from them could vote. This restriction would have guaranteed a docile electorate. But they found it hard to enforce the edict because voting was controlled by the individual towns. In 1699 the antiproprietors won control of the assembly and gave the right to vote to all "freeholders"—all those who owned property. This assembly also barred members of the governor's council and proprietary agents from its ranks. In a small body, a few of these men could tip the balance.

But the proprietors and their governors retained control of the courts. Their appointed judges repeatedly backed the proprietors in suits over contested lands, brazenly reversing the decisions of juries. The people retaliated with the only weapon they had left—mob violence. In East Jersey, courts were disrupted and prisoners freed in Newark and Elizabethtown. The climax was a brawl between Gov. Andrew Hamilton and the inhabitants of Middletown in 1701. The governor was trying a pirate named Moses Butterworth. A mob burst into the courtroom, freed the prisoner, and threw "ye Governor and ye Justices, the King's Attorney General, and ye under Sheriff, and ye clerks of ye court" in jail. In West Jersey, another mob stormed through Burlington protesting a heavy tax imposed by the proprietors to pay the court costs of defending their land claims.

Another source of social unrest was continuing aggression from New York. In 1698, New York sent forty soldiers and a customs collector to Perth Amboy to seize a ship supposedly "smuggling" a cargo into that port to avoid New York's duties. It took another trial, this one before the lord chief justice of England, to free Amboy and other New Jersey ports from the obligation to pay duties to New York.

More and more Jerseyans began to think that the only answer to the prevailing chaos was direct rule by the crown. Among the leaders of this movement was Lewis Morris, a wealthy landowner in his midtwenties. His father was an ex-Cromwellian soldier who had put the money he made as a merchant in Barbadoes into 3,500 acres in Monmouth County and some 2,000 acres north of the Harlem River (called Bronck's Land) in New York. Outspoken and ambitious, young Morris owed nothing to either party. The proprietors' ineptitude and arrogance aroused the Cromwellian side of his heritage. He persuaded the assembly to refuse to recognize the right of any proprietor-appointed governor to act without "approbation"—specific approval of his right to rule—from the crown. In an era when governmental wheels turned slowly and ships sailed even slower, this policy meant more than one proprietor-appointed governor had to sit around powerless waiting for this approbation to arrive. If the governor attempted to rule, Morris challenged him to his face. The young rebel also denounced quitrents and the proprietors' control of the surveyor general's office, which gave them the right to roam New Jersey "pinching pieces of land from honest men."

The proprietors kicked Morris off the governor's council. But they were growing weary of Jerseyan pugnacity. Pondering the riots, the aggression of New York, and mounting criticism in London, they began to see that a surrender of the right of government, if properly managed, would relieve them of enormous headaches and simultaneously protect the property they already possessed. The distinction between the "right of soil" and the "right of government," and the abortive abrogation of their governing powers by James II, contributed to this decision. In 1699, even before the disorders in New Jersey reached their height, the proprietors quietly offered to surrender their powers.

When the royal government indicated a readiness to accept the offer, the East Jersey proprietors surprised everyone by selecting Lewis Morris to come to London and negotiate for them. Morris accepted the offer because he hoped to talk the Board of Trade into appointing him the first royal governor of New Jersey.

In London, Morris abandoned the Cromwellian side of his character and sided with the proprietors. Politically he had no alternative. When he arrived he found the lords of trade discussing a proposal to divide New Jersey between Pennsylvania and New York. The aristocrats only wanted this obscure, distant colony to stop bothering them. Morris could hardly afford to start bickering with the proprietors, whom he was representing. Anyway, like too many men, Morris became an instinctive aristocrat when he smelled power. Exerting all his formidable charm and concealing his large abrasive ego, Morris talked the lords of trade into giving the proprietors almost everything they asked for in their memorial of surrender to the crown. The assembly was ordered to confirm the proprietors' "right of soil." The lords also confirmed their right to annual quitrents from ev-

eryone holding land they claimed. The assembly was forbidden
to tax the proprietors' "unimproved" lands—which meant they
could hold thousands of acres until the price rose high enough to
suit them. Only the proprietors were permitted to buy additional
land from the Indians. The proprietors controlled the governor's
council, which functioned as a combination senate, cabinet, and
supreme court. Only the proprietors could appoint surveyors,
crucial factors in land disputes. Only those with a hundred acres
of land could vote, and a man needed a thousand acres to qualify for the assembly. These property qualifications, Morris
smoothly assured the Board of Trade, would guarantee that the
"tag, rag and rascality" would be kept in their places.

To his chagrin Lewis Morris failed to get the crown's agreement on only one major point—the proprietors' right to nominate the governor. Their nominee would presumably have been
Morris. Though he politicked desperately, Morris was unable to
get much encouragement from the lords of trade on his chance
for an appointment from England's new ruler, Queen Anne. Already, the British had discovered that the governorship of a colony was a nice job to bestow on some broke and bothersome
minor aristocrat. It got him out of sight as well as out of mind.

If Morris was unhappy, the proprietors were delighted with
the deal. They soothed his disappointment by giving him the
sole right to cut timber and manufacture pitch, resin, and tur-
pentine on a swatch of well-forested land between the Shrewsbury and Manasquan rivers. The proprietors might not have
been so generous to their spokesman if they could have foreseen
the dangers in his failure to win control of the governorship.

The year was 1702. Partly because of her instability, partly
because of a lack of a major port, New Jersey's population
grew slowly. New York with 20,000 and Pennsylvania with
15,000 subjects had already outdistanced her. New Jersey had a
population of about 10,000—7,500 in the east and 2,500 in the
west. Almost everyone was a farmer, most living on about 50 to
150 acres of land. There was also a number of large proprietary
estates in the thousand-acre range, but nothing in New Jersey
compared to the huge manors of the Hudson River lords in New
York. The Hardenbergh tract, south of Albany, for instance,

was larger than the entire colony of Connecticut. More than one New Yorker worried about the power these huge estates gave their owners. "What man will be such a fool," wrote one New York official, lamenting the development, "as to become a base tenant to Mr. Delius, Colonel Schuyler, Mr. Livingston . . . when, for crossing Hudson's river that man can for a song purchase a good freehold in the Jersey's?"

In East Jersey there were nine well-established towns, six of them principally inhabited by emigrants from New England; one, Bergen, predominantly Dutch; and two others, Perth Amboy and Freehold, mostly Scottish. In West Jersey, towns were smaller and fewer and Quakers were still dominant, except for an active group of Anglicans in Burlington.

The Anglicans were led by John Keith, a former Quaker and one of the first members of the Society for the Propagation of the Gospel in Foreign Parts to reach America. He brought with him another Anglican priest, John Talbot, who became the minister of Saint Mary's Church in Burlington and joined Keith in trying to change Quakers into Anglicans. Talbot wrote home urging the appointment of a bishop and even bought a house large enough to accommodate one, obviously hoping he would be the first to wield the shepherd's crook. This campaign was an obvious step toward legally establishing the Anglican church in New Jersey, an idea that aroused intense antagonism, not only among New Jersey's Quakers, but among the Congregationalists, Presbyterians, and Baptists as well. In England, dissenters from the established Anglican religion had lost the right to vote and other privileges.

Diversity slowly but steadily became the rule in New Jersey religious life as the sects abandoned the idea of creating a New England-like purity and homogeneity in the towns where they were dominant. Newark, settled by rigorous Congregationalists from Connecticut, at first refused to let visitors stay in town overnight without a permit. By the time the century turned, the "watchmen of the Lord" were permitting people to settle in the town without even joining the church. In town after town, the requirement that each freeholder must contribute to the support of the dominant church slowly lapsed.

After religion, politics was the chief preoccupation of the average Jerseyman in 1702. Each town already had a vigorous tradition of self-government. Although the right to vote was somewhat restricted by property qualifications, almost every adult male was able to participate in town meetings and did so. The close connection between politics and economics was the chief reason. Towns disposed of surplus lands at these meetings, and they also elected a representative to the assembly, where the battles with the proprietors were chiefly waged.

In thirty-eight years of proprietary government, Jerseymen had had their political consciousness raised by their struggle to protect their rights and property. They soon discovered that the change to royal government only meant more of the same harsh lessons in power politics.

2

The Art of Taming Governors

*A*FTER thirty years of turmoil, climaxed by the upheavals of 1700–1701 that everyone in New Jersey called "the Revolution," until the term was co-opted by a much bigger uproar, the first royal governor was welcomed as a potential savior. He turned out to have a closer resemblance to the biblical character who wrecked the Garden of Eden. Like Lucifer, Edward Hyde, lord Cornbury, had a fondness for startling changes of costume. He was a forty-one-year-old transvestite who enjoyed prancing about in copies of gowns worn by his cousin, Queen Anne. Bankrupt, he came to the New World for only one reason—to renew his personal exchequer. To complicate matters even more, the queen had made him governor of New Jersey as an afterthought. He had already arrived in America as governor of New York when Anne decided to add New Jersey to his domain.

In May 1703, only a few weeks after the news of Cornbury's appointment reached New Jersey, the struggle for his favor began. A representative of the proprietors hustled from Perth Amboy to visit the governor in New York and make sure that he obeyed the royal instructions that came with his commission. These orders numbered 103 and contained the substance of the deal the proprietors had made with the crown. To guarantee Cornbury's co-operation, his visitor left a hundred pounds in his house—the first documented bribe in New Jersey's political his-

21

tory. Several weeks later another hundred pounds was delivered—substantial sums in 1703, when the pound was worth at least a hundred 1976 dollars.

Cornbury began playing the game the proprietors' way. The sheriff was the crucial man in the voting process, and Cornbury appointed the sheriffs. In East Jersey on election day, when the sheriff showed up to open the polls, he saw several hundred determined antiproprietary voters and only a handful of proprietary men. He suddenly found fault with the "accommodation"—the house where the voting was to take place—and left the voters standing outside all day in bitter weather. At the end of the day, only forty-two proprietary voters led by Lewis Morris had appeared, and more than 300 antis were still very visible. But the sheriff had the power to "make the choice upon the view"—instead of letting everyone vote. This English idea was intended to save time and money when one side's voters clearly outnumbered their opponents. So the sheriff made his choice. He "viewed" the proprietors' candidate as the winner. The antis furiously protested to the assembly, but they were ignored.

New York had voted Cornbury a hefty salary for seven years. He wanted a similar deal from New Jersey. When the proprietary assembly balked, Cornbury switched sides. He was also impressed by some coin of the realm delivered to him by the antis. Alarmed at rumors that Cornbury had been extravagantly bribed by the proprietors, the leaders of the antis roamed New Jersey collecting what was called the "blind tax." People were told to pay up for "the good of the country" and were promised the governor's support. No one knows how much was collected or whether the collectors took a cut. But a nice piece of cash—as much as 1,500 pounds in some versions of the story— was rushed to New York and left in the hands of a Cornbury henchman. In 1704 Cornbury disqualified three Quakers elected from West Jersey and gave his new friends a majority in the assembly.

They rewarded him by voting 2,000 pounds a year for two years to support the government. Cornbury responded by persuading the crown to liberalize the voting laws. Once more the franchise was extended to all freeholders, instead of a 100-acre-owning elite.

Cornbury gave the antiproprietors control of the colony's road building—a power they used to settle political scores. According to Lewis Morris, they "pull'd down their enemies' inclosures, laid waies through their orchards, gardens and improvements." They got even with Morris, who when the proprietors were riding high had once fenced in the road between Middletown and Freehold. The antis built a bridge across his millpond, forcing him to demolish a dam and mills on which he had spent a hundred pounds. To get even with the pacifist Quakers, who were the supporters of the proprietary party in West Jersey, the new majority passed a militia bill that required every man to own a gun, muster four times a year, and pay a one-pound fine if he failed to turn out.

Watching these antics, with his two-year support bill in his pocket, Cornbury decided to ignore both parties and build his own political machine. He handed out jobs to a collection of unsavory characters who became known as the "Cornbury ring." Many of them, like Roger Mompesson, had dual jobs in New York—in Mompesson's case he was chief justice of both colonies. Several of Cornbury's appointees were land speculators eager for a quick killing, and at least one, Peter Sonmans, was an embezzler. With the province secretary on their team and ready to certify every deal, they managed to grab a half-million acres, most of it from the proprietors. They sanctified these machinations by taking a "High Church" or "Tory" line toward dissenters, particularly the Quakers. In this they reflected events in England, where conservatives were trying to regain control of the government and were making extreme claims on behalf of the established church—largely as a device to increase their power. In New Jersey the Cornbury men were mindlessly supported by the Anglicans in Burlington. Sixty years later, the Anglicans would regret the reputation for power-hungry greed that became attached to them in this struggle.

By 1707, almost everyone in New Jersey—and in New York, for that matter—was desperate to get rid of Cornbury. Lewis Morris and the proprietors hated him most, however, and they organized for a mighty political effort, which won them control of the New Jersey Assembly in spite of the liberalized voting law. Undaunted, Cornbury coolly demanded support for the next twenty-one years. The assembly replied by investigating the blind tax. Lewis Morris turned Cromwellian again and decided that royal instructions to governors, which Cornbury repeatedly cited to get his way, had no validity unless Americans could send representatives to Parliament. Cornbury replied by kicking him off the council.

The assembly, under Morris's behind-the-scenes direction, drew up a list of grievances and descended upon Lord Cornbury. In spite of glares and maledictions from the governor, the assembly speaker, Samuel Jenings of Burlington, read every word of the document. With twenty-five years of experience in New Jersey's political wars, Jenings was not going to let a pipsqueak like Cornbury intimidate him. At times, Jenings stopped his account, took off his hat (a sign of contempt), sat down with his hands on his hips, and stared Cornbury in the face, then returned to his diatribe, which listed all of Cornbury's faults in acerbic detail. "So odious an insult, so Detestable a Pride has never before been offer'd to the Person of a Governour," huffed Cornbury's council.[1]

On that spring morning, the American Revolution was sixty-nine years away. But a spirit of independence was already very visible in New Jersey. Morris shipped scathing reports of Cornbury's sins to the influential friends he had made in London and the "detestable magot" was recalled in 1708. But he left his ring of Anglican friends entrenched in the offices of government. John Lovelace, the new governor, was a do-nothing cipher who died eighteen months after taking office, leaving one of Cornbury's henchmen, Richard Ingoldsby, in charge as lieutenant governor. In the year before he was replaced, he more than matched Cornbury's corruption record. He gave licenses to his friends for huge land purchases from the Indians and handed out 196 jobs. One of his friends got eleven offices and another, nine.

Royal government was clearly no panacea. It was not much better than proprietary government, when the power was used to

---

1. Donald L. Kemmerer, *Faith in Freedom: The Struggle for Self Government in Colonial New Jersey, 1703–1776* (Princeton: Princeton University Press, 1940), p. 70.

satisfy the greed of the few at the expense of the many. But the next governor of New Jersey demonstrated the danger of condemning any system of government in terms that are too sweeping. Robert Hunter was a good artistocrat, a soldier who had served with the great English general Marlborough in the European wars against King Louis XIV of France. Hunter was also an urbane, cultivated man, who numbered among his friends two of the best English writers of the day, Jonathan Swift and Joseph Addison. The possessor of a modest fortune, Hunter was free from Cornbury's venality. But this did not mean that New Jersey was free from turmoil.

Members of the Cornbury or Anglican Ring remained in positions of power, particularly on the governor's council. The Scottish East Jersey proprietors and the West Jersey Quakers controlled the assembly. The result was a political stalemate. The Anglicans reiterated their call for a bishop and urged the crown to disfranchise Quakers for their refusal to take oaths and serve in the militia. They used their control of the council to veto acts of the assembly that, in accordance with the original crown instructions, would permit Quakers to hold office and sit on juries by making a simple affirmation of their loyalty. The Ring also resisted bills that attempted to control their fraudulent land grabs.

To complicate matters, many of the men who backed Hunter at home were swept out of office by a shift to the High Church Tories. Hunter did not dare move against the Ring. But he coolly declined to side with them. Hunter let the assembly display some of the independence it had learned under Cornbury. Instead of voting a lump sum for the expenses of the province and giving it to the governor to dole out as he pleased, each official's salary was stipulated by an assembly resolution and the amount entered in the house journal. Daniel Coxe, Jr., son of the West Jersey speculator and a power in the Ring, huffed that there was a plot to make the governor and other officers "tools of the Assembly." But Hunter mildly remarked that the assembly had to be "humored."

Hunter waited and listened to various advisers, then made a difficult decision. He took Lewis Morris's advice and formed an alliance with the East Jersey proprietors. In the spring of 1711, the governor struck hard at the Ring. He dismissed Coxe and three other Ring members from his council for blocking legislation. They retaliated with a ferocious campaign against him in London, in the assembly, and in the village streets and country lanes of West Jersey. Daniel Coxe, Jr., was a gifted politician. He rode about the colony telling people not to pay their taxes. Hunter retaliated by calling his enemies "Jacobites"—supporters of the exiled James II. He said the Reverend John Talbot, the Anglican priest at Burlington, had formed them into a church.

Hunter's decision to side with the East Jersey proprietors was not entirely admirable. They were as eager to become the land monopolists of New Jersey as the Anglican Ring. But the governor had to back some organized group in the assembly if he hoped to pass any legislation. It was by no means the last time that Jerseyans were to learn the relevance of the adage that politics is the art of the possible.

Over the next five years, Hunter relentlessly cut away the members of the Anglican Ring until he had a council and a chief justice who were in harmony with him. The assembly began passing important laws, forbidding judges to accept gifts or high fees, banning malicious prosecutions, limiting the length of lawsuits. One can see proprietary influence in some laws, such as one limiting jurors to those who were worth 100 pounds. This kept poor men off juries, which played a large role in deciding land disputes. On the other hand, another law ordered the records of land transactions to be maintained in each county in books that were open to public inspection. This last law particularly enraged the Anglican Ring. They had fought it for a decade.

Under the leadership of Daniel Coxe, Jr., the Anglicans turned their High Church conclave in Burlington into a political machine. They used Hunter's alliance with the proprietors to corral voters among the Nicolls patentees. Coxe had a ready-made core of supporters among men who had bought land from him or his father and still owed him money. He was also free with a "large dram bottle." Whiskey was already an active ingredient in American elections, as it was in England.

The proprietors were no paragons of electoral purity. In 1710 the two proprietary candidates in Middlesex were trailing badly at the end of the first day's poll. The sheriff suspended the election for three days to give the proprietors a chance to round up some voters. When the poll was reopened and the tally started to go against the proprietors' men again, the sheriff began summoning for jury duty each man who called out his vote for the antis. This tactic frightened away a lot of voters and the proprietor's candidates finally edged ahead. The sheriff then "shut up the Pole [poll] so Suddenly & abruptly that the very Clarks [*sic*] at the Table knew not of it but lost their votes." [2] The assembly rejected forty-one irate petitioners who tried to have the election set aside.

Another favorite proprietary trick was "colonizing." The proprietors imported dozens of men from distant counties to Perth Amboy on election day and deeded each a sliver of land, making them all freeholders. Sheriffs also had the power to "move the pole" around the countryside at will, an easy way to influence an election. A biased sheriff simply moved the poll as far away as possible from a section that was not supporting his candidate. In one Burlington election, the sheriff moved it to the very edge of the county.

To Hunter's dismay, Coxe won control of the assembly in 1715. Hunter dissolved it and ordered another election. Coxe won again. Once more the governor dissolved the assembly without letting it meet. Coxe won the next election and insisted that the assembly convene in Burlington. Hunter refused. He had picked up rumors that the Anglicans were planning an armed insurrection and he did not intend to become a victim.

Coxe overreached himself. To cripple the assembly, he ordered his party to stay home. Hunter again showed how tough he could be. He had the sergeant at arms arrest thirteen assemblymen, enough for a quorum. They voted that Coxe, who had been elected speaker, had committed a "Breach of Trust" and expelled him. Eight other members were expelled for similar reasons. Hunter regained control of the assembly and the

---

2. Richard C. McCormick, *The History of Voting in New Jersey* (New Brunswick, N.J.: Rutgers University Press, 1953), p. 48.

Anglican machine, in disarray as rumors of their "wicked design" (the armed revolt) circulated through the colony, collapsed.

Robert Hunter sailed home in 1719, a tired man. His political battles in New York had been as strenuous as those in New Jersey. In London he told the government that there was a definite trend toward greater and greater independence in the colonial legislatures. "Ye colonies were infants sucking their mother's breasts," he warned. "But [they] would weane themselves when they came of age." He recommended that the crown pay the governor's salary, freeing him from dependence on the assembly. The advice was ignored.

This inaction was to prove unfortunate for the British Empire, but fortunate for the inhabitants of New Jersey and other American colonies. Already the New Jersey assembly had perceived that the people's representatives could limit, if not control, the governor's power by pulling tight on the purse strings. This maneuver worked particularly well with the next several governors of New Jersey because they were either bankrupt or genteelly impoverished and in their hunger for cash were ready to agree to almost anything.

Hunter's successor, William Burnet, the son of a famous bishop, lost his modest fortune when the London stock market took a historic nose dive in 1720. The assembly used the leverage Burnet's poverty gave them to solve a vexing New Jersey problem—the shortage of money. Without a major port, New Jersey did most of its export and import business through New York and Philadelphia. This meant that New Jersey's cash supply was constantly draining off to these two cities. Without ready cash it was hard to buy or sell land or do any other kind of business. The American colonies had been short of cash from their foundation because they depended on British specie, supplemented by Spanish and French coins from the West Indies. The supply was always inadequate because, like developing countries today, the colonies owed more than they earned. Experiments in paper money in some colonies, like South Carolina, had been halted because reckless overprinting led to depreciation and protests to Parliament from influential London merchants, who refused to accept the make-believe money as legal tender.

Beginning in 1709, New Jersey had tried to solve this problem by issuing paper money called "bills of credit." These were offered to individuals in amounts up to 100 pounds; the borrowers promised to repay them within a stated period of time. According to one Jerseyman, they were only borrowing from themselves. At the end of the loan period, the assembly was supposed to call in the bills and "sink" them. In the meantime they passed from hand to hand as currency and were acceptable in New York and Philadelphia. Unfortunately, retiring the bills was not as popular as issuing them, and the assembly repeatedly dragged its feet on making the borrowers pay up. Instead the assembly issued new bills to help pay off the old ones.

Governor Hunter had warned that this practice could lead to trouble. The Jerseyan answer was not a reduction in paper money but a demand for more. Under Governor Burnet the assembly backed the money with something called a land bank, or loan office. Each bill of credit was to be secured by a mortgage on the borrower's property for twice its value. The interest rate on these bills of credit was 5 percent—considerably lower than the going rate of 8 percent on ordinary loans. The borrowers had twelve years to repay. With these liberal provisions, the assembly foresaw no difficulty in disposing of 40,000 pounds of these new bills of credit. They could be used to retire 4,000 pounds in outstanding bills that constituted a debt the province owed itself. But would the governor approve the bill?

Burnet had begun his tour of duty with a high handed attempt to tighten the voting laws. The assembly had resisted him by refusing to honor his request for a bill paying his salary for five years. With the loan office bill at stake, the assembly suddenly breathed sweetness and light on the cash-hungry governor. They voted him support for five years, raised the salaries of other provincial officers, and gave Burnet an extra 1,000 pounds for "incidentals." Burnet not only signed the paper money bill; he also wrote a strong letter to the London government, persuading them to approve it.

In the original act, the assembly had promised to use the interest payments to retire bills of credit as fast as possible. Two years later, in 1725, they reversed themselves and began using the interest to pay the expenses of the government. Burnet, softened by another 500 pounds for still more incidentals, approved this policy, too, and New Jersey cruised into something approximating a financial golden age. The already-low taxes were cut almost in half, land taxes declining from ten pounds per hundred acres to five, and a per capita tax on all freemen from six shillings to four shillings a year. New Jersey paper money did not depreciate as the crown feared, and an increase in taxes became as rare in New Jersey as an earthquake—rarer, in fact: there were at least four significant quakes in the colony between 1700 and 1776. Whenever money grew tight as bills of credit were retired, the assembly voted a new issue, which enabled cash-short debtors to pay their old debts. The day of reckoning foreseen by Robert Hunter seemed subject to indefinite postponement.

In 1725, with the proprietors and their foes roughly equal in the assembly, the two parties showed a commendable interest in cleaning up the colony's voting practices. A new law stripped the sheriff of his power to "make the choice upon the view." It also forbade him to move the poll without the candidates' agreement and made the sheriff liable to a suit for as much as 300 pounds in damages if he misbehaved. Colonizing was restricted by requiring from a challenged voter a formal oath that he had been a legal resident of the town or country for a full year. Jerseyans obviously did not like electoral corruption any more than they liked the rioting and anarchy of the closing years of the proprietors' rule or the executive corruption of a crown governor. They wanted a government that was an honest expression of the popular will.

Other things troubled the colony. Above all New Jersey chafed at the idea of sharing its governor with New York. The larger colony, with its booming port, its lucrative fur trade, its border with French-held Canada, inevitably got most of the governor's attention. The New Jersey Assembly began petitioning the crown for a separate governor in 1728. It was ignored until 1732, when a hustler named William Cosby wangled the joint

New York–New Jersey governorship from the somnolent Board of Trade. Cosby arrived with a bad reputation from a try at governing Malta. He told the New Jersey Assembly he would spend half his time in the colony. The delighted assembly voted him support for five years and a bonus of 200 pounds. Cosby left for New York, and New Jersey only saw him once in the next four years.

Two prominent Jerseyans, Lewis Morris and James Alexander, the latter a Scotsman who had become a power in the East Jersey Board of Proprietors, became antagonists of Cosby in a dispute that involved money and power in New York. For ruling against him in a court case, Cosby removed Morris as chief justice of New York. Cosby borrowed a large sum of money from Alexander and refused to repay it. The two Jerseyans launched a ferocious newspaper attack on Cosby, literally annihilating the governor's already-shaky reputation. When Cosby attempted to prosecute the printer of the verbal vitriol, John Peter Zenger, for seditious libel, the jury refused to bring in a directed verdict of guilty. With Cosby reeling from this defeat, Lewis Morris decided to go to England and administer the coup de grâce. Tension between the governor and his chief enemy ran high. When Cosby learned that Morris was going to wage war on his home front, the governor sent soldiers to New Jersey to arrest him. The wily Morris eluded them and reached a London-bound ship off the coast of Shrewsbury. He was escorted to it by "a Convey of armed boats"—a good indication of what Jerseymen thought of Cosby.

Arriving in London early in 1735, Morris soon learned how little interest the great lords had in a "plantation governor, or all of them put together." But the duke of Newcastle, who ran the government's patronage machine, found it hard to ignore the abrasive Morris. At one point, exasperated by Morris's persistence, the duke wanted to know what would shut him up. The governorship of New Jersey, he was told. Meanwhile, pleas from Jerseymen for a separate governor continued to arrive by every ship. When Cosby died unexpectedly in 1736, Morris gave up and departed from the "noisy, stinking and very expensive town, London." But the duke of Newcastle did not forget him. After eighteen months of lackadaisically shuffling the job among minor bureaucrats, none of whom wanted it, in 1738 the duke appointed Lewis Morris the first separate royal governor of New Jersey.

3

An Explosive Melting Pot

A T last, Jerseymen exulted, when they heard the news of Morris's appointment. After so many decades of coping with corrupt outsiders sent by the proprietors or the crown, we have one of our own to govern us. It was Lewis Morris who had freed them from the proprietors. It was Lewis Morris who had played a powerful role in freeing them from Governors Cornbury and Cosby. Justice and peace were at last arriving in New Jersey. Surely one of their own would govern them with moderation, restraining the avaricious lawyer, the land-greedy proprietary board member. With his defiant remarks about royal instructions and parliamentary representation, Morris had repeatedly demonstrated his abhorrence of overweening authority, of using power for personal profit.

Within a month, the owners of these soaring hopes were suffering from acute disappointment. Lewis Morris swiftly demonstrated that Jerseymen were no more immune to the corruption and arrogance of power than anyone else. He began brawling with the assembly over the crown's prerogatives, which were now his prerogatives. He said that he was not satisfied with his salary of 1,000 pounds, almost twice what recent governors had received, and insisted on 500 pounds for incidentals connected with his trip to London. He appointed his son, Robert Hunter Morris, chief justice of the colony. Next the governor astonished the assembly by refusing to approve a 40,000-pound

issue of bills of credit, even though the members sweetened it
with a promise of 500 pounds for that familiar persuader, "incidentals." He had the gall to lecture the assembly on trying to
bribe him. He then made the quarrel public by flooding New
Jersey with lengthy extracts from the minutes of the assembly
session. The assembly fought back with a nasty pamphlet entitled, "The Note-maker Noted."

Morris also opposed the assembly's attempt to regulate the
high fees charged by crown officials, particularly judges. The
cost of a lawsuit often made it prohibitive for a poor man to
defend himself when the board of proprietors claimed his land.
With his son as chief justice, Morris lost interest in changing the
system. The assembly insisted they had a right to set these fees
at reasonable levels. The argument was a political disaster for
Morris. Almost all his supporters were beaten in the next election, and he was reduced to the feeble gesture of warning London that the assembly was "fond of the example of the Parliament of 1641"—the Puritan Parliament whose defiance of
Charles I had led to the English civil war and Oliver Cromwell.
Morris's control of the governor's council created another legislative stalemate that practically brought the wheels of government to a dead stop. Morris took to calling the assemblymen
"idiots" in public. They responded by halving the salary of his
son, the chief justice.

Less amusing was the revival of the explosive quarrel between the proprietors and the middle-class descendants of the
Nicolls purchasers, now called the Elizabethtown Associates.
This conflict had been sputtering for the better part of fifteen
years with Morris, as a power among both the East and West
Jersey proprietors, one of the chief antagonists. Depending on
who had won the most recent court test, the two parties alter-
nated between offense and defense.

The real battle was between the so-called "clinker lot right
men" and the proprietors. "Clinker" meant crafty fellow, and
the proprietors maintained that this was a good description of
the way they claimed their land. In court they talked vaguely of
Indian titles. One group swore that its title had been destroyed
when the house of the man who was minding it had burned

down. Complicating matters was the transformation of the Elizabethtown Associates into a land company in its own right. Flourishing Indian titles, by 1730 they were selling real estate as far away as Somerset County. Hundreds of squatters without even a pretense to an Indian title occupied land on a 15,000-acre tract claimed by the West Jersey proprietors in Hunterdon County. Before he became governor, Morris had been president of the West Jersey Council of Proprietors, and had launched a highly effective legal campaign that ejected hundreds of families from this land and threatened similar treatment to thousands more.

Hoping to further demoralize their opponents, the East Jersey proprietors announced they were going to try to collect some 10,000 pounds in back quitrents. A showdown came when allies of the Elizabethtown Associates began cutting valuable timber on proprietary land in Somerset County and selling it in New York. The proprietors filed a suit in the court of chancery where Governor Morris would be the presiding judge. The associates saw the handwriting on the wall and tried an appeal to the king that got two of them a free trip to London, but otherwise was a waste of time. As the suit was on the brink of decision Lewis Morris died. He was succeeded by the president of his council, another leading proprietor. When the associates failed to reply to the suit, the proprietors started ejecting more farmers and arresting anyone caught cutting timber on proprietary land.

A Newark mob freed the arrested men. When the leaders of the mob were arrested, a bigger mob freed them after an eye-ball-to-eyeball confrontation with some local militia. The rioting soon spread into Somerset and Hunterdon counties. Samuel Nevill, a proprietor and former speaker of the assembly who had made a speech against the rioters, was threatened with assassination. By the spring of 1747, the rioters were on the offensive, demonstrating their own brand of the arrogance of power. The clinker men used threats and midnight raids to drive people off land they coveted. Anyone who bought land from the proprietors was considered fair game for violent tactics. The assembly, dominated by antiproprietors, declined to vote enough money to support an adequate militia—the only police force

outside of the county sheriffs and their deputies the colony possessed. Chief Justice Robert Hunter Morris called for British
troops to restore order.

The governor who replaced Lewis Morris, Massachusetts-
born Jonathan Belcher, was another crown servant in desperate
need of cash. He had come to New Jersey after an acrimonious
tour of duty in his native colony, thinking of his new job as
early retirement. He tried going along with the assembly to get
his salary, but his co-operation only encouraged the rioters.
Chief Justice Morris departed for London to plead the proprietors' case. He did it so well that the home government
frequently gave the best jobs to people he recommended, over-
ruling the mortified governor. Morris also managed to kill
paper-money bills passed by the assembly and approved by the
governor.

Meanwhile, the rioters grew bolder. Their ringleader, Amos
Roberts, was "reverenced as much as if he had been a king,"
according to one somewhat biased commentator. In the assembly, John Low, another rioter, dominated the discussions,
leaving Governor Belcher practically helpless. For a while,
Amos Roberts looked as if he were setting up an independent
state. He had his own courts, a militia army with elected officers, and tax collectors and assessors. When Belcher attempted
to disarm them by offering a pardon to anyone who came forward, confessed to the crime of rioting, and promised to remain
peaceful henceforth, only twenty-three men took advantage of
it. Class overtones were clearly involved in the uproar. The
rioters were referred to as "capmen and mobmen" and the proprietors as "wigmen and gentlemen."

The home government, spurred by Robert Hunter Morris, ordered Belcher to crack down on the rioters or prepare to lose his
job. The Board of Trade seriously considered sending a new
governor backed by a regiment of regulars. News of this determination chastened the rioters and their supporters in the assembly. Meanwhile the proprietary boards lost interest in trying
to win their war with the common man and adopted a policy of
getting rid of their remaining land as profitably and expedi-
tiously as possible. Rioters who applied to the assembly for a

pardon were let off with a slap on the wrist, once they posted bonds to guarantee their future good behavior. Many of the leading rioters left the colony when their support melted away.

In spite of this acrimony, New Jersey prospered and grew. By 1760, the population had passed the hundred-thousand mark. Religious and ethnic diversity remained a dominant characteristic of the colony, even increasing with the arrival of large numbers of Germans in Hunterdon County. Farming and its natural corollary, livestock breeding, remained the chief occupations. There were no fewer than 144,000 sheep and at least as many hogs. New Jersey ham rivaled that of Virginia, in the opinion of some diners. Horse breeding was prominent enough to inspire Jerseymen to place a nag's head on the crest of the great seal adopted in 1776. Notable sires were constantly advertised in the papers, and Jersey racing stock, particularly from Monmouth County, was famous. As farmers, Jerseyans made money from timber, flax, and hemp, but most of their cash came from grains—wheat, corn, rye, oats, and barley sold in New York and Philadelphia for shipment to Europe.

As early as 1739, Casper Wistar began making bottles and other kinds of glassware in Salem County, with the assistance of four Dutch glassblowers. In the wooded northern hills, the iron industry boomed, and it was soon flourishing in the south, when large deposits of bog iron were discovered in Burlington County. Only the very rich could venture into this business. It took 20,000 acres of woodland to produce enough charcoal to keep a single blast furnace going.

Also emerging was a rudimentary transportation industry, which took advantage of New Jersey's pivotal position between the two most dynamic American cities, New York and Philadelphia. Bringing the products of the burgeoning iron industry, as well as cash from crops, to these two markets made the development of a road system one of New Jersey's first priorities. Jersey Wagons, one of the first indigenous vehicles, emerged in the 1730s. They were huge, with enormous wheels and cloth-covered tops. Teams of four to six horses were needed to keep them going.

New Jersey also got into the business of transporting people.

The Jersey Wagon, somewhat reduced in size, became the stage wagon. As early as 1733 an advertisement in a Philadelphia newspaper announced that Solomon Smith and James Moon were running two stage wagons between Burlington and Perth Amboy. Their schedule was once a week "or offt'er if . . . business presents." This was the first regular public transportation service in American history. Rivals soon appeared on alternate routes. By 1738 other wagons were running between Trenton and New Brunswick. In 1740 a third route ran from South Amboy to Bordentown on the Delaware. At each end, boats brought the traveler to his destination in New York or Philadelphia.

By 1765 New Jersey probably had more roads than any other colony in British America. Along them taverns multiplied amazingly. The iron industry also added to the number of these hostelries. Each forge was a miniature industrial village, usually in a hitherto-unsettled part of the country in order to provide access to needed timber. A tavern, which, incidentally, was the correct legal term and was used in granting licenses, was frequently little more than a private house, which explains why Jerseymen usually spoke of them as "houses." But "well-located" taverns soon became substantial affairs with large ballrooms, perhaps a dozen bedrooms, resident fiddlers for dancing, and innkeepers who were usually among the wealthiest and most influential men in the community.

At Princeton was the Hudibras; in Elizabethtown, the Rose and Crown, the Wheat Sheaf, and the Unicorn; in Perth Amboy, the Black Horse; in New Brunswick, the White Hart and the Indian Queen; on the road to Cooper's Ferry on the Delaware, the Death of the Fox. These taverns served a startling variety of liquors with equally picturesque names. Stonewall was a potent mixture of rum and hard cider. Scotchem consisted of applejack, boiling water, and a good dash of ground mustard. Stewed Quaker consisted of cider with some cider oil in it and a hot roasted apple floating on top. Most devastating of all was rum-fustian, which had no rum in it. The word *rum* was also an adjective meaning "very strong." Rumfustian consisted of a bottle of wine or sherry, a quart of strong beer, half a pint of gin, the yolks of a dozen eggs, nutmeg, orange peels, sugar, and spices.

With this kind of stuff going down, it was hardly surprising to hear some Jerseymen declaiming against the colony's taverns. In 1754, the grand jury of Hunterdon County issued a furious blast, calling them "public receptacles and seminaries of vice, irreligion and profaneness." Jerseyans apparently kept on drinking. By 1784 there were 443 taverns in the towns and along the main roads and byroads. This was roughly one tavern for every hundred and seventy male inhabitants in New Jersey. The taverns were, of course, also used by the growing number of travelers passing through New Jersey.

In the taverns, Jerseyans thrashed out their ethnic, political, and religious differences. Taverns were the one social institution where everyone was welcome. They played a part in fostering an atmosphere of social equality that was one of New Jersey's most striking characteristics. A young Presbyterian minister, Philip Fithian, who spent a year as a tutor to the children of a wealthy family in Virginia, found the Old Dominion's aristocratic society in sharp contrast with his native state. With evident pride he recalled how "gentlemen in the first rank of dignity and quality" associated freely with "farmers and mechanics" in New Jersey. Fithian was proud of the way Jerseymen considered "the laborious part of men"—those who worked with their hands—"the strength and honor of the colony."

The young minister put his finger on the reason for this equality. "The levil which is admired in New Jersey government, among people of every rank, arises, no doubt from the very great division of the lands in that province & consequently from the near approach of an equality of wealth amongst the inhabitants." [1] As early as 1748, New Jersey had acquired this essentially middle-class style. New England–born Governor Belcher

---

1. Philip Vickers Fithian, *Journal and Letters,* edited with an introduction by Hunter Dickinson Parish (Charlottesville, Va.: University Press of Virginia, 1968), p. 160.

said the colony was "the best country I have seen for midling fortunes, and for people who have to live by the sweat of their brows."

New Jersey also had more than its share of rich men. Its proprietary heritage made wealth inevitable. In most northern colonies, about 10 percent of the population were worth 2,000 pounds or more. In New Jersey the figure was 14 percent, and this wealthy elite owned more than a third of the land. William Alexander, son of James Alexander, long a power in the East Jersey Board of Proprietors, had a splendid estate at Basking Ridge and traveled in an opulent coach ornamented with the coat of arms of the lords of Stirling, whose title he claimed. Peter Kemble of New Brunswick imitated the New York manor lords, such as the Schuylers and Van Cortlands, to whom he was related. Kemble had a large farm near New Brunswick and outlying properties leased to tenants. Arent Schuyler of Bergen County needed fifty field hands to work his estate.

There were poor people in New Jersey, notably in the south along the fringe of the pine barrens and on the banks of the Delaware. There were growing numbers of landless agricultural laborers. "Considerably over half" of the men in Burlington County owned no land. Elsewhere about 30 percent of the white adult males were landless. There were also thousands of servants leading bleak restricted lives. Some were white—signers of "indentures" that bound them to work for nine or ten years to pay for their passage across the Atlantic. Some were black. New Jersey had about 8,000 Negro slaves by 1760. Most were field hands. Large landowners such as Peter Kemble and Arent Schuyler depended on them almost exclusively. But slaveholding was common among a wide range of middle-class farmers, particularly in Bergen County.

In Mount Holly, Quaker John Woolman, meditating on the lifetime of servitude to which slaves were condemned, found their fate revolting to his conscience and began the antislavery movement in America. In 1754 he published a pamphlet, *Some Considerations on the Keeping of Negroes: Recommended to the Professors of Christianity*. Woolman anticipated Thomas Jefferson's observation that slavery was a burden for both the slave and the owner. He was even more prophetic in his warning that "the ideas of Negroes and slaves" were becoming "interwoven in the [American] mind." [2] In the years before the Revolution, Jersey Quakers presented a number of petitions to the legislature asking for new laws prohibiting the importation of slaves and permitting them to be freed without a financial penalty. The New Jersey code was as harsh as that of Virginia on this point. Anyone freeing a slave had to post a bond of 200 pounds to guarantee the government that he would not become a public charge.

Along with its problems and complications, New Jersey by 1760 had also acquired another attribute, summed up in its nickname, "the Garden Colony." The superbly cultivated farms in the Raritan and Hackensack valleys drew repeated praise from travelers who often remarked that the beauty of the New Jersey countryside equalled England's rural districts. People marvelled at the richness of New Jersey soil, which produced corn eight feet high and peaches in such abundance that the ground of many orchards was covered with them. Another attraction was the falls of the Passaic, which drew numerous visitors from New York. These visitors frequently remarked on the hospitality they received on their journey. Jerseymen, wrote one English traveler, were typical country gentlemen, good-natured and generous.

Behind this peaceful prosperous facade lay a potentially serious problem. Since 1751 the London government had disallowed most of the paper-money bills the assembly had passed, causing painful deflations in the New Jersey economy. Only the French and Indian War persuaded the home government to relent and permit the assembly to issue hundreds of thousands of pounds of paper money to finance New Jersey's part in the conflict. This flood of currency and the presence of a large British army and fleet in America drove up the price of everything, creating an unreal prosperity in New Jersey and in other colonies.

---

2. John E. Pomfret, *Colonial New Jersey* (New York: Charles Scribner's Sons, 1973), p. 213.

Compared with the blows inflicted on the frontiers of New York, Pennsylvania, Virginia, and other colonies, the war scarcely touched New Jersey. A few dozen people in the northern mountains were killed by marauding Indians, but a system of forts and patrols put a stop to these raids. About a thousand volunteers, the "Jersey Blues," did some minor fighting. But Jerseyans, like most colonials, let the British regulars do the real fighting. They exulted in the capture of Quebec in 1759 and in succeeding victories that swept the French off the American continent. Along with almost everyone else, Jerseyans were proud to be part of the triumphant British Empire. Within its protected trading area, they saw no reason why their prosperity would not continue to grow.

Of course, they were still dependent on distant men of power in London for permission to deal with their economic problems. Only London could create the easy money that allowed poor men to pay their debts and enjoy a few of life's pleasures. These same faceless lords, acting in the name of an equally unknown king, selected their governors. But after sixty-two years as a royal colony, it was hard to imagine a different system. So in 1763 most Jerseyans reacted favorably when they heard that William Franklin, son of the famous Benjamin Franklin of Pennsylvania, had been named their latest governor. He was American-born, which most people considered a good thing, in spite of the memory of Lewis Morris. Franklin was young—only thirty-three—and had a pretty West Indian wife. His father had reportedly spent a thousand pounds to buy the job for him. A few moralists carped about his illegitimate birth. But this was not so unusual in England or America during the eighteenth century. Robert Hunter Morris, New Jersey's chief justice, had at least three illicit offspring. When William Franklin arrived in February 1764, Jerseyans turned out to welcome him. No one dreamt that they were greeting the last royal governor of New Jersey.

4

Across the Rubicon

NEW JERSEY'S hundredth birthday year, 1764, brought the worst possible news from England. Parliament had voted to bar all future issues of paper money in America. This decision meant instant deflation at the worst possible time—the end of the French and Indian War. Like other colonies, New Jersey had made large requisitions to support the war. But the assembly had relied on the old dependable device of paper money to make the payments relatively painless. By 1764 they had issued some 300,000 pounds—a debt they hoped to repay by issuing more paper money. The news that Parliament had banned such currency resounded through New Jersey like the knell of doom. Jerseyans had the largest per capita debt of all the mainland colonies, and they were now faced with paying it by direct taxation.

The cries of anguish were many and acute. But they were mild compared to the uproar that ensued when the British Government compounded this stupidity by attempting to extract hard cash from the Americans to pay the expenses of the empire. Jerseyans felt it was bad enough to be faced with heavy taxes from their own legislature. To be waylaid at the same time by a distant Parliament that had never before taxed so much as a shilling from Americans was too much. The Stamp Act, an imitation of a law already more than fifty years old in England, taxed newspapers and a wide range of legal documents. "Unless we are allow'd a paper currency without severe restrictions, they need not send Tax gatherers, for they can gather nothing," wrote one outraged West Jerseyan. "Never was Money so very Scarce as now."

"Discontent was painted in every man's face, and the distress of the people very great," wrote Cortlandt Skinner, a wealthy member of the East Jersey Board of Proprietors and speaker of the assembly. "The distress of the people [was] very great, from an amazing scarcity of money." Even more ominous was a letter to the colony's agent in England written by three prominent members of the New Jersey Assembly, functioning as a "Committee of Correspondents." They instructed the agent to "humbly & Dutifully Set forth In the name and on Behalf of this Colony that we look upon all Taxes laid upon us without our Consent as a fundamental infringement of the Rights and privileges Secured to us as English Subjects and by Charter."

Although the proprietary promise to pass no taxes without the approval of the general assembly had been theoretically repealed by the transfer to royal government in 1702, Jerseyans still regarded this clause as one of their fundamental rights. The correspondents also told the agent to remind the lords of trade that "our paper Currency hath always kept its [value] and being prohibited from having any more . . . let the Necessity be ever so pressing we esteem a very great provincial hardship." Another Jerseyan who signed himself "Caesarienis," went even further in his rejection of Parliament's right to tax Americans. Caesarienis said he saw no point in petitioning Parliament to repeal the Stamp Act, as many colonies were doing. In fact, he commended the New Jersey legislature for not bothering to do it,

> for it is to me a plain and evident absurdity to petition any body of men against the passing a law to bind me, when at the same time, I can see that such law, if passed by them cannot bind me. If the inhabitants of the moon, for instance, should happen to hear that the Commons of Great Britain had resolved . . . that their vellum should be stamped; no one would expect them to petition the said Commons against it.

New Jersey protests were mild compared to the violence that erupted in New York and other colonies. But Jerseyans made it very clear that they were opposed to the Stamp Act. Even the lawyers of the colony, gathered in a respectful conclave at Perth Amboy, presided over by the chief justice, denounced the act as "that Enemy of our Peace" and declared they would cease all legal activity in the colony, except for criminal proceedings, rather than pay the tax.

The continental uproar and a boycott of British goods persuaded Parliament to repeal the law. But repeal did not solve New Jersey's chief problem, the shortage of money, nor did it end the tension between the colonies and the mother country. Repeated attempts to get crown approval for additional paper-money bills met with stony vetoes, based on the Currency Act of 1764. Attempts to get the act repealed proved equally futile. By 1770, a resident of Hunterdon County described two-thirds of the people of New Jersey as debtors who "do not know how to extricate themselves. . . . A man possessed of an estate worth five thousand pounds will have it torn from him, tho' all his debts amount to but a hundred pounds; a situation which will naturally make a man feel desperate."

At the same time, another act of Parliament forced New Jersey and other colonies to support the British regulars stationed among them. Ostensibly maintained in the colonies to deal with Indians, the troops were considered an attempt to intimidate Americans, and the New Jersey Assembly joined the New York Assembly and other colonial legislatures in an extreme reluctance to pay for their support. A new attempt to tax Americans, the so-called Townshend Acts of 1768, added more turmoil and another round of boycotts against British manufacturers. As the uproar and unhappiness mounted, more and more people began to wonder what had gone wrong. One of the best explanations came from New Jersey Assemblyman Aaron Leaming. In a letter to his Cape May constituents, he gave a down-to-earth but essentially accurate explanation of how the shift in the relationship between Great Britain and her colonies had occurred.

Leaming began by pointing out that "the People in Great

Britain had little knowledge of these Colonies before the commencement of the [French and Indian] War in 1755." The war brought numerous officers and men to the colonies. "All of them had been bred up in the belief that America was a mere desart of poverty and distress, and the Inhabitants little if any better than savages." These Englishmen were astonished by the wealth they saw everywhere in America. "From one extreme they immediately fell upon another. From considering us the Seat of Poverty and distress, they immediately eyed us as the Seat of riches and happiness." The officers in particular did not make allowances for the fact they they were entertained by the wealthiest men in the various colonies. Nor did they take into account the heavy expenditures the colonies had made to support the war, which meant, Leaming said, "we had Mortguaged our Country for twenty years to come." When these warriors went home to England, they found the home government staggering under the enormous debt created by the war. They decided that the Americans, "rich and almost free from Taxes," were the answer to their problems. "It then became a matter of Patriotism that they Should ease themselves of their Taxes and lay their burthen upon us." On this plan Parliament "midwifed into the world the Stamp Act." [1]

In New Jersey the tension between colony and crown was accentuated by an awareness that the imperial tight-money policy favored people who belonged to the descendants of the old proprietary party. Many of the lawsuits for debt were brought by these wealthy Jerseyans, most of whom live in and around Perth Amboy. They were known as "the Group," and through a web of interlocking political and marital alliances they dominated the judiciary, the governor's council, and to some extent the assembly. Through the East Jersey Board of Proprietors, they still owned about a million acres in the state, which they sold or leased at a pace steady enough to guarantee each member of the twenty-four-man board an income of some 1,200 pounds a year.

1. Larry R. Gerlach, ed., *New Jersey in the American Revolution, 1763–1783: A Documentary History* (Trenton: New Jersey Historical Commission, 1975), pp. 61–63.

Gov. William Franklin needed all the political skills he had inherited from his father to cope with uneasy New Jersey during the first ten years of his governorship. Agitation against the foreclosure policies of creditors as well as a revival of the old argument between the proprietors and holders of Indian and Nicolls land titles boiled up to cause riots in Newark in 1769 and 1770. Every time the assembly met there was a flood of petitions for paper money, accompanied by reports of hundreds in jail for debt. To prevent the prosecution of debtors, a mob stormed the Monmouth County Court House in January 1770, sending the lawyers fleeing for safety and effectively halting all legal business in the county.

This unrest did much to polarize New Jersey before the Revolution began. Believers in law and order began to view all forms of protest with suspicion. Talk of natural rights, or a display of slogans like "Liberty and property," only made the Group and their numerous adherents link such cries with the tendency to claim property from vague Indian titles and the widespread refusal to pay lawful debts. On the other hand, many Jerseyans outside this moneyed group perceived that something was wrong with an imperial system that let aristocrats in London decide on paper money and other policies that drastically affected the peace and prosperity of New Jersey. But many who responded to this natural resentment were distracted by New Jersey religious divisions. These conflicts were visible from the lowest to the highest levels of the colony.

Converted by his devout wife, Gov. William Franklin became a member of the Church of England and its missionary arm, the Society for the Propagation of the Gospel in Foreign Parts. This made him a political enemy of the Presbyterians. It was not an unfamiliar role. In Pennsylvania his father had been fighting the powerful Presbyterians who supported the proprietary descendants of William Penn. Governor Franklin revealed his hostility to the Presbyterians by several attempts to take over their stronghold, the College of New Jersey at Princeton. In 1766 he offered the trustees government support if they would make him—the royal governor—the real ruler of the school. When the trustees demurred, Franklin granted an advantageous charter to

Queen's College in New Brunswick, creating a competing school only fifteen miles from Princeton. Presbyterians denounced "the schemes of Governor Franklin . . . with regard to the College." [2]

Queen's was designated to educate the liberal wing of the Dutch Reformed clergy and thus block a potential alliance between them and the Presbyterians. But Franklin's shrewd political maneuvering was nullified by the tactics of other Anglicans in New Jersey and elsewhere. In 1760 the Anglican clergy petitioned the governor to deprive justices of the peace of the right to perform marriages. This would have made it impossible for Quakers to marry—since their creed forbade all ceremonies conducted by "hireling priests."

Even more alarming to those religionists who dissented from the Church of England were the continuing Anglican attempts to procure a bishop for America. Political power was not the sole motive; the church's requirement that all priests had to be ordained by a bishop made it difficult to recruit clergy among Americans. Not many young men could afford the expense of a trip to London to be ordained. But the dissenters feared that the arrival of a bishop would be the signal for a campaign to imitate England and Ireland and disfranchise everyone who was not a member of the established church.

The Reverend Thomas Bradbury Chandler, the Episcopal pastor at Elizabethtown, was a skillful writer who published a number of pamphlets in favor of an American bishop. Public agitation was intense. One historian of the controversy wrote that people grew "almost frenzied in the course of it." [3] Few colonies were as exposed to the devisive effects of this quarrel as New Jersey, with her uneasy balance of fifty-two Presbyterian, thirty-eight Quaker, twenty-one Anglican, nineteen Baptist and fourteen Dutch Reformed churches. Adding to the tension was the memory of the Anglican political machine that had created turmoil in the past.

2. Melvin Buxbaum, *Benjamin Franklin and the Zealous Presbyterians* (University Park, Pa.: Pennsylvania State University Press, 1975), p. 182.

3. Sidney E. Ahlstrom, *A Religious History of the American People* (New Haven: Yale University Press, 1972), p. 362.

Another factor in reducing the level of New Jersey's revolutionary fervor was the colony's rural lifestyle. Elizabethtown, the largest town, only had about 1,200 inhabitants. There were no mobs of sailors and workers who made upheaval easy in Boston or New York and no rabblerousers such as Boston's Samuel Adams or New York's Alexander McDougall. New Jersey also lacked a newspaper, the other indispensable engine of eighteenth-century agitation.

All these facts explain the startling ambivalence with which the Revolution was greeted in New Jersey. Depending on who is quoted, a writer can make New Jersey sound like a volcano of revolutionary ardor—or a swamp of unenthusiasm for life, liberty, and the pursuit of happiness.

If we focus on that center of militant Presbyterianism, the College of New Jersey, we find resistance to British oppression and fiery speeches on behalf of patriotism and liberty being made as early as 1765. After the Boston Tea Party, the college's students burned the steward's supply of tea and issued "spirited resolves." No one knows who burned a shipment of tea that had been secretly landed in the Delaware River hamlet of Greenwich, but at least one Presbyterian minister was among the "Indians."

In January 1775, New Jersey Quakers joined their brethren in Pennsylvania in a blunt denunciation of the growing Revolution as not only contrary to the nature and precepts of the gospel, but destructive of the peace and harmony of civil society. As for the Anglicans, Thomas Bradbury Chandler, ignoring the hostility he had already incurred by his call for an American bishop, wrote *The American Querist,* in which he declared that anyone who challenged Parliament's authority was "in the high road to open rebellion." The Dutch Reformed church, split between two long-feuding groups, showed a similar tendency to divide on politics, with the conservative Conferentie faction loyal to the king and the liberal Coetus faction following the rebellious Presbyterians. New Jersey's numerous Baptists joined Presbyterians in their suspicion of an Anglican bishopric and generally supported resistance to the crown.

But not even fervent Presbyterians thought that resistance justified a vote for independence. As one of the smaller colonies, sandwiched between two large aggressive neighbors, New Jersey was instinctively wary of that idea. To most Jerseymen the protection of the British crown looked far more reliable, in spite of Parliament's new inclination to encroach on traditional liberties.

There was plenty of room for a skillful politician to maneuver, and Gov. William Franklin decided to use it. He tried to halt the drift to independence by blunt warnings. Simultaneously, he worked on the New Jersey Assembly to respond to heavy-handed British attempts at reconciliation. On January 13, 1775, Franklin warned the assembly against destroying "that form of government of which you are an important part, and which it is your duty by all lawful means to preserve." He urged them not to approve the resolutions of the First Continental Congress, which had adjourned the previous month in Philadelphia, and advised them instead to propose a meeting between delegates of the royal assemblies and negotiators appointed by the king. The assembly preferred the arguments of the delegates to the Continental Congress, and voted to approve that body's rebellious resolutions and back the boycott of British goods it recommended. Town and County Committees swiftly enforced the boycott. They were soon enforcing a prorevolutionary conformity that went far beyond economics.

On May 15, 1775, with the crisis deepened by bloodshed at Lexington, Massachusetts, and the Second Continental Congress gathering, Governor Franklin attempted to persuade the assembly to consider in a friendly light a conciliatory resolution passed by Parliament in February. The resolution proposed to exempt from all taxation any colony that agreed to pay its share of the imperial defense bill by an annual "requisition" that Parliament would compute each year, as it did when parceling out the expenses of the Seven Years War. Franklin pointed out how badly the British navy was needed to defend the long New Jersey coastline against French or Spanish fleets based in the West Indies. He noted that the assembly was not being asked to abandon the boycott of British goods that the First Continental Congress had decreed. He vowed that all the king wanted was a chance to settle the dispute "consistently with his own dignity." As proof of the royal benevolence, Franklin announced that New Jersey had received permission to print 100,000 pounds of paper money. If the assembly failed to respond to such generosity, Governor Franklin said he would be forced to conclude that the quarrel was not about taxation "but that the Americans have deeper views, and mean to throw off all dependence upon Great-Britain."

Although many assemblymen were obviously impressed by Franklin's reasoning, a majority voted to withhold an answer to the conciliatory proposal until the Second Continental Congress had responded for all the colonies. Three days later, New Jersey's first Provincial Congress met at Trenton. Only nine members of the old assembly were in it. The congress was dominated by Presbyterians, particularly by the delegations from Somerset County, led by the College of New Jersey president, John Witherspoon, and Essex County, home of the original Nicolls settlers, led by William Livingston. This scion of the New York manorial clan was married to a New Jersey woman. He had moved to Elizabethtown in 1772. A brilliant lawyer and talented writer, his presence was significant to Jerseyans for an even more important reason. He was a devout Presbyterian and in his New York days had been the leader of the dissenters' attack on the Anglican proposal to import a bishop.

After opening with a pledge of allegiance to the king, the Provincial Congress voted to raise companies of volunteers from every town. Taking advantage of the king's conciliatory gesture on the paper-money issue, they voted to tax ten thousand pounds worth of these paper dollars to pay for the troops, surely a peculiar form of gratitude.

But New Jersey's ambivalence was no worse than that of the Second Continental Congress, which adopted the New England army besieging the British regulars inside Boston. Congress appointed George Washington of Virginia as commander in chief of the army. Before Washington could take command, this army fought one of the bloodiest battles in American history on Breed's and Bunker's hills opposite Boston. But Congress proceeded to draft an olive branch petition to the king, pleading for reconciliation, and dispatched it on July 8. On July 31, Congress approved a report of John Adams, Benjamin Franklin, Thomas Jefferson, and Richard Henry Lee—all determined, but for the time being, secret, independence men rejecting the British conciliatory proposal. No one in America was quite ready to accept the consequences of this steadily escalating resistance to the king and his government.

In New Jersey throughout most of 1775 a precarious calm prevailed. The Provincial Congress, at a second meeting on August 5, reorganized the militia, requiring all able-bodied men between sixteen and fifty to join or pay a fine of four shillings a month. Because its representatives were having trouble collecting the ten-thousand-pound tax, orders were given to condemn or sell goods or possessions belonging to anyone who refused to pay. A Committee of Safety was organized to deal with recalcitrants while the Provincial Congress was not in session. Plans were laid to raise sixteen regiments, seven independent battalions, and a company of rangers. But when the Provincial Congress was asked to back these plans with thirty thousand pounds in new taxes, the answer was a resounding no. Jerseymen were as loath to pay taxes to the new government as they had been to the old one.

Beyond New Jersey the crisis deepened with Congress's decision to invade Canada and the king's refusal to receive the olive branch petition. Instead His Majesty issued a proclamation declaring the American colonies in rebellion. It amounted to a declaration of war. Two of New Jersey's delegates to the Continental Congress, John DeHart and James Kinsey, resigned. They were convinced that there was now no alternative to independence. But they could not in conscience vote for such a step.

In this atmosphere, William Franklin played a daring card. Historians without an adequate knowledge of New Jersey have regarded it as an odd, almost fanatical move, but Franklin was astute enough to see that the worse the crisis grew, the better became his chances of influencing the assembly to resist the pressure for independence. He knew how little enthusiasm there was for the idea among a majority of Jerseymen. Deepening the personal poignancy of the situation was the presence of Governor Franklin's father in the Continental Congress. By this time Benjamin Franklin and his son had had a long talk in which the elder Franklin had candidly declared himself in favor of independence and urged his son to resign and join the growing Revolution. William had refused this advice, to his father's intense chagrin. At forty-seven, Governor Franklin could no longer play the dutiful worshipping son.

On November 15, 1775, William Franklin convened the New Jersey Assembly and opened one of the most dramatic, least-known episodes in the Revolution. As never before, he had primed and positioned his supporters in the house, and he exerted every iota of his gifts as an orator and politician. He reminded the assemblymen of their failure to accept the British conciliatory resolution, mournfully declaring that "in all probability it would have led to some plan of accommodation." Now they saw grim evidence of the king's "firm resolution." Boldly playing for sympathy, he asked them if he should leave the colony and take refuge on a British warship. He asked the question because "sentiments of independency are, by some men of present consequence openly avowed, and essays are already appearing in the publick papers to ridicule the people's fears of the horrid measure. . . . If, as I hope, you have an abhorrence of such design, you will do your country an essential service by declaring it in . . . full and explicit terms."

The assembly's reaction proved that Franklin's timing was superb. A committee was appointed to petition the king for "a restoration of peace and harmony with the parent state." This was obviously a first step to implementing the conciliatory resolution—a move which would have ripped New Jersey out of the shaky American confederacy. The assembly also approved three resolutions declaring that there was no ground for the governor's concern about a plot for independence, warning the colony's delegates to the Second Continental Congress to vote against any motion for independence, and urging them to seek reconciliation with Great Britain as soon as possible.

When the news of these resolutions reached the Continental Congress in Philadelphia, consternation reigned. Three of the most effective speakers available, John Jay of New York, George Wythe of Virginia, and John Dickinson of Pennsylvania, rushed to Burlington and pleaded with the assembly to withdraw the resolutions and the petition to the king. It is significant that Jay and Dickinson were avowed opponents of independence. They were able to reassure the Jerseymen that the Continental Congress was equally reluctant to cut the cord of loyalty and law with the mother country. But there was no hope of forcing Great Britain to acknowledge America's rights if one colony started dallying with the conciliatory resolution. Such a move would reduce the continental union to a "rope of sand." Governor Franklin could only grind his teeth as the assembly succumbed to this reasoning and withdrew the petition to the king.

William Franklin had come too close to success to be left unchallenged by the revolutionary party. On January 2, the Continental Congress passed a resolution recommending "speedy and effective measures to frustrate the mischievous machinations and restrain the wicked practices" of those who were "misrepresenting and traducing the conduct and principles of the friends of American liberty." Unaware of this exhortation, which had the force of law to pro-Congress men, Governor Franklin was finishing a long report of his struggle with the assembly for his superiors in London. He was still confident that most of the people of New Jersey (and Pennsylvania) detested the idea of independence. "But the danger seems to be that the design will be carried on by such degrees and under such pretenses as not to be perceived by the people in general until too late for resistance" he wrote. He also included in this thick report a letter from his friend, Attorney General Cortlandt Skinner, to Skinner's brother William in London, containing a number of hostile remarks about the revolutionists.

The governor's packet never reached its destination. It was intercepted by William Alexander, commander of the rebel armed forces in East Jersey, acting in response to the January 2 resolution. Alexander, whom everyone called Lord Stirling in deference to his claim to this Scottish title, had resigned from the governor's council to side with the revolution. After a quick reading of the packet's contents, Stirling ordered his soldiers to arrest both the governor and the attorney general.

Skinner fled to a British warship in New York harbor. Governor Franklin stood his ground while militia under Lt. Col. William Winds marched into Perth Amboy. Franklin had recently moved into Proprietary House, a handsome mansion refurbished for him by the East Jersey Board of Proprietors. At 2 A.M. on the night of January 8, 1776, he was awakened by "a violent knocking" at the front door. Looking out of his bedroom window, he saw the house was surrounded by armed men. His wife Elizabeth became hysterical. A servant answered the door and was handed a letter from Colonel Winds with a demand for "an immediate answer." Winds wanted Franklin to promise that he would not leave Perth Amboy until the colonel knew "the will & pleasure of the Continental Congress."

Franklin replied that he had no intention of leaving the province, unless he was "compelled by violence." Winds retreated, and after more negotiation Franklin was permitted to remain in his mansion under an informal house arrest. The assembly still paid his salary, although most of the apparatus of royal government had ceased to function. It was a symptom of New Jersey's ambivalent attitude toward the Revolution. Another reason was a steep decline in enthusiasm for independence both in and out of the Continental Congress. The collapse of the American invasion of Canada and ominous evidence that the British were arming for war made many people feel a negotiated settlement was the wiser course.

In April 1776, at a secret caucus of local committees of correspondence in New Brunswick, John Witherspoon delivered a ninety-minute harangue in favor of independence. The reaction of his audience, composed of New Jersey's revolutionary elite, was overwhelmingly negative. An agitated Elias Boudinot, a leader of the Presbyterian "junto" from Elizabethtown, confided to his diary that he was

> at my wit's end, to know how to extricate myself from so
> disagreeable a situation . . . two or three Gent' [*sic*] of the
> Audience came to me and desired that I would inform the doctor

that if he proceeded any farther they would not be answerable for his safety . . . out of 36 Members, there were but 3 or 4 who Voted for the Doctor's proposition, the rest rejecting it with great warmth.[4]

The British, out of touch with events in America, decided to crush the rebellion with a massive use of force. The news that the king had ordered the fleet to seize American vessels on the high seas as contraband of war, that he was hiring Hessian mercenaries, did far more to change the minds of most Americans than the aggressive arguments for independence in Tom Paine's *Common Sense*. In fact, Governor Franklin believed that in New Jersey *Common Sense* had an opposite effect—it opened the eyes of many people "of sense and property" to the real intentions of the independence party.

A similar backlash was probably the chief effect of a contentious pamphlet by the Reverend Jacob Green, pastor of the Presbyterian church in Hanover. Disturbed by the state's lackadaisical progress toward independence, Green published "Observations on the Reconciliation of Great Britain and the Colonies" in April 1776. Green aimed the pamphlet at the hesitant Whigs who abounded in New Jersey. "I do not pretend to reason with professed Tories," he declared. The pamphlet is chiefly interesting today for the way it unintentionally revealed many of the illusions that emboldened the proindependence men in 1776.

Agreeing with Tom Paine's bland dismissal of the British army and navy in *Common Sense,* Green argued that the mother country could not support an army of 25,000 men and 10,000 sailors in America without going bankrupt. Even if they managed this feat, Americans could raise "five to one against this number." [5] On paper this was true. But the realities of the next seven exhausting years, during which Britain stubbornly supported far more than 25,000 men in arms in America, were to prove Green (and Paine) poor prophets.

---

4. Elias Boudinot, *Journal of Events in the Revolution* (Philadelphia: n.p., 1894), pp. 5–8.

5. Jacob Green, *Observations on the Reconciliation of Great Britain and the Colonies* (Trenton: New Jersey Historical Commission, 1976), p. 16.

In New Jersey, the fight for independence was won by brute force more often than it was won by persuasion. The Presbyterian-led revolutionists tightened their grip on the province by taking the offensive against all forms of opposition. Men who spoke out against the rebel government were arrested, fined, and required to post a bond guaranteeing their future good behavior. Thomas Randolph, a barrelmaker of Quibble Town (present New Market), criticized the revolutionists and got a coat of tar and feathers that made him "duly sensible of his offense."

The Second Provincial Congress met at New Brunswick on January 31, 1776. At the request of the Continental Congress, it ordered a battalion of Jerseymen to join New Yorkers in suppressing a counterrevolution in Queens County. The lawmakers were informed that the men could not march. They lacked guns and there was no money to pay them. This situation finally embarrassed the Provincial Congress into voting 50,000 pounds in bills of credit that would serve simultaneously as paper money and taxes. Severe fines were ordered against anyone refusing these bills. But all was not well with this Congress, from the viewpoint of the Presbyterian leadership. Too many delegates were lukewarm on independence. A call for a new Congress to be elected on May 28 was a first step toward solving this problem.

The proindependence men were in close touch with the New England–Virginia coalition in the Second Continental Congress. These radicals were determined to move the recalcitrant Middle Colonies—especially Pennsylvania and New Jersey—into the independence column. On May 10, the radicals maneuvered through the Continental Congress a resolution directing colonies to create new governments wherever royal authority had ceased to function. The colonial government was still operating in Pennsylvania. Royal authority was also alive in New Jersey as long as Governor Franklin remained in the state. But the independence faction eliminated this obstacle by adding a preface to the resolution, written by John Adams, declaring it was "absolutely irreconcilable to reason and good conscience" for any American to take an oath or make an affirmation of loyalty to Great Britain and "the exercise of any kind of authority under the said Crown [of Great Britain] should be totally suppressed.'' As John Adams candidly admitted to one protesting delegate, this statement was tantamount to a declaration of independence. In New Jersey and Pennsylvania, it effectively abolished British government. Significantly, the three New Jersey delegates in Congress voted against it, accurately reflecting the attitude of the Provincial Congress that had chosen them.

When Jerseymen voted for a new Provincial Congress on May 28, everyone clearly understood that the real issue was independence. But the election was hardly a genuine test of New Jersey's sentiments on the great question. In most counties, loyalists and moderates had been cowed into silence by rebel tactics of violent reprisal. Voting was in the English style, by voice, which meant a man had to publicly state his allegiance—exposing him to the kind of tar-and-feathers ''correction'' that had chastened Thomas Randolph, the loyalist barrelmaker of Quibble Town. In Burlington, where a large Quaker presence guaranteed an anti-independence majority, the polls were not even opened.

In populous Morris, Middlesex, and Somerset counties, the intimidated anti-independence men did not put up a slate. Only in counties where loyalists were numerous enough to protect each other from rebel reprisals—Hunterdon and Monmouth, for example—was this pattern significantly altered. There a few loyalists ran and won. Predominantly Dutch Bergen, where Presbyterians were few, elected a loyalist majority. Overall, an estimated two-thirds of New Jersey voters stayed home, in spite of a new law giving the vote to everyone with fifty pounds of real or personal property—a provision tantamount to universal suffrage.

Nearly half the sixty-five delegates elected to the Third Provincial Congress were new men, ready to vote for independence. Middletown, where there was a Baptist majority, and Shrewsbury, where Anglicans and Quakers predominated, sent petitions to the Provincial Congress urging them to remain loyal. But the legislators ignored them and sent to the Continental Congress four strongly proindependence Presbyterians, Richard Stockton of Princeton, a prosperous lawyer; Abraham Clark of Elizabethtown, former Essex County sheriff; Francis Hopkinson of Bordentown, musician, poet and propagandist; and John Witherspoon of Princeton, president of the College of New Jersey, who was their unquestioned leader. The fifth delegate, John Hart, was a Baptist.

To his considerable dismay William Livingston was dismissed as a delegate, reportedly because he was reluctant to vote for independence before an alliance with France had been secured. It is a comment on the urgency felt by the revolutionary party that they would risk alienating such an influential man, lest the independence juggernaut have even a single balky wheel. To salve his pride, Livingston was given command of the New Jersey militia.

At that point, William Franklin played a wild card. He called a meeting of the general assembly at Perth Amboy on June 20 to inform the members that the British Government was sending a peace commission to the colonies. But there was no hope of Governor Franklin repeating his performance of the previous December. On June 14, 1776, the Provincial Congress voted that the "late Governor's" proclamation was null and void. The Congress also decided that the proclamation was in "direct contempt and violation of the resolve of the Continental Congress of the 15th of May last." Franklin had thereby "discovered himself to be an enemy of the liberties of this country."

Col. Nathaniel Heard of Woodbridge was ordered to obtain from Franklin a signed parole in which he agreed to remain on his farm on Rancocas Creek in Burlington County as a neutral. The Congress also ordered the royal treasurer to stop paying the governor's salary. Colonel Heard was told to carry out the order "with all the delicacy and tenderness which the nature of the business can possibly admit"—a recognition of Franklin's popularity and a reflection on the tactics of Colonel Winds in January. Franklin had done his utmost to portray himself and his fragile, nervous wife as martyrs.

The governor refused to sign the parole. The Provincial Congress ordered Heard to bring him to Burlington under guard. After an acrimonious hearing at which Franklin refused to answer any of the questions asked him before "this illegal assembly,'' the Provincial Congress resolved that the governor was an enemy of the country and guilty of ''gross and insolent'' conduct. They might also have reproved John Witherspoon, the president of Princeton, who sneered that Franklin's conduct was ''every way worthy his exalted birth.'' But this outburst of Presbyterian hatred passed unnoticed in a Congress dominated by Presbyterians.

The Continental Congress ordered Franklin deported to Connecticut, where he became a prisoner of war. On July 1, while the royal governor was en route to this exile, New Jersey militiamen standing watch at Sandy Hook noticed a startling number of ships on the horizon. Within a few hours a huge British fleet approached the coast. There was no doubt that it carried the main British army which had retreated from Boston to Halifax, Nova Scotia, in March. Lt. Col. Nathaniel Scudder of the Monmouth County militia mounted his horse at 11 P.M. on the night of July 1 and galloped for Burlington to warn the Provincial Congress. He rode all night and burst into the deliberations of the state's founding fathers on the morning of July 2, thereby staking a claim to the title of New Jersey's Paul Revere.

The Provincial Congress rushed the news to the Continental Congress in Philadelphia. There, after a night of frantic negotiation, the radicals had finally put together a twelve-to-nothing vote for independence, with the New York delegates abstaining. The previous day, Pennsylvania, Delaware, and South Carolina had voted no. In Burlington, the New Jersey Congress took an equally momentous step on that same July 2. They ratified a constitution, drafted by a ten-man committee formed on June 24. But the vote cast a doubt on the strength of the state's affirmation of independence. It was twenty-six to nine. No less than thirty of the handpicked delegates to the Provincial Congress decided it was politic to depart before the final vote. Another indication of the attitude of the Congress was a clause which stated that ''if a reconciliation between Great Britain and these colonies should take place . . . this charter shall be null and void.''

But it is doubtful if many Jerseyans noticed these legalistic quibbles—or even bothered to read the state's constitution. The crucial document was issued in Philadelphia, from the brilliant pen of Thomas Jefferson. There were many things in the Declaration of Independence to which Jerseyans instinctively responded. The call for a government that concerned itself with the liberty and happiness of the individual was essentially the goal for which they had contended with royal governors and distant aristocrats in London. The bold assertion that all men, rich and poor, were created equal, struck another responsive chord. Jerseyans had seen too many examples of how wealth or privilege could destroy the equality every man should have in a courtroom or a polling place. Like other Americans, Jerseyans did not put a fanatical stress on the word *equal*. In a land of opportunity, where a man could improve a middling fortune by the sweat of his brow, no one was inclined to call for a ruthless levelling of wealth. But Jerseyans were emphatically ready to endorse a government that sought to keep wealth under control of the law, to make it responsive to the will of the people. This was the moderate goal of the Revolution, so well summarized by John Adams of Massachusetts: "A more equal liberty than had prevailed in other parts of the earth must be established in America." A great many Jerseymen were ready to fight for that.

5

Into Civil War

*A*FTER the Revolution, John Adams estimated that a third of the Americans were in favor of independence, a third opposed, and a third neutral. Widely quoted and implicitly accepted by many historians, these figures have little relevance for New Jersey. Recent studies indicate that at least half the citizens were active or hidden loyalists. Although economics played some part—poorer men, many of them young, tended to side with the Revolution—religion was the primary factor in the choice of sides. The Presbyterians ran the Revolution in New Jersey, controlling all aspects of it, from the distribution of political jobs to the appointment of New Jersey officers in the Continental Army.

Graphic evidence for this Presbyterian influence is visible in a conversation between Constable William Tatem and Joseph Cogil, a suspected loyalist. Tatem served Cogil with a summons to appear before a local court for examination. Cogil told Tatem he did not care for the new chief justice "nor none of the rest of the Devils, that the Presbyterians were trying to get the Rule into their own hands and that he never would be subject to a Presbyterian Government, that he was as good a Whig as ever sat upon a pot till Independency was declared." [1]

1. Quoted in Robert McCluer Calhoun, *The Loyalists in Revolutionary America, 1760–1781* (New York: Harcourt Brace Jovanovich, 1973), p. 404.

In Cumberland County the sheriff resigned, declaring he did not want to "distress poor people in these times of public calamity." In Monmouth and Hunterdon counties, loyalists organized for self-defense, and 400 militia from other parts of the state were sent into Monmouth to disperse a band of about a hundred loyalists who were hiding in the cedar swamps, waiting for assistance from the British army. The colonel of the revolutionary militia in the town of Shrewsbury resigned, abandoning all hope of recruiting enough men to make a regiment. Sixty men from Shrewsbury and Freehold slipped past the haphazard network of guards along the shore and joined the British army on Staten Island. Another forty-eight arrived from Perth Amboy. They assured Cortlandt Skinner, whom Governor Franklin had commissioned major general of the Loyal Militia of New Jersey, that there were hundreds, even thousands, more Jerseymen ready to fight for the king.[2]

The revolutionists responded with wholesale arrests of suspected loyalists, particularly in the Perth Amboy area, and their deportation to the interior of New Jersey. Even the wives and children of refugees like Cortlandt Skinner were moved. The energetic executor of these harsh measures was William Livingston, who was the militia general in command of eastern New Jersey defenses. On August 27, this vigorous man was chosen by the Provincial Congress as the first governor of the state. It was the wisest decision made by New Jersey legislators during the Revolution. Livingston's attitude toward the war was supremely realistic. "Whoever draws his sword against his prince, must fling away the scabbord," he wrote. "We have passed the Rubicon, and whoever attempts to cross it will be knocked in the head by one or the other party, on the opposite banks." [3]

Livingston did not have much chance to exercise his gift for wartime leadership in 1776. The British battered Washington and his army around New York until it was only a shadow of its

2. Leonard Lundin, *Cockpit of the Revolution* (Princeton: Princeton University Press, 1940), p. 118.

3. Lucius Q. C. Elmer, *Reminiscences of Bench and Bar During More Than a Half Century* (Newark: n.p., 1872), pp. 61, 71.

original strength—some 27,000 men. No fewer than 8,000 Connecticut militiamen picked up their guns and went home. Another 4,000 Massachusetts militiamen, many of them no doubt men who had fought well at Lexington and Concord, or their cousins or brothers, went home in late November, in spite of desperate pleas by American generals to defend their country in extremis. Washington brought few more than 2,500 men with him into New Jersey—expecting the state's 16,000 enrolled militiamen to turn out to defend their home soil.

By now, events had demonstrated the fatuity of the American reliance on militia. These men were not regulars who enlisted for a year or more and were trained to accept army discipline and battlefield brutality. Militia stayed home until a crisis called them into action. They were supposed to train at least once a month and keep their weapons and themselves ready for swift response. But the enforcement of these regulations was as haphazard as the average militiaman's willingness to turn out when summoned. Congress had been deceived by the lies told by Massachusetts leaders about the fighting at Lexington and Concord and Bunker Hill. To win sympathy and support from the rest of the continent, Sam Adams and his lieutenants had carefully concealed the training and weaponry that made their minutemen an embryo army. They pictured them as simple farmers who whomped the British with pure courage and enthusiasm. The congressional politicians thus missed vital differences in the situation around Boston in 1775 and the crisis that confronted them in 1776. In Massachusetts, the minutemen and militia had outnumbered the tiny British garrison army of 4,000 at least 5-1. The Americans had been training intensively for eight months and were spoiling for a fight with the redcoats. Massachusetts was religiously and politically united on the contest; loyalists were a tiny impotent minority. In New York and New Jersey, religious divisions abounded. Every second man was a loyalist, ready to counter the Revolution's ideology with a firm belief in "British liberty" and tout good King George as the "father of the country." The British army had swelled from a small garrison to an aggressive host of 34,000 men.

By mid-December 1776, these grim realities meant that en-

thusiasm for the Revolution had dwindled to the vanishing point
in New Jersey. A large body of New Jersey militia had joined
Washington's army early in the summer. When the British,
awaiting reinforcements from Europe, did not open the campaign until August 27, most of the Jerseymen obtained permission to return to their native state, ostensibly to protect it. There
they soon persuaded Brig. Gen. Hugh Mercer, in command of
the Flying Camp at Perth Amboy, the headquarters of eastern
New Jersey defenses, to let them go home. By August 4, Mercer
had only 274 rank and file in his command.

To persuade the militia to return, the New Jersey Provincial
Congress divided them into two classes, each of which would
serve alternate months. This tactic turned out a sizable body of
men. But their numbers dwindled with each rotation. On September 15, when Matthias Williamson accepted a commission
as brigadier general, he warned Governor Livingston that his
forces would "dwindle away to a mere nothing in three or four
relieves more." This was precisely what happened.

When the British sent a formidable army into New Jersey to
pursue Washington, the American commander had no alternative but humiliating retreat. By the end of the first week in
December he was forced to abandon the state for the Pennsylvania side of the Delaware. About a thousand New Jersey militiamen responded to desperate exhortations from Governor Livingston and the Provincial Congress. But all these volunteers
were individuals or small groups. Not a single unit except a
company of artillery turned out. The disorganization of these
volunteers made them practically useless. Meanwhile a whole
militia brigade decided to go home on December 1, when their
term of service expired. Washington had good reason to write,
"The conduct of the Jerseys has been most infamous." But
with the realism that was the hallmark of his greatness, he demonstrated his clear understanding of a major reason for it. "The
defection of the people . . . has been as much owing to the
want of an army to look the enemy in the face as to any other
cause."

Meanwhile, the British were busily occupying the state and
laying plans to turn New Jersey into the first "loyal colony."

Agents reached Gov. William Franklin, who was living in Wallingford, Connecticut, under a parole that included a promise to take no part in the war. He began signing pardons which the British issued to ex-rebels who took an oath of allegiance and promised "to remain in peaceable obedience to His Majesty." The pardons were part of the pacification plans of the British commanders, Adm. Richard Lord Howe and Gen. Sir William Howe. In Monmouth County, prominent loyalists were appointed commissioners to administer these oaths of allegiance. Loyalists in northern New Jersey seized their guns and exploded into an orgy of looting and burning the homes of their Whig neighbors, revealing the deep resentments that the rebel policy of violent repression had created.

As 1776 drew to a close, leading Whigs were being hunted down in the woods by gleeful loyalists. Samuel Tucker, the president of the Provincial Congress, surrendered to General Howe in a vain attempt to prevent the British troops from looting his fine house. Richard Stockton, a signer of the Declaration of Independence, was captured in Monmouth County and broke under brutal treatment in a New York prison. He, too, signed a loyalty oath and withdrew from the war.

The Provincial Congress, after a last pathetic appeal to the militia, had long since dispersed. At Morristown on December 22, Brig. Gen. Alexander McDougall of New York wrote: "This state is totally deranged, without government or officers, civil or military, in it that will act with any spirit. . . . When I anticipate the bad consequences that will result to the common cause from the submission of this state, it renders me almost unfit for any business."

Sporadic resistance continued in some parts of New Jersey with Washington's assistance. Three Continental regiments operated out of Morristown to support the fairly good turnout of militia in that area. Another largely militia army gathered in Springfield. British dragoons were ambushed on the road. Near Elizabethtown a British commissary, George Brindley, was badly wounded as he rode through the country buying forage. This guerrilla resistance should not be exaggerated. In few parts of New Jersey could the militia seriously threaten British control. One of Washington's aides told him that in Burlington

County the British and Germans were "scattered through all the farmers' houses, eight, ten, twelve, fifteen in a house, and rambling over the whole country." This was not the conduct of troops under constant guerrilla attack.

Nor should too much stress be placed on the plundering of the British and Hessian troops, which purportedly turned thousands of neutral or loyalist New Jerseyans into rebels. As Washington's aide, Joseph Reed, a native of New Jersey, told his wife, "It is of little consequence which army passes. It is equally destructive to friend and foe." The motives of the Whig militiamen were an unstable mixture of patriotism and avarice, as a letter from the Presbyterian "rebel high priest" of Elizabethtown, the Reverend James Caldwell, made clear. Writing about the militia army from Morris and Essex counties that was operating around Springfield, he remarked that they were "rather fond of plunder and adventure." Caldwell was uncertain what to do about "the arms, horses, or other property taken with any of the enemy. The parties who take them think themselves entitled to these things." [4]

In the Hackensack Valley community of Schraalenburgh, Whigs, most of them from New York, looted the countryside with savage abandon, stealing furniture, clothes, hogsheads of rum, gin, and brandy, and more than 400 pounds of pelts from a tannery. It is clear that this kind of warfare was closer to old-fashioned Jersey rioting. It would not have lasted another month in the face of a countryside occupied by the Royal Army, backed by aggressive, Presbyterian-hating loyalist Jerseyans who were more than ready to be as nasty to their rebel neighbors as they had been to them.

The man who rescued Jerseyans—and the rest of America—from becoming a conquered people was George Washington, who supplied the state's "want of an army" on December 26, when he slashed across the Delaware to capture the German garrison at Trenton. A few days later Washington returned to complete his "nine days' wonder" campaign with another victory at Princeton. Those defeats panicked the British into abandoning

---

4. Charles Lee, *The Lee Papers,* 4 vols. (New York: Collections of the New York Historical Society, 1871), 2:346–347.

four-fifths of New Jersey. They concentrated their army in a fortified ring in the Raritan Valley between Perth Amboy and New Brunswick.

The stunned loyalists elsewhere in New Jersey were left without British protection, exposing them to looting and personal abuse. Some of them had provoked these attacks, but hundreds of neutrals and relatively innocent loyalists also suffered. An outraged Washington asked Governor Livingston to stop the depredations, but there was little Livingston could do beyond issuing orders to militia officers, who seldom obeyed them.

In a stinging letter to Governor Livingston on January 24, 1777, Washington reiterated his call for "a stop to this kind of lawless Rapine." The American commander in chief also told the governor what was wrong with the militia. "Their officers are generally of the lowest class of people; and, instead of setting a good example to their men, are leading them into every kind of mischief." Washington was also troubled by the poor response of the militia, even though they now had an army to look the enemy in the face. He urged Livingston to procure from the legislature a new militia law that would require every man capable of bearing arms to turn out "and not buy off his service by a trifling fine."

Livingston tried manfully to persuade the legislature to give him a tough militia law. He was finally forced to write to Washington, admitting, "I cannot make our Assembly sensible of the importance of an effectual militia law; or if they be, they are so unduly influenced by the fear of disobliging their constituents, that they dare not exert themselves with the requisite spirit for the exigencies of war." Washington and the Continental Congress were learning the hard way that New Jersey was not Massachusetts.

What New Jersey desperately needed was leadership—and William Livingston proceeded to supply it. With respect to its ability to equip the state to deal with the crisis, the government created by the new constitution was a disaster. The legislators of New Jersey looked back, not forward, when they wrote the document. Remembering the quarrels between royal governors and the assembly, they tried to eliminate the danger of such discord by emasculating the governorship. The governor was elected by the assembly, thereby making him beholden to it. He lacked the power to appoint a single official. The assembly chose them all, from the secretary of state to the justices of the peace. New Jersey was not unique in this aversion to executive power. Pennsylvania constitution writers declined even to create the office of governor. An executive council presided over by a president was supposed to do the job. The Virginia governor was also a creature of the legislature, as Thomas Jefferson discovered to his grief when that state was invaded later in the war.

A fifty- or sixty-man legislature cannot provide the kind of leadership that inspires men in a crisis. Such direction can only be delivered by one—at most, a handful—of dynamic individuals. For New Jersey, William Livingston was that man. Looking around him in the opening months of 1777, he saw that the ordinary machinery of New Jersey government was paralyzed. The British army on the Raritan was capable of devastating forays north, south, and west to retaliate against attempts to punish loyalists through the local courts. Moreover, the legislature had dispersed once in the face of a British advance and the potential for similar crises, not to mention unexpected developments when the legislature was not in session, made it imperative to give the executive arm of the government power to deal with these problems.

At Livingston's request, in March 1777 the legislature created a council of safety composed of twelve men. The governor was the president. The council was given the power to call out the militia if necessary, to draw funds from the state treasury, and, most important, to hear cases as justices of the peace and jail anyone "disaffected to, or acting against the government." On March 18, 1777, three days after the legislature created this new weapon, Livingston presided over the first meeting of the council of safety in Haddonfield. For the next eighteen months it was the voice of the Revolution in New Jersey, meeting no fewer than 400 times. Governor Livingston presided at every session.

Although the responsibilities of the council of safety extended to such matters as appointing militia recruiters and investigating abuses in the quartermaster department, its main role was the prosecution of the laws against loyalists. Even after the British withdrew from New Jersey in June 1777, loyalist raids made it impossible for the courts to function in many parts of the state. Operating from Staten Island and New York, and eventually from a camp on the tip of Sandy Hook, the loyalists kidnapped judges, sheriffs, and constables, or terrorized them into resigning from their jobs.

Backed by as many as 500 militia, Livingston replaced the local courts with the council of safety. Loyalists were summoned at gunpoint, examined, and offered an opportunity to take oaths of "abjuration and allegiance," abandoning their loyalty to George III and pledging it to the state of New Jersey. Those who did so were usually permitted to return to their homes without further punishment. Those who refused were required to post bonds for their good behavior. Loyalists caught trading with the British or trying to reach British lines to join the Royal Army were arrested and sent to jails in the interior of the state.

After the British left New Jersey in 1777, leading loyalists were seized in wholesale lots. Wives and children of loyalists serving with the British were deported to New York. Active loyalists were indicted for high treason, a hanging offense. An undetermined number—many judicial records are missing—were hanged. The minutes of the council of safety fill 287 printed pages, each one jammed with names of Jerseyans who resisted the Revolution and required the grim attention of Livingston and his council. It is an awesome record that cannot be read without acquiring a new attitude toward the struggle that created the United States of America. Outside homogenous New England, it was a civil war. The enemy, as this record amply proves, was not only obstinate King George and his army and navy. At least as much time and effort were spent fighting fellow Americans.

Livingston tried to temper revolutionary justice with mercy. He persuaded the legislature to pass an Act of Indemnity in May 1777, permitting loyalists who had previously resisted the new government to return home without fear of prosecution. He did not permit Quakers to be fined for failing to turn out for militia duty and permitted them to make simple statements of affirmation before the council of safety because their faith did not permit them to perform the religious ritual, particularly Bible kissing, involved in a formal oath. He frequently granted executive clemency to those convicted of high treason and sentenced to death.

The governor's correspondence reveals the agonizing dilemmas that often confronted him. In 1779, the chief justice of New Jersey, John Cleves Symmes, sent him a long list of convicted men. One of them had to be hanged as an example. Which one? Symmes recommended William Hammet. He had been warned by the council of safety for his loyalist activity, but he returned home and immediately joined the enemy. He proved himself a daring soldier and was captured with a gun in his hand. At no time did he express himself as regretting his decision. Finally, Hammet was single. One can safely assume that Hammet died.

Livingston could be very tough. When the loyalists kidnapped a leading Whig, John Fell, and abused him badly in prison, the governor arrested two leading loyalists, James Parker and Walter Rutherford, prominent East Jersey proprietors and former personal friends, put them in irons and fed them on bread and water until Fell's treatment improved. Livingston requested and got from the legislature authority for the council of safety to retaliate on a loyalist whenever a similar counter-revolutionary kidnapping occurred.

Serving simultaneously as governor, judge, and prosecutor, Livingston also found time to be a highly effective propagandist. He arranged for Isaac Collins, the official printer, to begin publishing the state's first weekly paper, the *New Jersey Gazette,* and the governor frequently contributed essays to it under the pen name Hortentius. His efforts ranged from patriotic exhortations to scatological satire and sarcastic verse deriding George III, British generals, and the loyalists. It is hardly surprising that Livingston became a focus of loyalist hatred. A price of a thousand pounds was offered for his capture, and at least four attempts were made to assassinate him. For six years, he did not sleep more than two consecutive nights in the same house. In 1780 he remarked, "My family for these four years past have not had fourteen days of my assistance."

Unfortunately, his herculean efforts did not prevent him from becoming involved in New Jersey's habit of internecine quarreling. Within the Whig ranks there was almost as much dissension as there was between the rebels and the loyalists. The source of the division is interesting for the light it sheds on future as well as previous developments in New Jersey. The governor's chief opponent was Abraham Clark of Essex County. A self-educated man, Clark called himself the "poor man's counsellor," and was one of those Jerseyans who had intensely resented the high fees charged by lawyers who practiced in the royal courts. Since Governor Livingston was one of the most successful of these lawyers, with numerous clients among the proprietors, the root of their mutual antagonism is easily discerned.

Clark was a fervent admirer of Samuel Adams and his fellow New Englanders and regularly voted with them in the Continental Congress. Clark even wrote apostrophes to "the genius and political ideas of the New England states and New Jersey." Livingston intensely resented New England's attempts to dominate the Continental Congress by voting as a bloc under the leadership of Sam Adams. Another reason for his reluctance to vote for independence may well have been his fears of New England's aggrandizing power. In 1780 Livingston told the French minister to America that he would like to see a confederation of the American states that excluded New England. Livingston believed that "the interest of New Jersey is intimately connected with that of the middle colonies . . . & I could therefore never see the policy or propriety of our delegates throwing themselves into the arms of those of New England & Virginia as has generally been the case."

Clark and Livingston also disagreed about George Washington. Between the general and the governor there was a mutual trust and understanding which deepened with the passage of the war years. In a humorous letter to the governor's daughter Susan, Alexander Hamilton remarked, "Whether the Governor and the General are more honest, or more perverse than other people, they have a very odd knack of thinking alike.'' Livingston admired Washington so much that he wrote an extravagant ode in his honor. It appeared in the *New Jersey Gazette* in April 1778. Clark followed the policy of Samuel Adams—almost pathological hostility to the army and its officers, rooted in a fear that they were dangerous to America's free society. When Washington issued a proclamation on January 25, 1777, giving those who had accepted pardons from the British a chance to turn in their papers and swear allegiance to the United States, Clark tried to have the general censured in Congress. He maintained that citizens should only swear allegiance to their native states. Clark ranted about the danger of giving Washington the extraordinary powers Congress had granted him in the crisis of late 1776. Livingston thoroughly approved of this congressional decision and told Washington he only wished that Congress had done it ''a twelve month ago.''

Clark and his party were undoubtedly behind a serious attempt to knock Livingston out of the governorship in 1779 when they and many other Americans thought the war was practically over. France's entry into the war on the American side had forced the British to abandon Philadelphia. Washington had pursued the retreating Royal Army across New Jersey and fought them to a bloody draw in 100-degree heat at Monmouth Court House. The British were on the defensive in New York and there was talk of a French invasion of England. The Clarkites decided they could win the rest of the war without William Livingston. An essay in the *New Jersey Gazette* condemned the governor for the bad taste he supposedly displayed in the Hortentius letters, complained of his sloppy dress, and called him a ''thorough and complete coward.'' These gross exaggerations backfired and Livingston was elected by the usual large majority of the assembly for another one-year term. A very good thing for New Jersey and the Revolution, because the British had by no means abandoned the war or their hope of seizing control of the state. A few weeks after the letter was published, a good half of the British army sailed south to assault and capture Charleston, South Carolina, and open a vigorous campaign to subdue the southern states, with their heavy proportion of loyalists.

While the British fought in the sunny South, Washington and his army suffered through the worst winter of the century in their camp at Morristown. Devastating blizzards piled snow twelve feet deep in the roads. The Hudson, the Raritan, the Delaware froze so solidly that carriages and even cannon rolled across the ice. Simultaneously, the army's supply system collapsed. Inflation had reached the ludicrous point where an "ordinary horse" was selling for 20,000 continental dollars. In a futile gesture to halt further depreciation, Congress stopped printing money. In a matter of weeks the army ran out of cash and Washington was soon getting letters from officials of the commissary department informing him that without money they could not buy cattle or anything else. The commissary general and his deputy resigned in despair. Moore Furman, deputy quartermaster general of New Jersey, also ran out of money to pay the wagon teams carrying provisions to the army. On April 12, Washington was writing, "We have not this day one ounce of fresh meat or salt in the magazine." On May 23, 1780, two Connecticut regiments, after having no food issued to them for three days, mutinied and came close to persuading the rest of the army to join them.

New Jersey soldiers were equally disgruntled. In 1779, twenty-one officers of the New Jersey Brigade informed the assembly that if they did not hear in three days that some action was going to be taken to relieve their poverty and hunger, they were resigning. "Nothing which has happened in the course of the war . . . has given me so much pain," Washington told their commander, Brig. Gen. William Maxwell. The officers replied that they were "very unhappy that any act of ours should give Your Excellency pain." With not a little sarcasm, they remarked that "few of us have private fortunes." They could no longer tolerate seeing their families "suffering everything that can be received from an ungrateful country."

The real trouble was that old New Jersey problem, taxes. No one wanted to pay them, and the legislature hesitated to impose them for fear of alienating their constituents. Governor Livingston raged at the lawmakers' "unaccountable timidity," but they ignored him. Collections were even more lackadaisical. In 1781, Monmouth and Gloucester counties had not completed their quotas for 1775.

Complicating everything was the depreciation of the continental dollar, which made a captain's salary of $480 a month worth thirteen real dollars, and a lieutenant's salary of $126.60 worth $3.30. "The pay of a colonel of your regiments will not purchase the oats for his horse, nor will his whole day's pay procure him a single dinner. A common laborer or an express rider receives four times as much as he," the officers informed the assembly in their letter of protest. General Maxwell backed them in equally vigorous terms, which also give us a candid glimpse of the way the Revolution was being fought in New Jersey.

> The farmer as well as the merchant has come to the knowledge that every thing is worth what it will bring, and notwithstanding he knows that the security of his property and privileges has cost the soldier dear in heats, colds, thirsting, hunger and watching, yet he will make no scruple to strip him of his month's pittance for a day's subsistance.

In New York, Gov. William Franklin had been exchanged for the rebel governor of Delaware, whom the British had captured. Profoundly embittered—his wife had died a forlorn refugee in New York in 1777—Franklin created a semimilitary organization that eventually became the Board of Associated Loyalists. He formed an alliance with a New York loyalist, William Smith, who was in charge of procuring intelligence for that colony's former royal governor, Maj. Gen. William Tryon. Together the three persuaded the British high command in New York that an invasion of New Jersey would restore the state to royal allegiance.

At Morristown, Washington's army had dwindled to 3,600 men. Lack of money had forced him to seize cattle and grain from New Jersey's farmers virtually at bayonet point, giving them nothing but vouchers to be redeemed at some indefinite future date. To William Franklin their complaints were further evidence that New Jersey was ripe for counterrevolution. A swift blow that seized the passes through the Short Hills behind Elizabethtown would enable the Royal Army to overrun Washington's camp at Morristown, where most of the American army's cannon and ammunition were stranded for lack of horses and wagons to move them. Without the Continental Army, the loyalists would rise and with the help of the Royal Army easily mop up the New Jersey militia.

It was a feasible plan. Down in South Carolina, the British commander in chief, Sir Henry Clinton, was working on an identical plan, with an addition that practically guaranteed its success. He intended to return to New York with the bulk of his southern army and land at Perth Amboy to seize the mountain passes behind that town. Washington would then be faced with two armies, each of which outnumbered his dwindling force. If he attempted to defend his camp at Morristown, he would almost certainly be overrun. If he chose to fight at one pass, the other pass would be undefended, and the second British army would soon be clawing at his rear.

But an incredible web of jealousy and noncommunication in the British high command prevented Sir Henry from executing his plan. Instead, thanks to William Franklin and his fellow loyalists, the general in command of New York, Wilhelm von Knyphausen, launched his own invasion of New Jersey on June 6, 1780, without waiting for Clinton's return. Facing the 6,000-man British-German army as it came ashore at Elizabethtown were 500 men from the four understrength regiments of the New Jersey Brigade of the Continental Army. They were "on the lines," as the forward positions along the Essex County shore were called. The rest of Washington's army was at Morristown. Eleven miles away was Hobart Gap, the crucial pass through the Short Hills that the British advance guard hoped to seize by dawn.

Outnumbered ten to one, Maxwell and his New Jersey regulars dug in on the nearest high ground—the village of Connecticut Farms, where a branch of the Elizabeth River had cut a long narrow ravine. Without support, they would have been quickly destroyed or dispersed. But now the effect of William Livingston's years of revolutionary leadership became dramatically visible. Alarm guns on the Short Hills boomed and signal towers built by Washington and supervised by the Reverend James Caldwell blazed into the dawn. Militia from Essex, Middlesex, Somerset, and Morris counties swarmed to support the regulars while Washington organized his army for a forced march from Morristown to defend Hobart Gap.

All day the New Jersey Brigade and the militia fought the Royal Army to a standstill in the village of Connecticut Farms. As dusk fell the Americans retreated across the Rahway River into the village of Springfield. Advance elements of Washington's army, led by his Life Guard, joined them for a spirited counterattack that broke up a last British-German attempt to seize the bridge across the river. The rest of Washington's army occupied Hobart Gap, and the threat of immediate defeat was over.

In the course of the day's fighting, Americans fired from windows and doors of houses in Connecticut Farms. Most of the inhabitants of the village fled, leaving the houses empty. A few stayed, with fatal consequences. One civilian was killed by a bullet in the head early in the day. Later, the wife of James Caldwell was killed by a British soldier who fired into the room where she and her children had taken refuge. The Whigs, led by Caldwell himself, cried murder. Later in the year, Caldwell published eyewitness testimony that purported to show that the killing was deliberate. A reading 200 years after the event, without the hatreds engendered by a civil war, makes it clear that it was a military accident. Yet the official seal of Union County still dramatizes the propaganda version of the event. Mrs. Caldwell stands on the porch of her house, being gunned down by a vengeful redcoat at point-blank range.[5]

The British and Germans belatedly learned from a Henry Clinton aide that he was on his way to New York with the southern army. They retreated to the shore of Elizabethtown Point to await these reinforcements. When they arrived, the

---

5. "Certain Facts Relating to the Death of Hannah Caldwell," *New Jersey Journal* (September 6, 1780).

Royal Army made one more try to break through Hobart Gap and reach the American camp at Morristown. Brushing aside a relative handful of militia, they got across the Rahway into the village of Springfield, where regulars under the command of Maj. Gen. Nathanael Greene did most of the fighting with some assistance from militia who responded to the new alarm.

In the vanguard of the Royal Army were two loyalist regiments. One was a battalion of the green-coated New Jersey Volunteers. The other was the Queen's Rangers, which had numerous New Jersey men in its ranks. Greene's army was forced to abandon Springfield and withdraw to high ground in the Short Hills. The British decided it would cost too many men to dislodge them and retreated—after setting ablaze every house in Springfield, except two that belonged to loyalists. It was grim evidence of the savage, revengeful nature of the war in New Jersey. On June 7 the Royal Army had burned most of the village of Connecticut Farms, including the Presbyterian church, and in a spirit of pure destruction chopped down whole orchards.

Most historians of the Revolution have failed to recognize the importance of the British failure in New Jersey in 1780. Even Washington admitted he was baffled by enemy intentions. Only in recent years, when we have had access to the diaries of loyalist William Smith and the headquarters papers of Sir Henry Clinton, have we been able to grasp its significance. More than a few Americans, including Alexander Hamilton, saw it as a defeat. "You have heard how the enemy made an incursion into the Jerseys and made an excursion out of it," he raged to a fellow officer. Washington praised the New Jersey Brigade and the New Jersey militia extravagantly for their performance. Others agreed with him. A Massachusetts major of the artillery, Samuel Shaw, declared it was "Lexington repeated." While the phrase gives the militia the credit they deserve, it is erroneous because it misses the interdependence of the militia and the regular army that George Washington and William Livingston had forged in four bitter years of revolutionary struggle in New Jersey.

A year later, when General Washington joined forces with the

French and began his march through New Jersey to Yorktown and the victory that guaranteed American independence, many loyalists, including Gen. Benedict Arnold, were sure that the British could smash the allied army to pieces, strung out as it was in a long exposed line moving parallel to the Hudson. Sir Henry Clinton remembered how well the New Jersey militia had fought at Connecticut Farms and Springfield and rejected the idea.

The British did not invade New Jersey again, but the civil war between the loyalists and the Whigs continued with unabated ferocity. It reached a climax of sorts when loyalists hanged a captured American militia captain, Joshua Huddy, in retaliation for the supposed murder of one of their partisans, Philip White, after White was captured during a raid. Prodded by Jerseyans, Washington demanded that the British surrender the officer who had hanged Huddy. He was Capt. Richard Lippincott, who said he had acted under orders of the Board of Associated Loyalists. On this plea he was acquitted by a British court-martial.

An angry Washington ordered a British captain selected by lot, and announced he would be hanged unless Lippincott or the man who had given him his orders was surrendered. At this point, William Franklin, the president of the Board of Associated Loyalists, decided it was prudent to leave America for England. The British officer chosen for revenge was Capt. Charles Asgill of the elite Foot Guards. His powerful family exerted all their influence to save him, finally persuading the king and queen of France to intervene on his behalf. To New Jersey's chagrin, Asgill was released and Lippincott sailed off with other loyalist refugees to Canada, where he died with no sign of a guilty conscience at the age of eighty-one.

The civil war continued to rage along New Jersey's coast, even after the British began peace negotiations in Europe. In the social chaos, unsavory characters came to the fore on both sides. David Forman, a militia brigadier general from Monmouth County who was active in the corrupt sale of confiscated loyalist estates, and was also a leader in the art of rigging elections, formed an Association for Retaliation. These forerunners of the vigilantes announced they would burn homes and barns and rob cattle and goods in exact proportion to the damage the loyalists did to them. Anyone not a member of the association was fair game for their mercenary vengeance. Even more vicious was loyalist Capt. John Bacon. He and his gang massacred thirty militiamen on the beach at Barnegat on the night of October 25, 1782. The militiamen had been unloading a British ship that had run aground. They had decided to sleep on the sand and finish the job in the morning.

In spite of these outbursts of greed and savagery, the war wound inexorably down. On March 13, 1783, the text of the provisional treaty of peace arrived from Paris and on April 11 Congress declared an end of hostilities. Governor Livingston issued a similar announcement to the people of New Jersey on April 14, and there were celebrations mingled with joy and disbelief in every town in the state. It was, said one Jerseyman in words that echoed the tensions of seven years of violence, "a very happy alarm."

But the end of the end was yet to come. The British army remained in New York, waiting for Parliament to ratify the treaty. Congress, unsettled by threats of mutinous unpaid soldiers, who at one point surrounded the Pennsylvania State House with fixed bayonets, retreated to Princeton. There George Washington joined them to discuss a peacetime military establishment and other matters. On October 30, 1783, from his headquarters at Rocky Hill, the general issued his final orders, bidding "an affectionate, a long farewell" to the soldiers of the armies of the United States. It seems fitting that the end of the end of the exhausting struggle came in New Jersey, the cockpit of the Revolution.

6

"Never" in Philadelphia

*O*N November 25, 1783, thousands of Jerseyans lined the heights of Bergen and the shores of Elizabethtown to watch the British evacuate New York City. Most of New Jersey's loyalists departed with that 400-ship armada. But some were soon seeking permission to return to their native state. They got a frosty reception. Petitioners from Monmouth County urged the legislature to bar in perpetuity "bloodthirsty robbers" and "atrocious monsters." The assembly concurred, and New Jersey laws against the loyalists remained on the books. But they were selectively enforced. Men like Richard Lippincott, the murderer of Captain Huddy, or William Franklin, who gave him the order, would have been promptly tried and probably hanged if they had showed their faces in New Jersey. The fighting loyalists of this stamp were wise enough to spend the rest of their lives in England or Canada. For those who had not borne arms against their neighbors, there was less rancor.

The Reverend Thomas Bradbury Chandler reported that he was treated "with remarkable kindness and respect" when he returned. Like most loyalists, Chandler remained myopic about the Revolution. After conversations with "some persons who made themselves conspicuous in the late rebellion," he concluded that "all of them feel, that the exchange of British protection for independency has been ruinous to the country." He was certain that Jerseyans were ready "to adopt the language of

81

the repenting prodigal in the parable, towards the parent country." [1]

Chandler was wrong about an inclination to play the prodigal. But there was no doubt that New Jersey was not a very happy place in the early postwar years. Devastation from opposing armies and Tory raiders and counterlooting by Whigs had left the state a wreck. Hard money to rebuild it was practically nonexistent. The small supply was sucked into Philadelphia and New York, where stores were flooded with long-scarce British-made products. The New Jersey legislature resorted to that old panacea, paper money, but the nostrum no longer worked. Although Americans had just fought a long war that theoretically united them as a nation, the individual states began to show alarming separatist tendencies. New Jersey was on the receiving end of one of the worst examples of this trend. The merchants of New York and Philadelphia refused to honor her paper money, and it soon depreciated to the status of wastepaper. The same thing happened to copper coins the state issued, nicknamed "horses' heads."

Then came even worse economic imperialism from New York. The gentlemen of Gotham and their friends in Albany decreed that any boat, no matter how picayune, that carried goods across the Hudson from New Jersey had to be inspected by a customs officer and pay duties on its contents. Recent historians have pointed out that New York was only punishing New Jersey for its refusal to tax British imports—something almost every other state had done. But this explanation misses several major points in the dispute. The amount of goods transshipped from New Jersey to New York was minimal. On the other hand, Jerseyans bought a heavy proportion of their manufactured goods in New York, where they had to pay higher prices created by New York's tariffs—all of which went into the treasury of the Empire State.

The New Jersey legislature retaliated by laying a thirty-pound

---

1. Mary Beth Norton, *The British Americans: The Loyalist Exiles in England, 1774–1789* (Boston: Little Brown and Co., 1972), pp. 248, 256.

annual tax on the Sandy Hook lighthouse. A pathetic gesture at best.

Jerseyans were enraged but not surprised by these New York tactics. They had been among the earliest critics of the Articles of Confederation, the toothless Constitution with which Congress was attempting to govern America. During the Revolution, when she was in desperate need of assistance from other states, New Jersey had been an early proponent of a strong central government. In 1777, she had urged the members of Congress to take an oath of loyalty to the United States. During the debates over the Articles of Confederation, New Jersey had insisted that large states like Virginia, which claimed vast areas of western lands, should surrender their claims to Congress so that the lands could be disposed with equal benefit to all the states. With not a little acerbity, New Jersey pointed out that some states with no western claims were suffering far more to win the war than others who would become fabulously rich if victory drove the British off the continent. When the Articles of Confederation were finally ratified, New Jersey scored their failure to give Congress the power to regulate foreign trade. She feared from past experience the tactics of her bigger, more powerful neighbors.

In 1785, when protests against New York's high handed tax tactics were ignored, the Garden State stunned the feckless Congress with a declaration of independence. The New Jersey legislature refused to pay its share of the latest taxes "requested by Congress" from the states. Twelve states had agreed to let Congress tax imports to raise the money the federal government needed to pay salaries and interest on the national debt. But New York had refused to join this compact. The Trenton lawmakers declared that they would, in the words of one startled Congressman, grant "not a shilling, until New York accedes to the impost." [2]

There was another reason for New Jersey's defiance, one that

---

2. Edmund Cody Burnett, *The Continental Congress* (New York: Macmillan Co., 1941; Norton Library edition, 1964), p. 644.

went beyond her traditional antagonism to New York. Because so much of the war had been fought in New Jersey, her citizens had acquired an extraordinary number of promissory notes from the U.S. Government. In 1790, these paper debts amounted to $2,431,845, one-eleventh of the total domestic debt of the nation. When Congress defaulted on these notes and stopped paying interest in 1782, the New Jersey legislature came under terrific pressure from the voters. The legislature responded by levying a tax that was paid to the continental loan officer in New Jersey, who in turn parcelled it out to New Jersey creditors. In 1784 the state treasurer began paying the interest on these notes directly to New Jersey creditors of the United States. This meant that Jerseyans were paying a disproportionately large share of the interest on the federal debt, which in turn explains why New Jersey was so anxious to see Congress acquire national taxing power so that it could take over these payments and relieve Jerseyans of an unjustly heavy economic burden.

New Jersey was not alone in its inclination to disregard Congress. Of the $6 million in taxes Congress had tried to collect since the end of the war, only $1 million had been paid. But no other state had so explicitly and publicly defied the national legislature. One historian of the Continental Congress described New Jersey's action as "one of the most stunning blows that body had at any time received."

On March 7, 1785, a jittery Congress repeated a drama it had enacted with New Jersey ten years earlier. Three distinguished members, Charles Pinckney of South Carolina, Nathaniel Gorham of Massachusetts, and William Grayson of Virginia, were hustled off to Trenton to talk the New Jersey legislators out of their economic secession from the confederacy. In his speech, Charles Pinckney admitted New Jersey's revolt was almost justified by Congress's deplorable weakness. He urged the state "to instruct her delegates to Congress, to urge the calling of a general convention of the states, for the purpose of revising and amending the federal system." He promised to support "any measure of that kind" while he remained in Congress.

William Grayson of Virginia took a different approach. "What is your object," he asked the legislators,

> in hastening the dissolution of a confederation that has cost us so dear? Do you suppose that in a new system of government you would be allowed the importance that you have had hitherto? Do you think that Virginia, South Carolina, Pennsylvania, and Massachusetts would be willing to stand on equal footing with the handful of citizens which inhabit your state? In a new confederation you will be put in your proper place.

These rough words were to haunt New Jersey in the Constitutional Convention that her revolt precipitated. Although the legislature agreed to rescind its resolution defying Congress, it refused to pay the tax. New York added insult to this fiscal injury by still refusing to approve a national tariff on imports, except in the most nominal fashion. In Congress, Charles Pinckney called for a general convention to overhaul the Articles of Confederation. An uprising of debt-ridden farmers in Massachusetts helped impress Americans with the need for a stable central government that could do something about the drift toward economic and political anarchy.

When the Constitutional Convention met in Philadelphia in 1787, the New Jersey delegation became the spokesmen for the small states. They did battle with the large-state political juggernaut led by James Madison and the delegation from Virginia. From the point of view of those in large states, the chief defect of the Articles of Confederation was the provision giving each state an equal vote. They argued in 1787, as they had argued in 1776, that the power of each state in the federal government should be in direct proportion to the taxes that she paid to it. The Virginia Plan, already embellished to the last detail by James Madison, the greatest political genius of the era, gathered irresistible momentum. It called for proportional representation in both houses of the new government. Lower house members would be elected by the people for three-year terms, the upper house by the state legislatures for seven-year terms.

These ideas had been approved by overwhelming margins in

test votes when William Paterson of New Jersey arose on June 14, 1787, to propose the "New Jersey Plan." Paterson, the wartime attorney general of New Jersey, spoke for "the members from the small states" who were "friends to a good national government but . . . would sooner submit to a foreign power . . . than be deprived" of equal votes in both branches of the legislature, an inequality that meant they would be "thrown under the domination of the larger states."

The New Jersey Plan was buried by a two-to-one margin in the ensuing vote. But the skill with which Paterson defended it during the debates and the grim determination with which New Jersey, supported only by tiny Delaware, voted no in the final count aroused sufficient concern among the delegates to launch the most crucial negotiations of the convention. The result was the great compromise that gave each state proportional representation in the House of Representatives and an equal vote in the Senate. With ten states voting, it was adopted by a vote of five to four (New Jersey, Connecticut, Delaware, Maryland, and North Carolina in favor of it, and Pennsylvania, Virginia, South Carolina, and Georgia against it, with Massachusetts divided). The keystone of the compromise was the way Jerseymen said, "Never," to the nationalist plan and proved they meant it.

Unlike some other states, such as Virginia and New York, where the Constitution was bitterly resisted, New Jersey's Constitutional Convention was a love feast. Although Paterson and the other delegates to the convention were personally disgruntled with the compromise, they were good politicians, and they knew that electoral sentiment in New Jersey was overwhelmingly in favor of ratification. The convention lasted a week, but there was never any danger of rejection. On Dec. 19, 1787, the thirty-nine delegates—three from each of New Jersey's thirteen counties—unanimously endorsed the new national charter at the Blazing Star Tavern in Trenton. There were cheers from a large crowd when the news was announced the next day. Everyone knew that New Jersey had got what she wanted —and coincidentally what the nation needed—a strong federal government in which she could participate with dignity.

7

Politics, Politics

*T*HE first election under the national government produced new variations on New Jersey's traditional divisions, in particular the century-old split between East and West Jersey. During the 1780s, voting in the assembly had repeatedly revealed this sectional rivalry, which had been equally visible during the Revolution and under the royal government. The West Jersey party tended to be somewhat wealthier, inclined toward creditor interests, and therefore hostile to paper money, and influenced by the high percentage of Quakers in the voting population. East Jerseyans tended to prefer spokesmen for small- and moderate-sized farmers who were often debt-ridden and fond of paper money.

The Revolution had banished the British aristocrats and their American supporters. But New Jersey had its own native aristocrats without titles, men of wealth who had handsome houses and lived on large estates. They gravitated instinctively to the West Jersey party, no matter where they lived. The East Jerseyans also had no difficulty recruiting some western spokesmen for their poor and middle-class voters. Thus the West Jersey four-man ticket for the House of Representatives in 1789 had two wealthy East Jerseyans on it—Elias Boudinot and James Schureman. The East Jerseyans called their opponents the "Junto ticket" and did their utmost to arouse class envy against them.

87

The election continued the tradition of keeping the polls open while the party leaders drummed up votes, both legal and illegal. Seven East Jersey counties closed their polls on February 23, 1789. West Jersey kept theirs open for another two months. Essex County riposted by doing the same thing. The governor's council certified the West Jerseyans as winners before Essex County could finish counting its equally fraudulent votes. Governor Livingston suggested that Congress should decide who really won. But that body showed no interest in an investigation and the Junto candidates were seated without difficulty.

In the summer of 1790, just as the new national government was beginning to operate, Gov. William Livingston died. He had been in failing health for some time—which may explain why he played such a minor role in the Constitutional Convention. He had been re-elected annually by the citizens of New Jersey since 1776—a record that no other governor will ever match. William Paterson, the man whose eloquence had made New Jersey such a potent influence at the Constitutional Convention, was chosen to succeed him. When Paterson accepted President Washington's appointment as an associate justice of the Supreme Court of the United States, he was succeeded by Richard Howell. Both men were members of the Federalist party, ardent supporters of a strong central government.

By that time, the Founding Fathers' dream of running the country without political parties was evaporating. The rich and their followers, who believed that only "men of virtue and talent" could govern the country, had formed the Federalist party, and they tried to pin a treasonous hostility to the Constitution on the opposition coalescing around Thomas Jefferson. When the French Revolution broke out and the Jeffersonians supported it, the Federalists added atheism to their list of accusations.

It was an effective political operation, while George Washington was in the White House, lending the Federalists the aura of his unbeatable prestige. The Federalists controlled New Jersey throughout the 1790s. They relied on prominent local names to carry them to victory. Boudinots, Stocktons, Daytons—these were their leaders. This government from the top down revealed some of its most interesting tendencies in New Jersey. Far more than the Jeffersonians, who by one of those curious twists in historical continuity are considered the ancestors of the twentieth-century Democratic party, with its emphasis on Big Government, the Federalists were bold advocates of government planning.

The Federalist leader, Secretary of the Treasury Alexander Hamilton, wanted to encourage American manufacturers, whom he considered timid and unimaginative. Hamilton had gone to school in Elizabethtown and knew New Jersey and her prominent men well from the years he had spent in the state during the Revolution, when he was George Washington's aide. In the economic program Hamilton submitted to the federal Congress in 1791, he recommended the creation of a factory city beside the falls of the Passaic, to be run by a corporation called The Society for Useful Manufactures. He proposed to allocate no less than $1 million dollars—a staggering sum in those days—in government bonds and shares in the Bank of the United States to pay for it.

The Jeffersonians in and out of Congress balked. They denounced the idea of industrializing the United States, a policy they predicted would create cities full of unruly degenerate mobs. It was the beginning of the city-versus-the-country debate, which was to have fateful consequences for New Jersey and the nation. In 1791, the agrarians had an overwhelming majority of the votes and Congress refused to support Hamilton's proposal. But the secretary's idea got a much warmer reception in New Jersey. Governor Paterson invited him to Trenton to confer with the Federalist legislature, and numerous members of that body bought stock in the S.U.M. The society was voted a perpetual monopoly on manufacturing in the new city, which was named Paterson. It was exempted from taxes and given access not only to the waterpower at the falls, but of the entire Passaic River—the chief water supply of north Jersey. The charter also gave the S.U.M. all the powers of government in the new city. This proviso theoretically banished the spectre of unruly workers.

At the head of the S.U.M., Hamilton placed New York capitalist and friend William Duer, who quickly sold some

$600,000 in stock to private investors. Then Duer began displaying some of the frailties of human nature to which even members of the party of virtue and talent were subject. He became involved in a tricky scheme to corner the government bond market and got caught short, precipitating a financial panic and the new nation's first depression. Duer wound up in jail and much of the capital pledged to the S.U.M. vanished. Hundreds of speculators, including many of the S.U.M.'s directors, were ruined.

Nevertheless, Hamilton and his fellow Federalists struggled desperately to save their industrial brainchild. The secretary of the treasury got the S.U.M. loans from New York banks and took personal charge of planning the factories. But none of the directors, including Hamilton, had any manufacturing experience, and the federal government, where Jeffersonians were rising to power, stubbornly refused to come through with any financial aid. The society spent too much of its scarce capital on building factories and importing expensive machinery from England, expenditures that one shrewd English visitor remarked "brings a heavy mortgage on the concern, before they actually begin." By 1795 the S.U.M. was awash in red ink and scalded stockholders abandoned it. The society relapsed to a paper existence and Paterson's population sank from 500 to 43.

When Washington left the White House, the Federalists were in trouble. There was a built-in backlash among equality-minded Americans to the Federalist anointing of themselves as the party of virtue and talent. In 1796, the opposition, who were beginning to call themselves Republicans, challenged them for the first time in New Jersey. They backed Thomas Jefferson against the Federalist candidate, John Adams. The New Englander handily won New Jersey in the presidential election, but the Republicans put a man on the governor's council for the first time, and the following year they were back, fiercely attacking "the Federalist ticket alias the Aristocratical alias the Lawyers' ticket," the last item being an old New Jersey war cry that apparently still aroused the average voter.

Capitalizing on national Federalist blunders, in particular the unpopular Alien and Sedition Acts, which gave Congress the power to muzzle newspapers for criticizing the government, New Jersey Republicans steadily narrowed the gap. In October 1798, they scored their first statewide triumph by electing three of the five-member New Jersey delegation to Congress. In 1799, Republican members of the assembly began living in the same boardinghouses during the legislative session and announced they were "determined to give [Governor] Howell a sweat." They also demonstrated considerable shrewdness by wooing from the Federalist ranks Joseph Bloomfield, a Burlington politician who had served in Congress as a Federalist.

The national election of 1800, pitting Jefferson against Adams once more, was a ferocious contest. Joseph Bloomfield rode through New Jersey urging Republicans to work for the author of the Declaration of Independence. Lucius Horatio Stockton toured the state warning churchgoers that Jefferson was an atheist and predicting an assault on religion if the godless Republicans won. A minister in Sussex County retaliated by putting a picture of Jefferson on the altar of his church, like an icon.

As a last-minute ploy, the Republicans called a state political convention, one of the first in America. It issued an address to the voters signed by Joseph Bloomfield and attacked the Federalists for rolling up the national debt and levying unpopular taxes. The Republicans were hampered by a population imbalance that gave them huge majorities in Sussex, Essex, and Morris counties and minority positions elsewhere. The Federalists won control of the legislature thirty-eight to twelve, and John Adams once more got New Jersey's electoral votes. But the Republicans won all five congressional contests. The race was extremely close, each candidate winning by only a few hundred votes.

Jefferson's election to the presidency gave the Republicans control of federal patronage, and this in turn gave their New Jersey followers the impetus they needed to take over the state. They soon organized the legislative caucus as a basic tool of party discipline. The state nominating convention also became an institution. The Federalists tended to sneer at the Republican passion for organization, which created township associations, county committees, and state committees. The Federalists continued to rely on big names, ignoring the power of Jefferson's democratic revolution.

New York and New Jersey Federalists had maintained the close ties they displayed during the creation of Paterson. As the Jeffersonian ascendancy gained momentum, many New York Federalists despaired of regaining control of New York City. There, the Tammany Society had already become a democratic colossus. Federalists began eyeing smaller, more manageable New Jersey as a potential promised land. Even though the party had lost control of the state, each election was still hotly contested. Moreover, the Republicans showed signs of splitting into West and East Jersey branches, continuing that prerevolutionary feud. In 1803 West Jersey Republicans had their own convention and party caucus.

With their wealth and commercial backgrounds, the Federalists instinctively gravitated to cities. Brooding over their loss of New York, they conceived the idea of founding a rival in New Jersey. Where? Right across the river, where there would be equal access to the Hudson's broad waters and the huge sheltered harbor. Alexander Hamilton was once more a prime mover in the project. He reportedly maintained that all great cities rose on the west banks of rivers. He also saw it as a potential ally of his stillborn brainchild, Paterson. A Federalist port might pump money into the abandoned factories of that ghost town and restore it to life.

On March 26, 1804, Anthony Dey, a New York lawyer, began the Federalist exodus to New Jersey by buying Powles Hook on the bank of the Hudson from Cornelius Van Vorst, whose family had owned the property for more than a century. Dey soon brought in partners, Col. Richard Varick, the former Federalist mayor of New York, and thirty-three others. Hamilton drew up a charter for "The Associates of the Jersey Company." Federalists from New Jersey, such as Elisha Boudinot and William Pennington, mingled with Republicans, such as Joseph Bloomfield, which no doubt explained why the charter sailed through the state legislature with scarcely a ripple of criticism. As in Paterson, the associates were given the powers of government and even more important, the ownership of the prospective city's riverfront.

In the midst of these negotiations, Alexander Hamilton took a trip to New Jersey on other, more fateful business. Early on the morning of July 11, 1804, he rowed across the Hudson to fight a duel with the vice-president of the United States, Aaron Burr, on the shore of the village of Weehawken. Burr cut him down with a bullet in the belly, and the "little lion" of the Federalists was dead the next day. The heart of the Federalist party died with him. It would take another decade for rigor mortis to overtake the corpse.

Meanwhile, New York Republicans took steps to abort Hamilton's last brainchild. While the Federalists laid out lots and named a square in Hamilton's name, the corporation counsel of New York produced an opinion that the city owned the Hudson River up to the high-water mark on the Jersey shore. The Republican city government put an ad in the newspapers warning anyone who "made improvements, constructed wharves, etc between high and low water mark on the west side of the Hudson without getting their [New York's] official consent did so at his own peril."

Shortly before his death, Hamilton called New York's claim preposterous. But businessmen are not noted for their courage, and no one had much stomach for taking on a tax-supported corporation, the city of New York, in a lawsuit that might last years. The sale of lots in the new city came to a dead stop. For the next thirty years it was moribund, one more episode in the saga of New York economic imperialism.

New Jersey remained in Republican control, and Jefferson's allies soon felt secure enough to launch another political tradition—taking care of themselves and their relatives at public expense. When William S. Pennington retired from the governorship in 1815, he was handed a federal judgeship. The court met only four times a year. The terms rarely lasted more than a day. No grand jury was ever sworn in his court nor were any indictments ever found. He held this workless job until 1827. When Ebenezer Elmer lost his seat in Congress, he was promptly made collector of the thriving port of Little Egg Harbor. During his twelve years as governor, Joseph Bloomfield appointed his nephew and ward, Joseph McIlvaine, to numerous high-ranking militia posts and four different state jobs. The champion office-holder was James J. Wilson, editor of the Trenton paper, the *True American*. He was clerk of the assembly, clerk for Hunterdon County, surrogate for the county, adjutant general of the New Jersey militia, and president of the New Jersey State Bank. He went to the U.S. Senate in 1815, and when he retired from that august body in 1820, was not above becoming postmaster of Trenton.

It was hard to attack these abuses of power because the Republicans practically monopolized the governorship and legislature during the long reign of the Virginia dynasty under Presidents Jefferson, Madison, and Monroe. Not until 1828, when the party split into "National" and "Democratic" Republicans, a break loosely corresponding to conservative and liberal, did New Jersey Republicans have any consistent challengers.

During these years, Jerseyans tried to improve their voting laws, to eliminate fraud and give the popular will a chance to express itself. There were numerous complaints about voting irregularities during the years when Federalists and Jeffersonian Republicans fought for control. Laws were passed limiting to two days the time when the polls could be kept open. Candidates were forbidden to offer liquor or money to voters and "weapons of war" were banned from polling places. A 1797 law shifted the voting to townships, eliminating the sometimes lengthy journey to the county seat. But no one bothered to confirm or deny the most curious aspect of New Jersey's suffrage law—it gave women the right to vote. The hastily written state constitution of 1776 granted the vote to "all inhabitants . . . of full age" with no reference to sex.

Relatively few women took advantage of the privilege. But the sectional nature of New Jersey politics inclined local election officers, eager to roll up a big majority for their candidate, to allow almost anyone to vote, including "slaves, aliens, and Philadelphians." The climax of this tendency was an election in Essex County in 1807 in which Elizabeth and Newark battled

over where the county seat—and an expensive courthouse—should be located. Women voted in huge numbers, possibly more than once. At any rate, Newark alone cast more
votes than had ever been cast in the county as a whole—279
percent of the eligible male voters—and incidentally won the
election.

This "saturnalia of corruption and abuse" shocked the legislature into revising the suffrage statute. The lawmakers barred
women, but widened the voting rights to include anyone who
had paid a state or county tax, dropping the requirement that a
voter had to be worth at least fifty pounds. The legislature also
paid some attention to the principle of proportional representation, which had been endorsed in the 1776 constitution. More
populous counties were granted additional representatives.

Only once did the New Jersey Federalists seriously challenge
the Republicans. When the War of 1812 exploded on a
thoroughly unprepared nation, New Jersey Federalists quickly
pinned the war party label on the Republicans. With Jefferson's
successor, James Madison, in the White House and the western
and southern Republicans—the War Hawks—calling for blood
in Congress, this was easy to do. The main quarrel with England—freedom of the seas—had little meaning for New Jersey,
which had virtually no merchant marine. Quaker disapproval of
the war was widespread in West Jersey and businessmen in East
Jersey saw ruin in a British blockade. The Federalists won control of the legislature and state house and on November 10,
1812, passed a resolution condemning the war as "inexpedient,
ill-timed and most dangerously impolitic." The New Jersey
militia followed this unpatriotic lead by refusing to serve outside
the state.

The Federalists, practically admitting their victory was a
fluke, introduced into New Jersey politics a maneuver they had
picked up from the Republicans in Massachusetts. It was called
the "gerrymander" in honor of Elbridge Gerry, the Bay State
politician who invented it in 1811. It consisted of dividing electoral districts to give the party in power maximum support at the
polls. The Federalists proceeded to carve out three districts for
the congressional elections, constructed to give them a dubious

victory. The next year counterattacking Republicans crying "unconstitutional" regained control of the state.

One unexpected by-product of the war was the resurrection of Alexander Hamilton's city of Paterson and its guardian spirit, The Society of Useful Manufactures. Peter Colt, treasurer of the state of Connecticut, had been hired as "governor" by the directors of the S.U.M. in 1793 and had been deserted by them two years later. Colt and his relatives survived the lean intervening years, and steadily bought up corporation shares, which a recent historian of the city has described as among the most valuable documents in the United States. When the war cut off English textiles, the Colts were ready to supply the nation's need for cotton cloth. Paterson's factories were still standing, the machinery was ready to go. The city began to boom. Colt's son, Roswell, became governor of the S.U.M. in 1814 and did not relinquish the post until 1856.

Fortunately for Republicans, the War of 1812 remained remote from New Jersey. The state Federalists shunned the Hartford Convention of 1814, the conclave called by New England Federalists to discuss the possibility of seceding from the Union. When the war ended on a triumphant note with Andrew Jackson's victory in New Orleans, followed by a treaty of peace that satisfied most voters, the Hartford Convention became a spectre that demoralized the already-dying Federalist party.

Federalists feared the Democratic-Republicans would unleash that "great beast," the people, on the better sort, creating a French-style revolution. (The name "Democratic-Republican" was itself at first a term of opprobrium.) But these fears proved groundless. Jefferson and his Republicans turned out to be just as interested as the Federalists in maintaining an ordered society. They made only minor modifications in the existing political system. But they grafted onto that system the political party, which surprised the Federalists and other pessimists by becoming one of the institutions that fostered rather than threatened order. The Republican organization in New Jersey was a remarkably complex and hierarchical affair, with township committees coalescing into county committees, and county committees coalescing into state committees that in turn worked closely with the Republican caucus in the assembly. All of these offices, from the largest to the smallest, gave Jerseyans a chance to participate in the political process and exercise varying degrees of responsible leadership. A man who belonged to a political party, it soon became evident, was much less likely to become a reckless demagogue because competition within the party put an automatic brake on his power and influence. He had to govern with a view to satisfying a majority of his party, a fact that generally discouraged drastic innovations. Thus the elaborate party organization of the Democratic-Republicans, which was soon imitated by other parties, became a conservative as well as a stabilizing force in New Jersey's history.

In New Jersey as elsewhere, politics did not exist in a vacuum. The struggle for political power was intimately connected with economic and social advantages. In postrevolutionary New Jersey, the old hunger for a monopoly on the sale of land vanished. With the opening of vast new western territories, land values in the East plummeted. Scientific agriculture was slow in winning followers in New Jersey, as it was elsewhere in America, and numerous European visitors made critical comments about the way New Jersey farmers cropped a field with grain year after year until its fertility was gone. "The corn fields, the meadows, the cattle, &c., are treated with equal carelessness," wrote one visitor. To depleted soil was added the problem of the high price of labor. It is significant that one commentator on farming in New Jersey remarked that the gardens kept by the wives of farmers were often "half the support of their families."

New Jersey's dream of creating a port to rival New York and Philadelphia died with the legal karate chop that New York gave the city Hamilton tried to found. Philadelphia and New York dominated the merchandising side of New Jersey life, selling, according to one estimate, about a million dollars in European goods and "West India articles" in the state annually. Jerseyans sold about this amount of grains, lumber, native apple cider, and a small amount of manufactured goods to merchants in both cities. But the cost of transporting these goods to market left them approximately a hundred thousand dollars in arrears each year. More than a few alert Jerseyans noted the importance of transportation in the state's economic posture. Steamboat routes, bridges, toll roads, and canals became new prizes in the political struggle for power.

Perhaps most dramatic was the fight over steamboat routes. In 1807, Robert Fulton built the first commercially successful steamboat in America. Fulton and his partner, the wealthy New York manor lord, Robert R. Livingston, obtained a twenty-year monopoly on steam navigation from the New York legislature, and they tried to run all boats belonging to Jerseymen off the waters of the Hudson and New York harbor.

When the Federalist politician, Col. Aaron Ogden, unexpectedly became governor during the party's 1812 resurrection, he persuaded the legislature to give him a monopoly on steamboat transportation in New Jersey waters. This enabled him to negotiate a deal with the Livingston-Fulton monopoly, under which both companies ran steamboats to and from New York. Thomas Gibbons, a high-spirited Georgian who had moved to Elizabethtown, challenged both monopolists with a steamboat piloted by a daring New Yorker named Cornelius Vanderbilt. He puffed about New York harbor flying from his masthead a flag that proclaimed: "New Jersey must be free!" Sheriffs' writs, lawsuits, and countersuits flew in all directions. The argument finally ended in the U.S. Supreme Court, with Daniel Webster pleading Gibbons's case. Chief Justice John Marshall accepted the great orator's arguments and wrote a historic decision giving the federal government power to regulate interstate commerce. The effect of this decision proved a tremendous stimulus to the growth of the national economy. No longer would state lines be barriers to business activity.

Bridges and toll roads were another source of the transportation dollar that required legislative approval and encouragement. Bridges came first. In the 1790s, the legislature chartered companies to build spans over the Passaic and Hackensack rivers and, later, the Raritan. The builders were organized as "proprietors" and were given a lease entitling them to collect tolls until 1889. The tolls ranged from four cents for a man and a horse to thirty-nine cents for a vehicle with four horses. To the bridge over the Passaic at Newark was added a toll road to the Hoboken ferry. There were numerous complaints about the high tolls that enabled the proprietors to earn as much as 10 percent annually on their investment. One by-product of the Newark-Hoboken road was the creation of the New Jersey commuter. Three stages a day carried those who "lived in Newark and carried on their business in New York" to the metropolis at 6 A.M. each morning and returned late in the afternoon.

Soon other bridges spanned the Raritan and the Delaware, each owned by private corporations. More and more stagecoach companies were chartered, and competition between them grew fierce. If the reader thinks the danger of high-speed travel in our era is unique, a glance through accounts of journeys in the stagecoach era may be consoling. Coaches frequently capsized, went out of control going down steep hills, and sometimes ran down pedestrians. The amenities were also frequently neglected. The ironic author of "Rules for Traveling in a Stagecoach," published in 1800, directs:

1. Let every man get in first with all his baggage and sit there firmly, let who will get in, and if any other complains that the trunk is too large for the inside, let him declare that it contains great value—that he has the promise of an inside passage, and that it shall not go out.

2. At every town, let every man light a segar, and continue smoking in the face of his fellow travelers, and cursing the driver, during each stage; then let him light his segar again.

3. If anything is said about the general government, let every man take his segar from his mouth, blow out a volume of smoke, and then curse the President. . . .

4. If ladies are present, double entendres are very convenient." [1]

In the first two decades of the nineteenth century, toll roads multiplied across New Jersey. The Morris Turnpike, chartered in 1801, connected the upper Delaware with Newark Bay. It soon had four competitors for the trade of the Delaware Valley. Another turnpike connected New Brunswick and Trenton. The

1. Wheaton J. Lane, *From Indian Trail to Iron Horse, Travel and Transportation in New Jersey, 1620–1860* (Princeton: Princeton University Press, 1939), pp. 132–133.

Middlesex Turnpike connected New Brunswick, Elizabethtown, and Newark. Between 1801 and 1829, the legislature gave charters to fifty-one turnpike companies. About half of these managed to raise enough money to build toll roads totalling some 550 miles. Their charters extended from fifty to ninety-nine years, and the tolls allowed by the legislature were usually high. Many of these turnpikes simply absorbed existing roads and agreed to maintain them to the financial and administrative relief of local communities.

Because there were so many of them, none of the turnpikes made much money until the War of 1812. Then Washington, D.C., started paying immense sums to ship supplies to the armies defending the frontier with Canada. Simultaneously, the British blockade cut off shipments by water, by far the most popular and cheapest form of transportation. By 1814, the federal government alone was spending $2 million dollars to transport goods across New Jersey. New England manufacturers and New York and Philadelphia merchants multiplied the traffic until 4,000 wagons and 20,000 horses were rumbling back and forth across the state. This appalling upsurge of traffic demolished the roads. A growing number of Jerseyans began to think there had to be a better answer to the state's transportation problems than the crude roadbuilding technology of the period. To some, the solution seemed to be canals. But in Hoboken, a Jerseyan was at work on a machine that would make both toll roads and canals obsolete. It would also make the struggle for power among steamboat owners and toll road and bridgebuilders seem trivial.

8

Turning Iron Horses into Gold

N 1811, Col. John Stevens of Hoboken petitioned the New Jersey legislature for a charter entitling him to construct the first railroad in America. It was to run across the state and make New York a market for the products of the Delaware Valley. The legislature thought it was dealing with a visionary and rejected the idea. Stevens responded by publishing a pamphlet entitled *Documents Tending to Prove the Superior Advantages of Railway and Steam Carriages Over Canal Navigation.* He predicted railroad trains would some day go as fast as a hundred miles an hour and argued that laying a set of rails was much cheaper than building turnpikes or digging canals. Stevens urged Congress to take charge of building the country's railroads. He pointed out that the steamboat should have become a national possession, as its inventor, John Fitch, had hoped. Instead, it had become a tool of local politics and state monopolies.

Stevens knew what he was talking about. He had been experimenting with steam navigation since 1787 when he saw the first American steamboat, built by John Fitch, on the Delaware. Fitch had obtained an exclusive right to construct, employ, and navigate steamboats from the New Jersey legislature the previous year. Stevens's first steamboat, the *Phoenix,* was launched in 1808, a year after Robert Fulton's *Clermont.* But Fulton and his backer, Robert R. Livingston, blocked the operation of the *Phoenix* on the Hudson. Stevens retreated without a fight, sending the *Phoenix* around Cape May to operate on the Delaware. He was more interested in railroads anyway.

Throughout the next decade, while Ogden, Gibbons, and Livingston fought for control of the Hudson and New York harbor, Stevens continued to push railroads as the best answer to New Jersey—and national—transportation problems. But he was unable to raise the money he needed, even when he got the legislature to grant him a charter in 1815. Stevens saw that only a realistic demonstration would persuade Americans that a railroad was a practical possibility. So he built the first American locomotive and laid out a circular trackway in Hoboken.

On May 12, 1825, the *New York Evening Post* reported:

> Mr. Stevens has at length put his steam carriage in motion. It traveled around the circle of the Hoboken Hotel yesterday at the rate of about six miles an hour. His engine and carriage weigh less than a ton, whereas those now in use in England weigh from eight to ten tons. His original intention was to give the carriage a motion of sixteen or twenty miles an hour: but he has deemed it more prudent to move, in the first instance, with a moderate velocity. It will be in motion again tomorrow, from three o'clock to sundown.[1]

Other Americans had been converted to railroading by a visit to England, where the Stockton & Darlington was a commercial success. In the 1820s, charters were granted to the Mohawk & Hudson, the Baltimore & Ohio, and the South Carolina Canal & Railroad. John Stevens and his sons petitioned the New Jersey legislature for the right to build a railroad from a point opposite Philadelphia across the state to Raritan Bay. The Stevenses immediately found themselves embroiled in a political feud with the backers of the Delaware and Raritan Canal. This project had been discussed in New Jersey for almost twenty years. The huge cost and a depression that followed the War of 1812 had delayed the digging but the growth of New York consumption of Pennsylvania coal kept the idea alive. The legislature finally agreed to charter a private corporation to tackle the job.

Stevens and his railroad constituted a major threat to the

---

1. Lane, *Indian Trail to Iron Horse,* p. 283.

canal. Worse, the railmen now had the public image to win support. The legislature granted a charter to the Camden and Amboy Railroad on the same day—February 4, 1830—that it chartered the canal. The railroad's $1 million stock offering sold out in ten minutes. The canal had trouble selling 10 percent of its $1 million in shares.

Backed by the powerful Stockton family, the canal still had plenty of supporters in the legislature. But its future looked bleak—until the Stocktons and the Stevenses got together and decided to avert "suicidal competition." Instead of dueling unto financial death, they became the Joint Companies. This merger was blessed by an "act of union" in the legislature on February 15, 1831. The *Princeton Courier* commented sarcastically upon the marriage.

> The peerless pair their jealousies forego
> Unite their stocks, and thus their wisdom
>   show;
> Embrace the state within their circling arms,
> And teach the world the magic of their charms.

It looked like a cushy deal on both sides. The Joint Companies gave the state 1,000 shares of stock. In return, the legislature guaranteed that no other railroad would compete with the Camden and Amboy between New York and Philadelphia for the thirty-year life of its charter. This arrangement was to have fateful consequences for New Jersey.

The Camden and Amboy Railroad was fabulously successful. Its monopoly on traffic between New York and Philadelphia was bolstered by an absolute guarantee from the legislature in 1832. The state received as a gift an additional 1,000 shares of stock and a guarantee that the dividends on the 2,000 shares it then owned would never fall below $30,000—the cost of the state government at that time. This ready money neatly eliminated the need for statewide taxes. The parallel with the pre-revolutionary bills of credit whose interest painlessly paid the state's expenses is striking. States, like people, find it hard to shed bad habits.

As early as 1832, the Joint Companies stock was selling at 50 percent above par in New York. There was never any doubt about the state getting its $30,000 minimum each year. Often it received twice that sum. The Camden and Amboy was not content with its through line between the two cities in its title. It soon was operating from Bordentown through Trenton to New Brunswick. The railroad acquired steamboats on the Delaware and the Hudson to complete its monopoly of traffic between Philadelphia and New York.

The monopoly permitted the Camden and Amboy to charge extremely high fares. It cost $3 for a first-class seat between New York and Philadelphia in a period when the average laborer was lucky to earn a dollar a day. Second-class passenger riders paid $2.50. By the late 1850s, the railroad was carrying more than 450,000 through passengers a year. Newspapers frequently pointed out that transportation was less costly in the stagecoach era by as much as 50 percent. Accidents were frequent on the Camden and Amboy—its safety record was deplorable. One wreck almost killed ex-President John Quincy Adams in 1833.

More common were complaints about poor service. In 1844, forty-two travelers to Philadelphia published an open letter in the *Newark Daily Advertiser* complaining about their journey. Their steamboat to Amboy was "miserably dirty." The train ran off the track, causing an interminable wait in late summer heat, and their baggage was battered and in some cases lost. According to one newspaper, the Camden and Amboy regarded its passengers as nothing more than "live lumber."

Passengers were by no means the only people who got a raw deal from the Camden and Amboy. In spite of fat profits, the line remained a mostly single-track affair until the Civil War, when federal pressure persuaded the owners to build double tracks. Worse was the railroad's attitude toward any and all forms of criticism and opposition in New Jersey. Independent owners of steamboats who tried to compete with the monopoly's boats on the Raritan or Delaware found their crafts wrecked or their passengers threatened by hired toughs. Passengers who used the independent steamboats were ejected from railroad cars. Any politician who criticized the monopoly was guaranteed a short public life. The Camden and Amboy not only controlled the legislature and the governor's chair; it was also not above throwing its weight around in town meetings and city councils.

In the early years, the Camden and Amboy was very sensitive to the charge of being a monopoly. In 1836, the Stocktons, the Stevenses, and the other principal owners offered to sell the canal and the railroad to the state for $7,650,000. The legislature rejected the offer. The decision was influenced by newspaper editors who pointed out that this gave the owners a $2 million profit, long before they could hope to realize such a sum from operations. Other newspapers sarcastically asked if the legislature was going to buy up at equally inflated prices the stock of turnpike companies ruined by the railroad.

The failure of this gesture convinced the railroad owners that political control of the state was their only hope of survival. Led by the imperious Robert F. Stockton, naval hero of the War of 1812, they infiltrated the Democratic party and made sure, thanks to their ability to manipulate the state convention, that very few Democrats who did not support the Joint Companies got nominated for any office of importance. An astute politician, Stockton was capable of switching parties at the right moment. In 1840 he jumped to the Whigs, the conservative coalition that had emerged from the national Republicans. The Whigs were successfully blaming the Panic of 1837 on the Democrats and looked like winners. When the Whigs started to fade in the 1840s, the Commodore returned to the Democrats, who remained the dominant party in the state.

When New Jersey revised her constitution in 1844, the Joint Companies saw to it that a harmless-looking clause was inserted into the document forbidding the legislature to create any debt exceeding $100,000 without a referendum. This provision made it practically impossible for the state to purchase the railroad properties. The Joint Companies fended off attacks from outsiders by controlling the New Jersey delegation to the U.S. Congress and by arguing that the company made most of its money "from strangers, and persons not living in New Jersey." The Joint Companies were working day and night, according to this argument, as "agents and partners" of the people of New Jersey. Criticism tended only to "abate rather than to increase," the state's prosperity.

Strangers and persons not living in New Jersey took a more jaundiced view of the Camden and Amboy's fondness for picking pockets. Groups of businessmen, first in Philadelphia and later in New York, petitioned Congress to authorize a competing railroad across the state, no matter what the New Jersey legislature said about it. In the *New York Tribune,* Horace Greeley wrathfully pointed out that there were four railroads carrying passengers to Boston, and even more were available for a traveler to Albany. Philadelphia was closer to New York City than the Empire State capital, yet it cost a traveler four times as much to get to the City of Brotherly Love. Greeley called New Jersey "a free-booting baron."

These outside attacks only tended to consolidate Jerseyan support for the Camden and Amboy. Commodore Robert F. Stockton dismissed the complainers as "socialist speculators or demagogues." The fact that many of the squawkers were from New York did nothing to soften Jerseyan hearts. If anything it caused them to gloat that at last they were getting even for all the dirty things New York had done to them over the decades.

But Jerseyans found it harder to dismiss a wide-ranging attack on the companies by well-known political economist Henry C. Carey. Writing anonymously at first as a "citizen of Burlington," he accused the monopoly of bilking the people of New Jersey at least as much as it was plundering outsiders. He revealed that the railroad had failed to pay the state its share of a one-dollar fare rise—a sum amounting to a half-million dollars. The state was getting about $80,000 from transit duties and dividends, and the owners of the company were pocketing much more than a million in excess profits. Worse, the company was concealing the profits of its steamboat and canal lines.

Carey's attack created tremendous agitation inside New Jersey. The legislature was forced to appoint a commission to investigate the railroad. The commissioners were soon so cozy with the directors of the Joint Companies that they interrogated Carey like a criminal when he testified before them, and they refused his repeated pleas to let him see the railroad and canal company's books, so he could prove his charges.

The Camden and Amboy redoubled its efforts to consolidate its position politically—with astonishing success. It persuaded the legislature to extend its exclusive privileges to January 1, 1869, and by shouting the Democratic party war cry of states' rights, consistently strangled any and all attempts by outsiders to push a competing railroad through New Jersey. The story of the Camden and Amboy, which has never been completely written, is an amazing saga of an oligarchy at work. So triumphant were they that their supporters in the legislature could get together at midnight parties in Trenton and roar out a song which ended:

> *We are all a band of robbers,*
> *We are all a band of robbers*
> *From the Camden & Amboy State.*

This was not the more equal liberty for which the Revolution had been fought. Instead, technology had created a new class of industrial aristocrats whose arrogance would cause a century of conflict in New Jersey.

9

Conscience and Contradictions

*J*ERSEYANS did not devote all their attention and energy to battles with the iron horses and the men who owned them. In the first half of the nineteenth century the state developed in other directions as well. At first progress seemed torturous. In the thirty years between 1790 and 1820, the population rose a mere 95,000 to 227,500. New York, which was roughly equal to New Jersey in population at the beginning of the Revolution, soared past a million. The new state of Ohio went from zero to 581,000 in the same period. Kentucky and Tennessee exhibited similar growth.

Many of these westward migrants were from New Jersey. Numerous midwest towns such as Cincinnati and Dayton, Ohio, had Jerseyans among their founders. James Marshall of Lambertville was the man who discovered gold in California and started the great rush west to that state. In 1834, one New Jersey writer commented, "The state has been an *officina gentium,* a hive of nations, constantly sending out swarms, whose labors have contributed largely to build up the two greatest marts of the union [Philadelphia and New York] and to subdue and fertilize the western wilds."

New Jersey remained old-fashioned, dominated by farming and allied occupations, as indicated by statistics showing 857 gristmills, 655 sawmills, and 388 cider distilleries. People made shoes, boots, and harness equipment in the "leather towns" of

Newark, Bloomfield, and Rahway. Glass and iron were manufactured in Burlington, Gloucester, and Cumberland counties. But most Jerseyans with skills and a desire to play a role in the accelerating industrial revolution had to head for Philadelphia and New York. Manufacturing remained "insignificant," in the words of one commentator. "Few establishments contained more than a score of employees." Until 1830 New Jersey remained rural and agricultural. The largest city was Newark—with a population of 10,953, barely enough to fill a single New York City ward.

Jerseyans were well aware of their slow economic growth. At the constitutional convention of 1844 there was vigorous debate over whether the legislature should be free to grant charters of incorporation of any kind. A number of states had imposed constitutional restraints on their legislatures, after widespread abuse of this power, particularly in the field of banking. But a majority of the delegates to the constitutional convention contended that "the future economic prosperity of this state demanded an unfettered legislature." New Jersey's docile attitude toward corporations became official policy in these lean years.

An example of legislative meddling in the economy with disastrous effects was the silkworm craze of the late 1830s. Christopher Colt established a silk mill in Paterson in 1838. To back him, the legislature decided New Jersey could grow its own silk. It offered fifteen cents per pound for silk cocoons. Some 200,000 mulberry trees were planted across the state. Speculators swore that hitherto-barren soil in the southern part of New Jersey could produce forty to fifty dollars an acre in cocoons. Numerous silk companies were incorporated from Bergen to Trenton. For a few months it looked as if the state were going to become a forest of mulberry trees. Then someone realized that practically no one was producing silkworms. Without these little toilers, who could not survive the cold New Jersey winters, the 200 and 300 pounds of cocoons per acre projected from the mulberry trees were worthless. The bubble burst and glum farmers burned mulberry wood in their stoves and fireplaces for several winters.

Colt's silk factory failed in 1840, but it was not the end of silk in Paterson. An enterprising Englishman named John Ryle, with almost two decades of experience in English silk factories, took over the plant, imported raw silk from abroad, and by 1856 was hiring 500 employees, a huge number for that era. Paterson became known as the Silk City and Ryle became one of the richest men in America. For the city's seal, Ryle suggested a picture of a man planting a mulberry tree—an unintentional irony.

Waterpower was the key to Paterson's burgeoning industry. The canny Colts also lured skillful mechanics from England and Scotland to sustain their cautious progress in the cotton side of the textile business. From the machine shop of English-born John Clark came a host of talented mechanics who added technological expertise to the city's growth pattern.

The guns that conquered the West, Colt repeating rifles and pistols, were first manufactured in Paterson. Even more famous in its day was the Rogers Locomotive Works. One of John Clark's graduates, Thomas Rogers began as a builder of textile machinery in 1831. He switched to locomotive building in 1837 and produced the Sandusky, the most advanced engine yet built in America. Among its new features was a steam whistle. By 1850, Rogers was building two locomotives a week, and other men were building iron monsters of their own design. By 1860, Paterson passed Philadelphia as the locomotive-building capital of the world.

Thanks to some creative thinking by the city of Paterson and the New Jersey State Department of Transportation and some hard digging by industrial archaeologists, we have recently gotten a glimpse of how these early industrialists operated. Backed by a $340,000 grant, the archaeologists dug into the S.U.M. district of Paterson, now largely abandoned, and uncovered one of the three original raceways down which water diverted from the Great Falls poured to power the factories. The raceway, complete with old turbine pits, was amazingly intact. It had been simply covered over, instead of being destroyed when later technology replaced it and new factories were built. This massive hydraulic project, which included damming a major river and sending its power through a system of canals and raceways more than a mile long, is a unique monument to American industrial ingenuity. It represents the earliest planned engineering project in the United States using waterpower, antedating similar projects at Lowell, Lawrence, and Holyoke, Massachusetts. The city of Paterson, with the help of the state, has been making valiant efforts to preserve this monument. The creation of the Great Falls Historic District may well be the most notable result of New Jersey's bicentennial enthusiasm.

But nostalgia should not blur another side of Paterson's story. Beside the bright pages of advancing technology stands a somber narrative of human exploitation. Few cities in the nation matched the Paterson industrialists' absolute control of their workers. With the collusion of the legislature, which was as kind to The Society of Useful Manufactures as it was to the Canden and Amboy, Paterson did not even have a government until 1831. The S.U.M. owned and ran everything. When the legislature finally gave Paterson a town charter, it yielded only minimal powers to the people, and permitted S.U.M. to maintain its tax-free status. One of New Jersey's first strikes occurred in Paterson in 1794, when the workers asked for schools for their children. They were ignored. The Colt family insisted on having new streets named after them but declined to contribute anything to their cost. Jacob Rogers, son of the locomotive tycoon, refused to donate a small tract of land for a city hospital. "I don't owe anything to Paterson," he said.

This new industrial aristocracy was in many ways worse than the hereditary aristocrats—British and Federalists—who had ruled New Jersey in the past. The earlier aristocrats at least had a sense of noblesse oblige. They participated in the government of the nation and acquired some insight into the problems of their time. The industrial aristocrats were alienated from the government. Buoyed by a warped interpretation of American freedom as the liberty to get away with anything, they corrupted the legislature, the courts, and the newspapers to maintain their advantages. Like the land-monopolizing proprietors of the eighteenth century, they would reap a whirlwind of violence.

A similar story unfolded in the city Alexander Hamilton helped to found on the west bank of the Hudson. After three decades of stagnation, New Jersey finally won the legal right to use the Hudson waters and New York confirmed it in a treaty between the two states in 1833. By that time, as one historian of the episode wryly pointed out, the original Federalist founders of the city were either dead or "broken old men." In response to petitions from the inhabitants, the state legislature finally gave the community a name, "the City of Jersey," and in 1838, a charter that permitted them to elect a mayor and common council. But the associates of the Jersey Company, the city's founders, still retained their rights to the waterfront. When the board of aldermen challenged their control of this vital asset, the case went to the state's highest court, the New Jersey Court of Errors and Appeals, which decided overwhelmingly in favor of the associates. The court denied the city the right to widen or extend waterfront streets, or to establish a ferry to New York to compete with the one owned by the associates, and it confirmed their exclusive privileges of building docks and filling in marshland as they saw fit.

Not satisfied with their legal victory, the associates persuaded the legislature to write their monopoly into a new city charter in the following year, 1851. A clause stipulated that within the limits of the city, the local government had no control over "any docks, wharves, or piers used for ferries or other commercial purposes." The board of aldermen pleaded in vain with the legislature to give the people of Jersey City control over their most valuable natural resource. Two years later, the associates sold their rights to the waterfront and ferry service to the New Jersey Railroad for $485,000. The railroad, a local line connecting Jersey City, Newark, and New Brunswick, transferred Philadelphia passengers to the Camden and Amboy at the last city. Eventually the Camden and Amboy octupus absorbed the NJR and the rights to the Jersey City waterfront, making the city a corporate captive.

Industry came to other New Jersey cities. In Trenton, Peter Cooper and Abram S. Hewitt opened a factory to supply the Camden and Amboy Railroad with rails. They were soon joined by John Roebling, the Pennsylvania manufacturer of wire rope for suspension bridges. The wires that swung spans across Niagara Falls, the East River (the Brooklyn Bridge), and hundreds of other streams and gorges came from this plant. In Newark, the leather industry remained king, with the help of an ingenious New Englander, Seth Boyden, who invented a way to slit a cow's hide into several layers, magically multiplying its value and creating innumerable possibilities for its use.

Waterpower made towns such as Whippany and Milburn paper manufacturing centers. More than fifty New Jersey paper-mills fed the churning presses of New York's newspapers. Jersey City's Joseph Dixon produced the nation's first high-grade steel in a graphite crucible in 1848, and William Colgate produced tons of soap in his huge vats, which sent their uniquely nauseating odor through the downtown wards into which Irish immigrants were crowding.

Although New Jersey's population doubled to more than 600,000 in the antebellum decades, the state remained rural. There were only about 56,000 factory workers, and only three counties, Essex, Hudson and Burlington, that had populations grater than 40,000. But the steady accumulation of wealth and the rise of a small but nonetheless visible city proletariat created some social unrest. In the panics of 1837 and 1857, newspapers told stories of starving workers. Two thousand unemployed men held a mass meeting in Newark in 1857 to demand "not alms, but work."

To cope with these problems, some Jerseyans turned to utopian solutions similar to those developed by New Englanders. The best-known was the North American Phalanx, founded by ten families from Albany, New York, near Red Bank, in 1843. In the prime of its twelve-year life, the Phalanx had about ninety members. Bachelors lived on the third floor of the phalanstery and families on the second floor, and there was a community dining area on the first floor. They lived on the products of their 643 acres of land and made their own clothes and almost everything else they needed in communal mills and machine shops. Several dropouts from the Phalanx founded the Raritan Bay Union near Perth Amboy in 1853. Like more recent attempts at creating communes in individualistic America, enthusiasm dwindled slowly over the years, and by 1859, the Phalanx and the Union were only memories.

Other reformers tackled the state's wretched prisons and mental hospitals. A legislative commission called the state prison "a hatching ground for new crimes" in 1829. John Haviland, a prison reformer who doubled as an architect, designed a new prison that let in far more light and air. But Haviland added to this welcome innovation a weird conviction that solitary confinement was the best road to individual reformation. It took the state about twelve years to discover that solitary confinement was creating more madmen than repentants. This was bad news, because around the same time a pioneering study of the mentally ill in the state found them in far worse shape than the convicts.

Both the insane and the mentally retarded were usually parked in poorhouses or jails, often in chains. A commission urged the construction of a state asylum. But the legislature acquired instant deafness on the subject and remained that way until a determined young lady from Massachusetts, Dorothea Dix, assaulted them with a fiery address that demanded, not asked, a hundred and fifty thousand dollars for an asylum. A senator suggested instead that a thousand dollars be spent on getting Miss Dix out of the state. But this bravado soon faded in the face of Dixean fury. After three months of her ferocious lobbying, the legislators collapsed, and by 1848, New Jersey had a decent mental hospital in Ewing Township north of Trenton.

Similar agitation created free public schools in New Jersey—although this progress, too, took almost twenty years of backing and filling. The first statewide school law was passed in 1829. It was promptly emasculated by succeeding legislatures and revived only after another round of agitation. Not until 1854 did the state acquire a normal school for training teachers. The country schools were especially bad. The first state superintendent of schools wrote in 1848, "A merciful man being merciful to his beast would not winter his horse in places appropriated at present for district schoolhouses." State aid remained at a paltry level and the notorious reluctance of Jerseyans to pay taxes forced most school districts to charge tuition until 1871.

There was one subject on which Jerseyans with delicate consciences agitated in vain—the Negro. Because the state had more black slaves than any other northern state except New York at the end of the Revolution—some 11,000—New Jersey had no enthusiasm for antislavery ideas. Repeated Quaker protests finally prodded the legislature into passing an act in 1804 providing for the gradual emancipation of slaves. The act freed all children born into slavery at the age of twenty-five if a male; twenty-one, if a female. Slaveholders received a monthly cash payment for each child. As one historian put it, New Jersey managed "to harmonize as much as possible the interests of private property, social stability, and the ideological imperatives of the Declaration of Independence." The state's predominantly middle-class character, a trait that prevailed from its earliest days, had not a little to do with this intense respect for private property.

New Jersey's interpretation of the doctrine "all men are created equal" did not include the Negro. The Suffrage Reform Act of 1807, which excluded women from the franchise, also barred blacks from the polling booths. Petitions from free New Jersey blacks asking for the right to vote were ignored by the constitutional convention of 1844. The Republican party, born out of abolition agitation, was so unpopular in New Jersey that its members declined to use the official name and called themselves the Opposition party. This name also represented an attempt to meld the fractured remnants of the old Whig party and new-blooming Republicans into a united front against the Democratic party.

The dominance of the Democrats in New Jersey throughout the antebellum period, an era when party discipline and party loyalty were part of the social gospel, also contributed a strong southern tinge to New Jersey's attitude toward the Negro. Coupled with this influence was an equally strong economic factor. Many of New Jersey's industries were based on southern markets. It was a common saying of the period that the

South walked on Newark shoe leather. At least as important was the use of the states rights' argument to defend the Camden and Amboy's monopoly.

All of these things explain why New Jersey was the only northern state that never challenged the Fugitive Slave Law. Mobs of angry citizens never rose to rescue a captured black, as they did in Massachusetts, and no one harassed federal agents guarding the ferry landings on the Raritan, the Hudson, and the Delaware. But a substantial minority of Jerseyans sympathized intensely with the slaves. Along the Delaware, Quakers set out blue and yellow signal lights guiding runaways to stops on an underground railroad that ran across the state to New England. In 1859, members of the Raritan Bay Union almost caused a bloody riot by bringing north the bodies of two of John Brown's raiders for burial in their cemetery on the Eagleswood estate. At Perth Amboy, a furious mob met the steamboat that was supposed to be carrying the bodies. The utopians had wisely landed the caskets at Rahway and buried them secretly.

The furor was one more symptom of New Jersey's stance in the crisis that was about to divide the Union. In heart and mind, in politics and economics, New Jersey was a border state, separated only by an accident of geography from the rebellious South. For New Jersey this ambiguous status meant another decade of searing internal division.

10

The Madness of War

ON July 1860, the Democratic party convention in New Jersey declared that the looming sectional crisis had been caused by "the actual and threatened interference on the part of northern agitators with the rights and property of the people of the fifteen states of this union." The answer to the turmoil was the motto of the Democratic party: "The Constitution as it is, the nation as it was." [1]

Fortunately for the future of the nation, by this time New Jersey Democrats were as deeply divided as their national party. The Democrats had come apart during James Buchanan's presidency. The mini–civil war that had raged in Kansas, the incursion of northern abolitionists into Virginia under the leadership of John Brown, and the South's violent reaction to both these provocations had created chaos in the nation's dominant party. It was split between hawks and doves on both sides of the Mason-Dixon line. At the top, President Buchanan was determined to deny the presidential nomination to Stephen Douglas of Illinois. At the Democratic National Convention in Charleston, Douglas could not get the necessary two-thirds of the delegates.

Meanwhile, the Republican party had been growing steadily.

---

1. Larry A. Greene, "The Emancipation Proclamation in New Jersey and the Paranoid Style," *New Jersey History* 91 (Summer 1973): 110.

Its hard core of abolitionist fanatics had been quietly absorbed by seasoned politicians from the old Whig party, men like Abraham Lincoln of Illinois. Under their guidance, abolitionism was transmuted into a carefully articulated antislavery position that called for firm but peaceful opposition to the "peculiar institution." The growing Republican strength was well demonstrated in New Jersey, where William A. Newell became the first Republican (disguised as Opposition) governor in 1856. Three years later, the party edged Charles S. Olden of Princeton into the executive chair by a hairline margin of 1,600 votes.

But Lincoln lost the state in 1860 by 4,500 votes, in spite of the existence of three other candidates on the ballot. This reflected the national vote fairly well. John C. Breckenridge ran with the backing of President Buchanan and moderate southerners. Douglas ran as the candidate of northern Democrats. The third candidate, John Bell of Tennessee, representing the Constitutional Union party, sought the independent vote. Among them, the three outpolled Lincoln by more than a half-million votes nationally. The vote clearly proved that most Americans did not want a war over slavery.

In New Jersey, this attitude was stated explicitly. Aging Commodore Robert F. Stockton declared that New Jersey should "supplicate to the North to yield." Ex-Gov. Rodman Price went even further. "I say emphatically that New Jersey should go with the South for every wise, prudential and patriotic reason." Only the presence of Governor Olden in the executive chair stopped New Jersey from doing just that. The mind reels to think what might have happened if the state had voted to secede during the frantic early months of 1861. But Olden in his annual message was careful to talk like a Democrat. "The troubles connected with slavery," he said, "have in great measure been brought on by a few persons of extreme views both in the North and South." The governor then led a nine-man delegation, including pro-Southerners such as Stockton and Price, to Washington for the abortive peace conference that sought to work out one more compromise between the North and South. Abraham Lincoln also helped steady Union sentiment in New Jersey by traveling through the state on his journey from Springfield, Illinois, to Washington, D.C. In a speech before the Democratic-controlled legislature, he solemnly declared, "The man does not live who is more devoted to peace than I am."

Then the South committed its fatal blunder—firing on Fort Sumter and the American flag. Secession and armed rebellion, the appeal from the ballot to the bullet, became a fact of American life. Millions of moderate Americans, including thousands in New Jersey, responded with wild patriotism to Lincoln's call to preserve the Union. Governor Olden had no difficulty persuading the legislature to borrow almost two and a half-million dollars to finance New Jersey's share of the war. Prominent businessmen offered bonuses to volunteers. Soon the state had three men for every one it needed to fill its quota of 3,120 soldiers.

Everyone was convinced that the war would not last more than a month. The North would raise its mighty metal fist and smash King Cotton's plantation patricians into submission. Bull Run's shocking defeat and a call for five more regiments from New Jersey changed a great many minds. Suddenly people began remembering Democratic opposition to the war.

Ten days after the Battle of Bull Run, about 500 persons heard Bergen County Democrats meeting at Schraalenburgh demand that the South be recognized as a separate nation. They accused the Lincoln administration of "a settled purpose to destroy the rights of the states and individuals" and called on their fellow citizens to resist "in every legal and rightful way [that] the hatred of tyranny might suggest." [2] On September 5, 1861, a secession flag was flown in Hackensack. Federal marshals rushed from Jersey City to Schraalenburgh to seize the guns of the town's uniformed militia company, the "American Guards."

Even more shocking to Jerseyans was the sudden arrest of Col. James W. Wall of Burlington, a vocal Peace Democrat. Wall was jailed in New York for two weeks and released only

2. Adrian C. Leiby, *The Huguenot Settlement of Schraalenburgh, the History of Bergenfield, New Jersey* (Bergenfield: Free Public Library, 1964), p. 76.

after he took an oath of allegiance to the United States. These acts were a disastrous miscalculation on the part of the Lincoln administration. Wall was greeted by a torchlight parade when he returned to Burlington, and the Democrats rolled up heavier-than-usual majorities in the legislative election of 1861. The next year they put Joel Parker into the governor's chair. Less than two months later, Lincoln signed the Emancipation Proclamation.

The day after the proclamation, the stridently Democratic *Newark Daily Journal* asked: "Is not Negro insurrection here hinted at and countenanced?" The *Trenton True American* ran a story about a revolt of West Indian blacks who tried to massacre the white minority with the comment: "Here we have a foretaste of what may be expected to take place if the Emancipation Proclamation is carried into effect." The newspapers were seconded by Governor Parker in his inaugural address. He too expressed fears of servile insurrections. Like most northern Democrats, he insisted he had no sympathy for slavery. But he maintained that it was the southerner's business. "Slavery was introduced by our forefathers and incorporated in the institutions of both sections," he said. "Upon the establishment of our national independence and the formation of the federal government, it was recognized as a state institution and left by the framers of the Constitution to the people of the several states to manage for themselves."

It was the Constitution to which New Jersey's Democrats pledged their allegiance. Democratic Congressman Nehemiah Perry of Newark declared, "If we give up our defense of the Constitution, or yield one inch of the sacred territory upon which we take our stand, we seal our own fate, are accessory to our insignificance and aid in our own destruction." Historical echoes resound in Perry's words. The Constitution was the great compromise forged in part by New Jersey's demands, a compromise that rescued her from the fate of being crushed between two large neighbors. Insignificance and economic destruction—those were the threats New Jersey had fought for a long time.

Democratic politicians also expressed the fears of the working classes that the Emancipation Proclamation would flood the northern states with cheap Negro labor. Republicans were accused of "Negromania," which meant they were antilabor, which meant in turn they were anti-immigrant. A 10 percent rise in the price of sugar and molasses the day after the proclamation was blamed on the Republicans. This paranoid trend grew stronger as the battlefield casualty lists lengthened. The editor of the *Newark Journal* accused Lincoln of preferring war to a peaceful solution because war gave him control of the army and navy, which he needed in order to free the slaves.

Secretary of State William Seward's claim that there was a higher law that justified repudiating the Constitution's compromise on slavery aroused James Wall to find antecedents of such thinking in the dictatorship of Genghis Khan, in the invasion of Ireland by James II, and in the tyrannies of George III. After the Democratic triumph of 1862, twenty-four petitions were presented to the legislature calling on the lawmakers to produce a Negro exclusion act. Several bills were submitted. Today the debate sounds like something from a historical nightmare. The assemblymen wrangled over one clause that fined anyone who "knowingly" brought a Negro into New Jersey. Some assemblymen, obviously expecting a Confederate victory, said New Jersey should exempt vacationing Southern planters, who would be bringing their slaves with them. The bill passed the assembly but died in the senate.

In March 1864, the assembly passed a miscegenation bill entitled "An Act to Prevent the Admixture of the Races." Again, this effort to keep New Jersey white died in the senate.

A little perspective is needed on this subject, lest Civil War New Jersey appear to be totally deranged. There was a broad white supremacy belt that stretched across the southern two-thirds of Illinois, Indiana, Ohio, most of Pennsylvania, and the lower half of New York, as well as New Jersey. It was the northern area with the heaviest concentration of Negroes. Sad to note, historians feel this Negro presence is probably the best explanation for the virulent antiblack sentiments of the white population. In Indiana, antiwar sentiment was so strong the governor suspended the legislature and ruled by fiat. In Ohio

Congressman Clement L. Vallandigham, who regularly denounced Lincoln on the floor of the U.S. House of Representatives, came close to winning the governorship in 1863. But
nowhere else did the Democrats achieve such complete political
control as they did in New Jersey. In the presidential election of
1864, Lincoln lost the state by 7,600 votes to the man he had
fired as commanding general, George McClellan.

But ever-lengthening casualty lists and southern intransigence
began to radicalize many Democrats. The party split into Peace
Democrats and War Democrats. Governor Parker was one of the
latter. He wanted to end the war. But he also wanted to preserve
the Union, and it gradually became apparent that there was no
way out of this dilemma but victory.

By 1863 there were 30,000 Jerseyans in the Union Army.
The Democrats among them tended to be lukewarm about the
war. The 22nd Regiment, mostly Democrats from Bergen
County, never ceased writing home about the stupid way the
war was being fought. One officer published a letter complaining that the government owed him $500 in backpay while freed
slaves working for the army had pockets full of cash. He said he
and his men lived in tents and ate hardtack and salt pork while
the slaves lived in comfortable barracks and ate soft bread and
fresh beef. When the regiment was ordered to join the Army of
the Potomac on January 11, 1863, the men refused to march.
They said they did not have the training to qualify as frontline
soldiers. After six months in the army they remained convinced,
in the words of a correspondent who reported on their activities
to the *Bergen Democrat,* that the war would end only "when
the abolition nest is routed out of Washington, horse, foot and
dragoon. . . . So long as there is a dollar left in the public
treasury, there will be a nest of thieves, swindlers and contractors lounging around Old Abe." In June 1862, the regiment's
term of service expired and the men went home en masse.

Other New Jersey troops exhibited similar unenthusiasm for
the war. In July 1862, the state furnished 10,470 men for nine-
months' service. All eleven of these regiments came home in
June 1863, in spite of the fact that the Union Army in the East
was reeling and Robert E. Lee had invaded Pennsylvania in the

abortive campaign that became the high tide of the Confederacy. Governor Parker called on militia volunteers to join the Federal Army at Harrisburg. A Somerset County mass meeting responded with the demand that militia be forbidden to leave the state. They declared they had no confidence in the Federal administration. Another company disbanded the moment they received their marching orders.

The Union's victory at Gettysburg did not change many minds. When Lincoln responded to the dwindling flow of volunteers with a draft, riots flared in a number of northern cities, particularly in New York. On the same day that the Empire City was almost seized by rampaging mobs—July 13, 1863—Newark protestors broke windows in the offices of prowar newspapers and attacked the homes of Federal officials. Governor Parker hastily persuaded the Federal government to let him fill New Jersey's draft quota with volunteers. The following year, of the 6,981 men drafted in New Jersey, only 380 actually served. The rest either bought their way out or hired substitutes. No wonder the poor resented the Civil War draft.

On the battlefield, many New Jersey regiments fought well. The 33rd Regiment, mostly Democrats from Essex and Hudson counties, marched with Sherman to the sea and suffered 60 percent casualties. New Jersey had her Medal of Honor winners like fifteen-year-old Willie Magee, the Newark drummer boy who led a charge on a Confederate battery in Tennessee in 1863; her brilliant generals, notably one-armed Phil Kearney, commander of the 1st Brigade of New Jersey; and Judson Kilpatrick, who could surpass George Custer when it came to reckless cavalry charges. Two hundred and eighteen officers and 6,082 enlisted men from New Jersey died on the battlefields.

As the war wound down to its end at Appomattox, New Jersey Democrats remained stubbornly opposed to the Republican policy toward the South. Governor Parker told the Democratic legislature he did not approve of the Thirteenth Amendment abolishing slavery in the United States. Parker insisted that the restoration of the Union was the sole purpose of the war. The Democrats miscalculated the impact of the war's sacrifices, particularly when accounts of them were narrated by the thousands of Jerseymen who had fought in the ranks throughout the war. These veterans had a much tougher attitude toward Southerners and slavery, and their presence in New Jersey no doubt explained why Republicans elected Gov. Marcus L. Ward and took over the senate and the assembly in 1865. They approved the Thirteenth Amendment and the more controversial Fourteenth Amendment, which repudiated the Supreme Court's Dred Scott decision and guaranteed citizenship to all persons born or naturalized in the United States. It also denied a state the power to abridge the privileges of any citizen or deprive any person of life, liberty, or property without due process of law. But not even these Republicans were ready to eliminate the word *white* from the state's voting law.

With the death of the moderate Lincoln, the Radical Republicans took over the party. The Radicals were committed to a punitive approach to the conquered South and immediate equality for the Negro. By 1866 they had a two-thirds majority in both houses of Congress. Determined to ram through their program, the Radicals tried to make Congress the final arbiter of the government. They manipulated the Supreme Court, raising the number of justices to ten, and then reducing them to seven, crippling the court's power to rule on the Reconstruction program. They climaxed their grab for total control by trying to impeach President Andrew Johnson. Democrats said the Republicans were plotting to wreck the Constitution and cried, "I told you so." The Republican tactics healed the breach between New Jersey War and Peace Democrats, and they rode back to power in 1867, supporting President Johnson's insistence that the newly freed slaves were not ready to exercise the right to vote.

This issue also produced Democratic victories in New York, Pennsylvania, and Ohio. The New Jersey legislature rescinded the state's ratification of the Fourteenth Amendment. The Radical Republicans in Congress ignored this slap, which had no legal impact, and grimly pushed ahead with their program, passing the Fifteenth Amendment, which explicitly guaranteed the Negro's right to vote. New Jersey Democrats refused to ratify it. Again the Republicans aroused themselves and in November 1870 won control of the legislature to give the state's approval. But not until 1875 did the politicians of either party feel it was safe to strike the word *white* from New Jersey's suffrage law.

11

Old versus New Americans

$\mathcal{A}$FTER the Civil War, New Jersey grew at a stupendous pace. The population soared from 906,096 in 1870 to 1,883,669 in 1900. The number of factories increased by 230 percent. Villages such as Passaic and Bayonne were transformed into urban manufacturing centers. Few other states experienced the flowering of the industrial revolution more dramatically than New Jersey. With it came profound new divisions, as more and more Jerseyans began to identify with the powerless workers of Paterson.

Eras often overlap, and this one was no exception. In 1873, the decades of struggle against the railroad barons reached a climax. In March of that year the legislature voted to end the monopoly on transportation it had granted them. But it was a flawed victory. The vote was not against the Jerseyans who owned the Camden and Amboy, but "foreigners" from Pennsylvania. In 1871, the Joint Companies, which had become the United New Jersey Railroad and Canal Company with the absorption of the New Jersey Railroad in 1867, leased its $40 million worth of real estate and rolling stock to the Pennsylvania Railroad for 999 years. The Pennsylvania had been fighting hard for the right to build a line across New Jersey. Its owners found it impossible to penetrate the political power of the monopoly and finally accepted the "onerous terms" insisted on by the New Jersey railroaders.

But the Pennsylvanians could not sing the Camden and Amboy's old song—that it was only picking the pockets of strangers and persons not living in New Jersey. The Keystone State tycoons decided to acquiesce in the loss of their exclusive rights and settle for behind-the-scenes control of the legislature on such vital issues as taxes.

A holiday atmosphere, complete with brass bands and "jubilee meetings" swept New Jersey when the legislature killed the monopoly. It was a naive celebration. People thought that the free competition would bring badly needed prosperity to the state, which was already suffering from the economic woes that later in the year climaxed in the Panic of 1873. It soon became apparent that the struggle against the industrial aristocrats had merely shifted its focus.

In no place was this more visible than in Jersey City. By 1870, the city was being called "the Gateway to the West." Along with the New Jersey Railroad, the eastern arm of the Camden and Amboy's Philadelphia–New York monopoly, the city was the terminus of two other lines, the Jersey Central and the Erie. Because the New Jersey Railroad controlled the city's prime shoreline, thanks to its absorption of Alexander Hamilton's old Associates of the Jersey Company, the Central built its own shoreline by filling Communipaw Cove with garbage from New York City. The stench pervaded downtown Jersey City for a decade while citizens protested in vain. The New Jersey Railroad decided to expand in the same way and filled large parts of Harismus Cove with garbage. The state legislature gave the railroads permission to lay tracks at will throughout the city and exempted them from paying millions in local taxes. Wrathfully, Mayor Orestes Cleveland cried that the city had fallen

> into evil hands. . . . She is hedged round about, cut up and run over by the great monopolies; her commerical facilities [her waterfront] cut off; her natural energies crushed; her public spirit smothered; her growth retarded; the very air she breathes as a city dealt out to her in small quantities by one or other of these gorged institutions that have no souls and no eye for anything that does not fill up and protect their own plethoric purses.[1]

1. Quoted in Hermann K. Platt, "Jersey City and the United Railroad Companies, 1868: A Case Study of Municipal Weakness," *New Jersey History* 91 (Winter 1973): 252.

In 1882, Assemblyman George Farrier reported to the legislature that $19,934,546 in railroad property in Jersey City was exempt from municipal taxation. The sum exceeded the entire valuation of the county of Bergen with all its thriving towns and farms.

Jersey City was the worst but by no means the only sufferer. Around the same time, Charles L. Corbin, a well-known lawyer, read a paper at the Kent Club in Jersey City analyzing the public debt of New Jersey. He noted that the state ranked nineteenth in population but was fifth in the amount of red ink on its books. Only one other state—New York—had increased its public indebtedness as rapidly as New Jersey since 1870. New York City and Brooklyn had average tax rates of less than 1 percent. In Jersey City the tax rate was 2.94; in Brunswick, 3.63. Newark was $8,000,000 in debt. Elizabeth and Rahway had gone bankrupt in the preceding decade. There was only one explanation for these grim statistics. One-fourth of the property in the state was owned by the railroads and was therefore exempt from local taxation. Corbin maintained that the railroads in New Jersey were worth at least $250,000,000, although they claimed a net worth of $167,618,000. This meant they were beating the state government out of an annual $2,000,000 in taxes.

A glimpse of the underground resentment against railroad dominance is visible in the story of Thomas V. Cator, a lawyer who organized an antimonopoly league in Jersey City. He ran for the assembly in a Jersey City district populated by numerous railroad employees. A railroad appointee was running against him on the Republican ticket. A renegade Republican received a copy of a letter from Culver Barcalow, a slim, sly little man with a drooping eyelid who was the chief Pennsylvania Railroad lobbyist in Trenton. Barcalow urged the Republican (who was concealing his renegade nature) to do everything in his power to beat Cator. The renegade slipped the letter to Cator, who published it in the newspaper. It was all Cator needed to win the election. There were bonfires and dancing in the streets when the results were announced.

But Cator remained a relatively isolated example of an honest citizen beating the big shots. The railroads and other corporations were able to get away with their public-be-damned tactics because New Jersey voters were split by other issues that created new divisions in politics and geography. The spectacular growth in population focussed on a few counties and cities. By 1900, the biggest county was Hudson, which did not even exist in the era of the Revolution, followed by Essex, Passaic, and Camden. These four counties contained 50 percent of New Jersey's population. They were, predictably, the counties where industry had also shown enormous growth.

More than half the workers who manned the lathes and stoked the furnaces in the factories and swung the picks on the railroads were new Americans, immigrants and sons of immigrants. A staggering two-thirds of Hudson County's residents were foreign-born. Hudson and Essex counties alone accounted for 50 percent of these people, with another heavy concentration in Passaic County, thanks to the booming factories of Paterson. Cities such as Jersey City and Newark grew at incredible rates between 1850 and 1860. Jersey City's population quintupled, and almost doubled again in the next decade. Newark, already a substantial city, doubled in size. Hitherto-tiny towns such as Bayonne and Passaic showed growth rates of 144.4 and 145.8 percent.

This influx of immigrants swamped the native American voters in these cities. They were dismayed to discover that the newcomers, especially the Irish, were close readers of the Declaration of Independence and the U.S. Constitution and rapidly became contenders for political power. As early as 1850, a native New Brunswick man was expressing his exasperation at this phenomenon. "The simple truth is that the honest men of the county are tired of being voted down by the . . . foreigners in this city, a vast majority of whom were ten years ago the ignorant serfs of Ireland."

This reaction produced one of the more unlovely perversions of the American dream of brotherhood: nativism. In the 1850s it flowered as the American party, whose members were nicknamed the "Know-Nothings" because that was supposed to be their answer to all inquiries about their organization. In New Jersey they elected an alarming number of assemblymen and senators and at least two governors who echoed their views about "ignorant foreigners." The Civil War destroyed them as a party, but they resurfaced as The Order of United American Mechanics, the American Protestant Association, and the Patriotic Order of the Sons of America. Oddly, some of the loudest shouters for Americanism were British immigrants who were welcomed in these secret societies for their staunch Protestantism.

The ultimate expression of this trend was the American Protective Association, which blamed everything from unemployment to the destruction of democracy on the Roman Catholic church and Catholic immigrants. Anyone who submitted to the Papacy could not be a good American, went their argument. Catholics should be barred from public office and from teaching in the public schools. APA members also took a pledge not to hire Catholics. The writer's father was on the receiving end of this treatment in Jersey City. There the APA owner of a local factory solved an economic dilemma at the same time. He had promised not to hire Catholics. But Catholics were by far the cheapest available labor. So he forced each man or boy who looked for work to respond to the question: "Protestant or Catholic?" If the applicant answered Catholic he was told: "No work today." If he said Protestant, he was hired, even though the map of Ireland was on his face.

The APA also sponsored lectures by ex-priests and ex-nuns and delighted in the riots they caused in many New Jersey cities. They issued forged encyclicals from the pope, calling on Catholics to prepare for an armed revolution to exterminate heretics, and lurid exposés like Edith O'Gorman's *Convent Life Unveiled,* which purported to tell of her awful experiences in a New Jersey convent.

Such stuff did not go down well among the naturally pugnacious Irish, and religion again became an ingredient in New Jersey's political divisions. Protestant native Republicans locked horns with Catholic immigrant Democrats. Another division reinforced these ethnic and religious lines: country versus city. Outside the industrial counties, most of New Jersey remained rural. The state constitution required that each county had to have at least one assemblyman, and the senate remained a one-man-per-county affair. So the legislature never came near a one-man, one-vote standard of representation. The Republicans consistently controlled both houses, while the Democrats, the real majority in the state, consistently elected governors.

Only a few percentage points—ten or fifteen thousand votes—separated the two parties. This even division added to the political ferocity. When the Catholics tried to get permission for priests to say mass and distribute the sacraments for the inmates of state prisons and reform schools, the Protestants fought them in the legislature as if Armageddon were at hand. Catholics in Union Hill and other towns where they were the majority retaliated by voting the Bible out of the public schools. When the Catholics demanded state funds for their parochial schools, the Protestants responded with bills that tried to tax the schools out of existence, or forbade nuns to wear habits while teaching American children. Political careers soared and crashed on both sides of these issues.

Other aspects of the struggle revolved around voting. The Republicans invariably fought for a tough registration law to stop Democratic "naturalization mills," where immigrants were processed into voters at miraculous speed. The Democrats called for tough laws against bribery of public officials, the favorite ploy of the better-heeled Republicans. Both sides bought votes in wholesale lots. One legislative committee reported in 1889 that "a large proportion of . . . the voting population depend[ed] upon election day as a regular source of income." An estimated fifty thousand votes were for sale in the state with almost half of these in Essex and Hudson counties.

After the New Jersey legislature, imitating Congress, decided in 1852 that the legislature would be elected from voting districts, gerrymanders of wondrous size and shape were concocted to provide a temporary majority. In 1861 the Democrats carved Burlington County into one Republican district forty-six miles long and three small Democratic districts. These manipulations were intimately connected with the struggle between Protestants and Catholics, native Americans and immigrants. Perhaps the prime example of how these antagonisms coalesced in the struggle for political power was the Republican-nativist take-over of Jersey City in 1871.

Between 1860 and 1870, Irish Catholics became the dominant force in the city's Democratic party. They alone constituted 60 percent of all the foreign-born and 37 percent of the city's adult white males—almost equalling the 39 percent who were natives. Virtually to a man the Irish were Democrats. The other large immigrant group, the Germans, who made up 11 percent of the population, reacted by becoming Republicans. But neither the Germans nor the natives could match the Irish aptitude and appetite for politics. By 1869, the Jersey City Board of Aldermen was 70 percent immigrant, and almost half were Irishmen. They did not hesitate to exert their influence on the police department, permitting the city's saloons to stay open on Sunday and censuring patrolmen who protected strikebreakers in a clash between the Erie Railroad and some Irish machinists.

When the city's poundmaster captured a stray goat in the Seventh Ward, its owner, described as "a gigantic Celtic lady," called for help. Alderman John Maloney rushed from his saloon, grabbed one of the poundmaster's deputies, and shook him until his bones rattled. The poundmaster and his cohorts retreated "amid a terrific volley of stones, bricks, broken bottles &c.," without the goat.[2]

The answer to such populist politics, in the opinion of Jersey City's Protestants, was a new city charter. They were tacitly and sometimes vocally assisted by native Democrats who were as dismayed by the Irish takeover of the city's party as the Republicans. The idea of legislatures seizing control of city governments did not originate in New Jersey. Before the Civil War, the New York state legislature had taken charge of New York City's police department. Similar power plays had been made by legislatures in Illinois and Michigan. Almost invariably, the issue was nativist control of the police. But few legislatures went as far as the Republican politicians in Trenton.

2. Douglas V. Shaw, "The Politics of Nativism: Jersey City's 1871 Commission Charter," essay in *Urban New Jersey Since 1870,* ed. William C. Wright (Trenton: New Jersey Historical Commission, 1975), p. 89.

Responding to a Jersey City Republican convention on charter reform, the legislature placed the city's public works, police, and fire departments in charge of state-appointed commissions. The board of police commissioners was empowered to increase the force by 30 percent and give policemen summary powers of arrest. Backing them up were three police justices appointed by the legislature. The mayor and the aldermen became figureheads with little more than the responsibility for licensing saloons and street-corner salesmen. To guarantee continued GOP dominance, the legislature gerrymandered Hudson County into six tiny districts dominated by Republicans and one huge, grotesquely shaped district along the Hudson amalgamating most of Jersey City's Irish Democrats. On the map it looked like a horseshoe and that is what it came to be called.

The city's native Democrats remained mute before this Republican grab for absolute power. There were strong rumors that a number of leading Democrats, such as former Mayor Orestes Cleveland, had even had a hand in writing the new charter. The anti-Irish bias of the charter's originators became cruelly visible when a small group of middle-class Irish attended a Republican meeting and offered to join the charter coalition. The response was "deafening laughter, shouts and hisses." The city's leading paper, the *Evening Journal,* declared itself in favor of the charter "because it will give somebody besides Irishmen a chance to find employment under the city government."

Democratic Gov. Theodore F. Randolph vetoed the charter bill, but the legislature easily overrode his negative. The constitution of 1844 had given the governor a veto with one hand and emasculated it with the other hand. All the legislature needed was a simple majority to override.

In Jersey City, the legislature's appointees, all Protestant, all Republican, went to work. Irish Catholics were kicked out of city jobs by the dozen, particularly on the police force. One of the police commissioners blandly told a *New York Sun* reporter that he was in favor of appointing Americans and Germans "but Irishmen are nowhere." A camp of the Patriotic Order of Sons of America suggested that the fired Irish might now have time to "so improve their minds as to rise above the slavery of priest-

craft." There was a hullabaloo when one of the police commissioners recommended a new man with an obviously Irish name.
But the furor died down when he proved to be a good Protestant.

The police justices instituted a reign of Protestant morality.
Drunks were fined $5 instead of the traditional $2 and got three
months in jail instead of ten days.

Thanks to the gerrymander, native Democrats were able to
regain control of the party in Jersey City. At the local Democratic primary convention, five former Know-Nothings were
nominated for office. The *Evening Journal,* hoping for another
Republican victory, editorialized that the Democratic leaders
were "serving notice on the Irish voters to take a back seat—
telling them that they are good enough, as of old, to do the voting, but not the sort to put in the lead or be put into office."

The native Democrats were living in never-never land. The
Irish in the Horseshoe stayed home en masse and the Republicans swept the city election, winning control of the board of aldermen. The board members had little to do, but they testified
to their party loyalty by refusing to review the city's Saint Patrick's Day Parade. Elsewhere in the city, the agents of nativist
purity were having problems. There was one office that Republicans in their overhaul of the local government had missed—
that of the sheriff. He was elected by majority vote and he controlled the grand jury. The Democrats nominated a man named
John Rhinehardt. The Irish backed him to a man, and he also
ran well in German districts, although he was born in France.
He went to work on the Republicans. In January 1872, he em-
paneled a grand jury that was almost exclusively Democratic—and heavily Irish. Within a few months they had returned 148 indictments against the officials of the board of
public works, the board of police commissioners, and other
members of the Republican cabal. They condemned the police
justices for jailing people "for long terms for very trivial of-
fenses." It not only burdened the state; it was "depriving their
families of support." Most of the indictments were dismissed.
But the police commissioners were caught soliciting party con-
tributions from their newly appointed patrolmen, and one

member of the board of public works, an English-born contractor named William Bumsted, went to jail for rigging city real estate purchases to line his own pockets.

The following year the Panic of 1873 struck. The public works commission had launched an ambitious building program. Revenues dried up and the city teetered toward bankruptcy. On top of this disaster, the harried Republicans had to face a new round of indictments from the Democratic grand jury, which continued this annual rite for the next four years.

The climax to Republican demoralization was the disappearance of the city treasurer, named, with marvelous historical irony, Alexander Hamilton. At first everyone thought he had gone off on a spree with Winetta Montague, a vivacious variety actress who had recently appeared in Jersey City. This in itself was an interesting comment on the morality of these staunch Protestants. Then Hamilton's mortified fellow Republicans checked the vault and discovered that $60,000 had also disappeared. Newspapers plastered Hamilton's name and picture across the nation. Glimpses of him along his route suggested he was heading for Mexico. Police Inspector Benjamin Murphy of Jersey City pursued him. In Texas, Hamilton hired a desperado named Hutchinson to take him across the border. Hutchinson notified his cousin, Thomas Parker, chief of police in Corpus Christi, and together they relieved Hamilton of $7,500 in cash before they booted him across the Rio Grande.

When Inspector Murphy reached Corpus Christi, he learned that every outlaw in the region—and crooked cops like Parker— were hunting for Hamilton. The frantic fugitive hired another outlaw known only as "Happy Jack" to protect him. This cost him more money. Happy Jack handed him over to Cortinas, a Mexican bandit who had just proclaimed himself mayor of Matamoros. The dauntless Murphy pursued his man to the city hall of Matamoros where he negotiated gingerly with Cortinas. The bandit declined to co-operate with the lawman and Murphy went home.

A few months later, a shabby wreck of a man stumbled into Murphy's office at Jersey City Police Headquarters. It was Alexander Hamilton. Cortinas had "protected" him out of his last dollar and then shipped him to Brazil in a sailing vessel. Hamilton pleaded guilty to embezzlement and was sentenced to three years' imprisonment.

This caper finished the Republican experiment in Jersey City. Democratic Governor Parker had been attacking special legislation as one of the state's worst sins. In 1875, the voters approved an amendment to the constitution forbidding the legislature to regulate the internal affairs of municipalities. Jersey City promptly demanded the end of the state-appointed commissions. When the Republican legislature refused to act, the city easily won its case in court. But it was by no means the end of Protestant nativism in New Jersey. In fact, only by grasping its persistence as a motive force can the political and social history of the state for the next several decades be understood.

12

By the Beautiful, Purifying Sea

SYCHOLOGICAL analysis of another generation is a tricky business. But when one ponders the terrific tensions that surged through New Jersey on all levels of life during the post–Civil War decades, one wonders why the state did not explode. The answer may well have been New Jersey's ability to localize many of its problems in the industrial counties and the relatively remote state capital of Trenton. The grittier aspects of industry and politics seldom penetrated the tranquil suburbs in Essex, Morris, and Bergen counties, where the railroads encouraged thousands of New York commuters to settle. Beyond the commuting range, in Hunterdon and Sussex counties, and in most of Camden and Burlington counties on the lower Delaware, life remained much the same as it had been in the eighteenth century. "Thrift, wariness and stolidity prevail," wrote Walt Whitman on a trip through the southern counties. "In these parts more than anywhere else, yet linger the farback tracts, ancient hymn books."

"But to me," Whitman wrote, "it is the sea-side region that gives stamp to Jersey, even in the human character." It was a prescient remark, worthy of the Democratic poet, who spent the last years of his life in Camden; and it touches another reality that may have enabled New Jersey to escape its ugly problems. The miles of sunny beaches washed by the guardian Atlantic gave thousands and finally millions of Jerseyans a place where they could temporarily escape their searing conflicts and even achieve a spurious purity.

The hegira to the saltwater began when the railroads and steamboats put the shore within easy reach of the state's northern cities and suburbs, as well as New York City's restless millions. First among the shore towns was Long Branch. Today it sits sedately beside the blue Atlantic, just south of Sandy Hook and the Highlands. Here and there a rambling Victorian house hints at a former elegance. It is hard to believe that this narrow strip of sand was for almost twenty years the playground of the presidents, and that on the palmier days in the 1880s, the combined wealth of the congregation worshipping in Saint James Chapel on Ocean Avenue was calculated at $120 million. The story of Long Branch is nothing less than a forgotten American saga.

Around the turn of the nineteenth century, Long Branch began to acquire some reputation as a health resort. As early as 1830, it began to assume a gayer air. One visitor commented on the "card playing, billiards, bowling, and dancing, and fast driving on the beach." By 1860, there were enough hotels and boardinghouses along the shore to accommodate 4,125 persons, and celebrities such as actor Edwin Booth, actress Maggie Mitchell, and Gen. Winfield Scott, hero of the Mexican War and the losing presidential candidate in 1852, joined them. The first hint of greater things was an unexpected visit by Mrs. Abraham Lincoln in August 1861. The town turned out en masse to greet her and literally wrapped itself in American flags. Mrs. Lincoln went to a concert, attended a cricket match, and watched an exhibition of the latest lifesaving techniques, which included firing a lifeline to vessels in distress. It was not the sort of activity that attracted sophisticates, and to complete the aura of anticlimax, while she was there the Battle of Bull Run was fought and lost. Mrs. Lincoln departed, never to return.

With those kinds of notices, Long Branch might have moldered into insignificance. The combination of Saratoga's healthful spring waters and famous horseracing was a magnet that drew the best people in the opposite direction. But a number of capitalists had faith in Long Branch. They included people such as George F. Baker, Jay Gould, and George W. Childs, wealthy publisher of the *Philadelphia Public Ledger*. They financed Louis P. Brown, a promoter with more energy than money. In 1866, he acquired a mile and a quarter of oceanfront property, and the following year he laid out and constructed Ocean Avenue and landscaped a park behind it. Within another year, land values soared from $500 to $5,000 an acre. But the place remained discouragingly middle-class.

In the summer of 1869, George W. Childs had a brainstorm. President Ulysses S. Grant had just been inaugurated. A friend of the president, Childs knew Grant was miserable in the sweltering White House, besieged by hordes of officeseekers. It was a simple matter to persuade him to sample the cool breezes and relaxed lifestyle of the Jersey shore—at Long Branch.

The president and his plump but still-pretty wife Julia, their beautiful daughter Nellie, and their two younger sons, Jesse and Ulysses, created an instant sensation. Grant has been so downgraded by historians for being a mediocre president that it is hard for modern Americans to realize the magic of his name in 1869. After so many other generals had failed, he was the man who had achieved the apparently impossible and won the war that was threatening to destroy the nation. Thousands of people poured into Long Branch to catch a glimpse of him. Overnight, celebrities, society leaders, and men of wealth snapped up every hotel room in sight.

The Grants first tried two of the most fashionable hotels, the Mansion House and the Stetson. They hated the formality and ceremony and the staring eyes of the curious. The president felt compelled to dress in broadcloth and stand on the piazza, bowing and smiling to ladies who passed. On the dance floor he was a disaster. Finishing a waltz at a ball in his honor, he muttered to his footsore partner, "Madam, I'd rather storm a fort than attempt another dance."

But Grant liked everything else about Long Branch, and when he told his friend Childs that he had "never seen a place in all his travels which was better suited for a summer residence," Childs, George Pullman, and the New York financier

Moses Taylor purchased a cottage at 991 Ocean Avenue and gave it to Grant as a gift. With that almost charming (at this distance) simplicity that led Grant to trust too many captains and lieutenants of industry, the president accepted it. The house was soon being called "the summer capital." Two and a half stories high, it had an octagonal porch and an architectural style that a *New York Tribune* reporter called "a mixture of English villa and Swiss chalet."

Although Grant enjoyed the company of the rich and famous, as well as fellow generals such as Phil Sheridan and George Gordon Meade, who streamed into Long Branch in his wake, the president simultaneously displayed the simple tastes and casual airs that made the common man love him. In the army, he had never bothered to wear his general's insignia. At Long Branch, he sat on his porch in a white plug hat and linen duster, smoking a cigar, and swapping yarns with Len Van Dyke, the special policeman on duty at his cottage. Another favorite crony was Henry Van Brunt, who owned the bathing pavilion directly opposite the fashionable Mansion House. Several times a week, the president would come down the street with his highstepping horse and smart buggy, and Henry would stomp out of the pavilion with his pants rolled high above his bare, blistered feet, and away they would ride down Ocean Avenue in the afternoon carriage parade.

Aside from swimming on his private beach, Grant's favorite recreation was racing as many as twenty miles along the shore or over the roads around Long Branch behind two lively bays, Egypt and Cincinnati. In his West Point cadet days, Grant's horsemanship had been the talk of the school, and he still retained a passionate interest in improving the breed. Thus, in 1870, when several entrepreneurs opened Monmouth Park Race Track, the president immediately took a box and seldom missed a race.

Monmouth Park was sensationally successful, and it sent Long Branch's popularity soaring to unparalleled heights. Elegant new hotels were built at a frenzied pace. The Continental, advertising itself as "the largest hotel in the United States," commanded 700 feet of oceanfront and had 600 rooms, bowling alleys, and "the only shooting gallery on the shore attached to the house."

Grant returned to Long branch every summer for the two terms of his presidency, and except for a few summers spent traveling abroad, continued to come back every year until the end of his life. In fact, it was to the old "summer capital" that the ruined ex-president returned in 1884 after the Wall Street firm to which he had entrusted his reputation and cash collapsed. The Grants were so penniless that the ex-First Lady of the land had to cook and keep house. After a month of staring disconsolately at the ocean, Grant, at Mark Twain's urging, began writing his classic memoirs, which he finished in a heartbreaking race against cancer.

Grant's Republican successors followed his example and spent at least a part of every summer at Long Branch. Rutherford B. Hayes and his prim wife, called "Lemonade Lucy" because she barred all wine and liquor at the White House, carefully avoided the resort's more risqué activities. By the time they arrived in 1876, the little town had become the Las Vegas of the era. Col. John Chamberlain, an ex-Mississippi riverboat gambler, had opened his elaborate Pennsylvania Club on the corner of Brighton and Ocean avenues. A skillful French chef cooked magnificent dinners, which were served free to all the patrons. The house offered roulette, rouge et noir, birdcage, and many other games in rooms dominated by huge paintings, mantels crowded with vases, massive horsehair furniture, and marble-top tables in the most sumptuous mid-Victorian style. Other gamblers swiftly opened opulent imitations.

The action attracted characters like "Jubilee Jim" Fiske, Jay Gould's garish partner, who used to arrive accompanied by the entire regiment of 9th New York Guards, of which he was the colonel. They came on Fiske's 345-foot steamer, the *Plymouth Rock,* which Jubilee Jim commanded in an admiral's uniform. Just to make sure everyone knew who owned it, he had his face painted in rich colors on each side of the ship's boiler. Not far behind him in bad taste was Diamond Jim Brady, who enjoyed riding up and down Ocean Avenue at the head of a fleet of six electric cars, and who never failed to create a sensation by swaggering into the Pennsylvania Club or Monmouth Race Track with the statuesque Lillian Russell on his arm.

President James Garfield upheld Long Branch's reign in spite of the fact that it meant an uncomfortable confrontation with Ulysses Grant, whom Garfield had blocked in his try for a third term. Garfield arrived early for the 1881 season, settled his family, and returned to Washington briefly for some pressing paper work. On July 2, Lucretia Garfield received the terrible news that her husband had been gunned down by a half-crazed, disappointed officeseeker in Washington's Union Station. The badly wounded president was moved from sweltering Washington to Long Branch at his own request. Because doctors feared to transport him in a jolting carriage, a railroad spur five-eighths of a mile long was built in a single night directly to the front door of the cottage where he was to stay. Alas, the sea air did poor Garfield no good, and his blundering doctors did him a great deal of harm. He died on Sunday, September 18. Vice-President Chester A. Arthur, who had already rented a house that season in Long Branch, took over and returned to enjoy the playground each summer for the rest of his term.

But Garfield's death had cast a pall over Long Branch. The influx of the sporting crowd had also soured many of the haughtier millionaires, and they began retreating to Saratoga and Newport. When Democrat Grover Cleveland won the presidency in 1884, he scrupulously avoided imitating any and all aspects of his Republican predecessors, and Long Branch became an ex-playground for presidents. Republican Benjamin Harrison spent some time there during his single term (1888–1892) but "The Branch" was definitely in a state of decline.

Long branch's coup de grâce was a wave of puritanical reform that swept New Jersey in the nineties, closing down the gambling houses and the racetrack. Although President William McKinley, too, paid a visit, it was more in memory of his Republican predecessors than the pursuit of the social splendor a president deserved. By this time, another New Jersey resort had captured national attention. The Philadelphia & Atlantic City Narrow Gauge Railway began running to Atlantic City in 1877, bringing packed carloads of working-class Americans from the City of Brotherly Love for one-day bargain excursions. By 1890, there were more than 500 hotels, a vast boardwalk with fifty-seven commercial bathhouses, ten amusement-ride centers, and eighteen sellers of saltwater taffy. Streams of pamphlets, press releases, and newspaper stories pictured Atlantic City as "the national resort."

Although the city tried to portray itself as a mecca of the social elite, it was really a materialization of lower middle-class America's dreams. As one newspaperman put it, "The ultra swell and almost no one else go to Lenox, Bar Harbor, Newport. Swell and near-swell and folks 'just comfortable' go to places like Asbury Park. Into Atlantic City every day in the season are dumped ultra, almost, and near-swell, folks comfortable and uncomfortable, and absolutely every kind by the thousands."

Other publicity suggested the city tempered class conflicts and promoted social equality. Among the favorites were reports of salesgirls from Wanamaker's marrying wealthy scions from Colorado. The "pretty shop girls from the big [Philadelphia] Market Street stores" were taught to swim by "big athletic clubmen who would scarcely deign to notice them in the scurrying throngs along Chestnut Street after six o'clock," declared one of these puffs. "The most haughty and conservative of Walnut Street beauties in boldly negligee [*sic*] attire laughingly received the splashings of a denizen of 'de Fourt' Ward,'" wrote a *Philadelphia Inquirer* reporter. Rand-McNally's *Handy Guide* maintained it was "no uncommon sight to see the children of millionaires and the little ones of laboring men riding happily on the merry-go-round at the same time, and perhaps to find the parents fraternizing on the switchback railway."

Hardnosed historical research tends to prick these publicity bubbles. A comparison of names in hotel personal notices in Atlantic City and in the Philadelphia Social Register reveals that less than 1 percent of the guests worthy of report in the newspapers came from the upper crust. It was more accurate to say that New York might have had its 400, but Atlantic City had its 40,000. Anyone could join the throng.

America's pursuit of pleasure on a mass scale began in Atlantic City. A local newspaper remarked, "The Baltimore police have been instructed to arrest all young persons kissing or spooning in the public parks of that city and a fine of twenty dollars is imposed for each offense. A similar edict in this city would greatly swell the public revenues, but it would not be submitted to; it would raise a riot." Applegate's Pier had a Lover's Pavilion in the middle of its upper level.

The sport of girl-watching was already flourishing in 1897. One reporter wrote that bathing suits of light brown linen were becoming popular because "it clings to the body as tightly when wet as would a sticking plaster and the graceful contour of a Venuslike form is made conspicuous, but by no means obtrusive."

As for the sale of liquor on Sunday, the most Atlantic City tried to do was "make the liquor sellers show some respect for the day." Other less-innocent pleasures were also available. A series of exposés of Atlantic City's vice and corruption in the *Philadelphia Bulletin* of 1890 included one story about a very respectable lady who lived at Number 20 South on one of the leading crossavenues of the town. At Number 20 North lived a lady who had "brazen females" distributing cards bearing her "business" address along the boardwalk. "Gay young men and disreputable old men" unfamiliar with Atlantic City's system of street and house numbering frequently confused Number 20 North and Number 20 South. As a result, the very respectable lady in Number 20 South was awakened at all hours of the night by "drunken loafers" making "scandalous inquiries" to her.

Somehow, although everyone knew such things went on, the decadent side of Atlantic City was purified by the presence of the sea. It was no accident that the City by the Sea eventually became the resort's favorite title. As a city it had bustle and hustle and tremendous variety for the pleasure seekers. As a seaside resort it retained an aura of purity. One Atlantic City booster put this sentiment into poetry:

> The sea to our ills serves as balm and as lotion
> 'Mong its buffeting waves from our cares we are free.

Each day we return with a zealot's devotion
To kneel at the shrine of the god of the Sea,
And bow to the charms—'tis a pleasure and duty—
To the half-hidden charms of America's girls;
One feels as he looks on their grace and their beauty
The blue sea is showing its loveliest pearls.

A prose writer put it in more practical terms. "I would advise a man before getting married, to see his sweetheart in her bathing dress. There is no deception there. He can see exactly the size of the human nature he is in love with.

"And no harm . . . the salt water washes away all impropriety." [1]

1. Charles E. Funnell, "Atlantic City: Washbasin of the Great Democracy," essay in *Urban New Jersey Since 1870,* ed. William C. Wright (Trenton: New Jersey Historical Commission, 1975), p. 109.

13

The New Idea

*T*HE sea as a nostrum for New Jersey ills was hardly an answer that would satisfy serious men. There was a growing disgust with the excesses of the industrial aristocrats and their political partners in crime. At first this moral indignation expended itself on futile feuding between Protestant Republicans and Catholic Democrats. The high tide of the more obvious, Democratic-style corruption came in the 1880s and 1890s, when two Protestant Democrats from Jersey City, Leon Abbett and George Werts, learned a lesson from the nativist attempt to push the Irish around. Abbett in particular became the voice of the workingman and led the Irish into state politics, appointing them to important jobs in Trenton.

Carried away by an election triumph in 1893 that put Werts in the governor's chair and the party in control of the legislature, the Democrats overreached themselves. The proliferation of racetracks around the state had become a major issue. Bookmaking, prostitution, and numerous other violations of the law were openly condoned inside these establishments while the police force looked the other way. Frequently the tracks were owned by a local political boss like the notorious Billy Thompson of Gloucester.

When criticism mounted, the trackmen fought back. Taking a leaf from the Pennsylvania Railroad book, they elected numerous members of their own kind to the legislature. Thomas

Flynn of Passaic, a starter at Thompson's Gloucester course, became the speaker of the assembly, and the "boys" rammed
through a series of laws guaranteeing their gambling duchies.
When Republicans protested, Speaker Flynn dismissed them as
the spokesmen for "old women and dominies." The Republicans retaliated with their moral shock troops. No less than 5,000
indignant, mostly Protestant middle-class spokesmen and
women took over the assembly chamber on Washington's Birthday and denounced the "jockey legislature."

Before the year was over, the Panic of 1893 struck like a bolt
from an angry Jehovah, shriveling New Jersey and the rest of
the country. Grover Cleveland sat in the White House and the
Republicans had no difficulty blaming the economic disaster on
the Democrats. It was the beginning of a long Republican reign
both in the nation and in New Jersey. The Republicans took
over the legislature in 1894 and began exhuming loads of
Democratic corruption. In 1896 GOP voters elected their first
governor in twenty-seven years.

The application of business expertise to government and an
image of moral rectitude were the twin secrets of Republican
success. But their casual attitude toward conflicts of interest between the politician and the businessman left the industrial aristocrats untouched by reform. The state's economic policy reflected their pervasive influence. As American industry
matured, the primitive concept of unrestrained competition was
perceived to be less than a blessing. Monopolies of the sort enjoyed by the old Camden and Amboy barons looked far more
soothing to the nerves and beneficial to the wallet. The answer
was the trust, a combination that organized groups of companies
in a single industry into a monolith that set wages and prices. A
nationwide revolt against these tactics began in the late 1880s.
State after state passed antitrust laws. But New Jersey once
more displayed its talent for marching to its own special drum.
It not only refused to pass an antitrust law; it specifically autho-
rized holding corporations. These giant combines were less su-
ceptible to prosecution and were uniquely suited to issuing large
amounts of common stock, which simplified the takeover of
other companies.

Standard Oil absorbed the oil industry for John D. Rockefeller under the generous provisions of New Jersey law. Hundreds of other corporations rushed to imitate the performance. The costs were modest. All that was needed was a one-room home office and a few pieces of paper from the state purchased for 20 cents on each $1,000 of capitalization. The business neatly fitted the old rationalization—only strangers and persons not living in New Jersey were taking a beating, and the money, plus railroad cash, paid the expenses of the state government, once more staving off any need for a statewide tax. Enraged reformers like journalist Lincoln Steffens dubbed New Jersey the "Traitor State."

Anyone who took a close look saw that the boss of the Republican party, William J. Sewell, believed that what was good for the Pennsylvania Railroad was good for New Jersey and vice versa. To make the point even clearer, Sewell held court in the Pennsylvania Railroad office in Camden. He was a powerful man, both in the state and nation, an intimate of Bosses Thomas C. Platt of New York and Matthew Quay of Pennsylvania. Sewell's influence got Paterson's portly Garrett A. Hobart, known to his fellow Jerseyans as "Gus," on the McKinley ticket as vice-president in 1896. An amiable nonentity, Gus was extremely fond of the good life and expired after three years of enjoying it in Washington, D.C. If he had been more temperate, he would have probably been renominated in 1900 and become president when McKinley was cut down by an assassin's bullet in 1901.

Boss Sewell saw nothing wrong with requiring his first Republican governor, John W. Griggs, to appoint the chief lobbyist of the Pennsylvania Railroad Company as state commissioner of banking and insurance. The Republican state senate gagged somewhat, but confirmed him. Governor Griggs was later rewarded by an appointment as attorney general in McKinley's cabinet, from which he ascended to the U.S. Supreme Court. As New Jersey's two U.S. senators, Sewell chose John F. Dryden, president of the Prudential Insurance Company, and John Kean, chief executive of the Elizabethtown Gas and Light Company. Thomas McCarter, the state attorney general, resigned in 1903 to become head of the Public Service, a holding company that soon dominated gas, electricity, and inner-city transportation in much of the state. The legislature serenely appointed his brother, Robert H. McCarter, to replace him, with not a word said on the Republican side of the aisle about McCarter continuing to work as counsel for two of the state's railroads. To no one's surprise, Public Service was soon obtaining perpetual franchises to run its trolleys along city streets. When citizen groups asked the attorney general to test the legality of these franchises, they were ignored.

It was difficult to break the stranglehold of the corporations because they had powerful spokesmen in both parties who worked closely with political bosses to see that the "right" men got the nomination. The political bosses controlled the state and county conventions where nominees were selected. Thus Chandler Riker, the Essex County public prosecutor, refused to act against the North Jersey Street Railroad Company following a disastrous trolley accident at a grade-crossing in 1903 in which nine high school students were killed. Such attitudes and policies disgusted more than a few high-minded Republicans.

The big jolt to New Jersey's bosses and their business backers came from the most unexpected place in the most unexpected way. In 1901, a young Irish-Catholic undertaker named Mark Fagan ran for mayor of Jersey City on the Republican ticket.

His candidacy seemed an exercise in futility. The Republicans had only won two mayoral elections since the city was founded. Their 1871 grab for power with the help of the legislature and the gerrymander had left a stigma on the party that the average Jersey City voter found hard to forget. But Fagan knew precisely what he was doing. He was far from the "servant of God and the people"—a canonization given to him by Lincoln Steffens. Fagan was a political animal. He had grown up in Jersey City's downtown wards. He knew that even there, considerable dissatisfaction with the political status quo existed.

Uptown, the middle- and upper-class Protestants and a growing group of middle-class Irish and Germans simmered with even more discontent. Jersey City was governed by an unsavory alliance between E. F. C. Young, president of the First National

Bank, and "Little Bob" Davis, the Democratic boss. Young was the economic dictator of Jersey City. He was president of Dixon-Crucible, the city's second-largest industry. He was a director of the Public Service Company, and the First National was the city's and state's largest bank. He was often called "the father of Jersey City business." More cynical observers said, "All roads lead to First National."

Young's son-in-law was president of another bank as well as the eastern agent of the Pennsylvania Railroad Company. With Davis's help, Young made sure that the Public Service and other corporations got what they wanted—minimum taxes, perpetual franchises, and indifference from the city and county government on such sticky matters as plant safety and the right to organize unions. When Young persuaded the easygoing Davis to nominate his son-in-law, George T. Smith, for mayor in 1901, Fagan saw his opportunity. Running against bossism and in favor of such basic services as efficient police and fire protection, Fagan stunned the city and the state by beating the Democratic boss and his banker partner.

Except for his Irish-Catholic background, Fagan sounded at first like any other New Jersey Republican. He was not a reformer. He started out trying to deliver "good government" by applying business principles to the city politic. But Fagan soon discovered that he could not keep promises to build more and better schools and a city hospital or even pave the numerous downtown streets, which became lakes and quagmires after a rainstorm. Jersey City simply did not have the money. The railroads owned one-third of the city's property, including the invaluable waterfront. The state board of assessors valued the railroad holdings at $25,830,000. The city said the real estate was worth $67,450,000. The utilities were getting similar deals. In 1903, after winning re-election as mayor in spite of an all-out effort by the Democratic machine, Fagan asked for help from the state Republican party. With the assistance of corporation counsel George L. Record, a tall, lean, philosophic Maine Yankee who had been fighting bossism in New Jersey for a decade, Fagan submitted to the legislature a program proposing equal taxation and a limitation on public utility franchises. The legislators ignored him. The infuriated Fagan responded with an open letter of protest against corporation control of the Republican party.

This bombshell exploded across the state with startling effects. It launched the New Idea movement, which soon attracted outspoken and independent Republicans in Newark like the millionaire Everett Colby. When the Republican boss of Newark, Major Carl Lentz, tried to purge Colby from the assembly, Colby retaliated by running for the state senate in 1905. He won by an amazing 20,000 votes on a platform demanding prohibition of perpetual utility franchises, equal taxation for railroads and other corporations, and the replacement of the convention system by the direct primary. The success of Fagan and Record in Jersey City and Colby in Newark inspired dozens of other Republicans and Democrats to join the New Idea movement, which soon blossomed into the New Jersey version of the Progressive party. A People's Lobby surfaced in Trenton to check undue corporate influence.

With their uncompromising denunciation of boss rule—"It is impossible," Mark Fagan said, "for a public official to get along with a boss, except upon terms of abject obedience and the sacrifice of self-respect" [1]—the New Idea men seized the initiative and fired the voters with faith in their cause. When the Essex County Republican boss, Major Lentz, tried to manipulate the re-election of U.S. Sen. John F. Dryden, Colby denounced the president of the Prudential Life Insurance Company as a man who bought elections, and the voters sent eleven hitherto-unknown Democrats to the assembly with orders to vote against Dryden's re-election. In 1906, U.S. senators were still elected by the legislature. The New Idea men thought they should be elected by direct vote.

When Mark Fagan won re-election for a second time in Jersey City, running as both a Republican and a New Idea independent, the *Newark News* called his victory "an unqualified endorsement of his fight against bossism and an acknowledgment

---

1. Quoted in Eugene M. Tobin, "The Progressive as Politician: Jersey City, 1896–1907," *New Jersey History* 91 (Spring 1973): 22.

that he is the leader in the struggle for equal taxation throughout the state of New Jersey." But the New Idea men were promising more than they could deliver. They probably never had more than 1,200 hard-core supporters. The father of the Progressive movement, Robert La Follette, came to New Jersey in 1906 to support them. But like Lincoln Steffens's naive canonization of Mark Fagan, La Follette's support probably did the New Idea men more harm than good. The *Jersey City Evening Journal* declared that La Follette "reminded Republicans that anarchy, socialism, confiscation and destruction can never become Republican issues." In the primary elections of 1906, Republican regulars routed the New Idea men everywhere. Previously an enthusiastic supporter of Fagan, the editors of the *Evening Journal* turned against him and accused him of building his own personal machine.

In one sense they were right. Fagan had discovered he could not survive without patronage and city jobholders to support him. At the same time, almost in defiance of his critics, he became more radical, calling for municipal ownership of trolley lines and minimum fares. The Roman Catholic church, unhappy with Fagan's attempts to build public schools, moved in with cruel finesse to destroy him for the bosses. First the pastor of Fagan's own church, then a prominent monsignor speaking for the bishop in Newark, discovered that Fagan was failing to enforce the Sunday saloon closing law. This so-called "bishop's law" had been enacted with the backing of both Catholic and Protestant temperance advocates. "You cannot serve church and saloon," cried the clergymen, and accused Fagan of violating his oath of office. Simultaneously, the priests began praising Fagan's Democratic opponent, Protestant H. Otto Wittpenn. With the bosses of both parties, the city's leading newspaper, and his own church against him, Fagan lost by 9,500 votes. The New Idea was dismissed by the *Jersey City Evening Journal* as "a mixture of idealism and humbug."

Republican progressivism was dead in Jersey City, but it was by no means dead in New Jersey. On the contrary, Fagan's opponent, Wittpenn, was a tribute to the vigor of the New Idea and its appeal to the voters. Wittpenn was a young German businessman who said he was just as much opposed to bossism as Fagan and co-opted almost all of Fagan's progressive causes. The Republican party soon did the same thing. Gov. Franklin Murphy called for and got from the reluctant legislature primary election reform and strong child labor laws. His successor, John Franklin Fort, declared himself in favor of controlling the public utilities by law, abolishing the county tax boards that favored the railroads, and regulating the state's chaotic civil service, which still operated largely on the spoils system. But the Republican legislature, which had put Fort in the governor's chair largely as New Idea window dressing, insisted on business as usual with the railroads and the utilities.

In 1910, with the two leaders of the New Idea, Hudson's Mark Fagan and Essex's Everett Colby, beaten to the political sidelines, the Republicans decided they could go back to a safe conservative governor. Democratic bosses were thinking along the same lines. James Smith of Essex and Robert Davis of Hudson ignored two progressive volunteers, H. Otto Wittpenn of Jersey City and Frank Katzenbach, the former mayor of Trenton. They decided they would be happier with a college president named Woodrow Wilson.

Wilson was not just any college president, of course. He was president of Princeton. There he had led a widely publicized fight for democratization, to be achieved largely by curriculum reform and the abolition of the aristocratic eating clubs. Wilson had been defeated by alumni conservatives. But he had won a national reputation in the process. He was in demand as an afterdinner speaker and a facile writer of magazine articles on the issues of the day. A glance through these articles and speeches had assured Boss Smith that Wilson was a "safe" candidate. He had been outspoken in his opposition to the regulation of public utilities and other corporations by state or federal commissions. In an article in the *Atlantic Monthly* for November 1907, he had called attempts at federal regulation of corporations a compound of "confused thinking and impossible principles of law." He blamed the panic of 1907 on "the aggressive attitude of legislation toward the railroads.'' That same year he branded the ''rough and ready reasoning of the reformers'' as socialistic.[2]

James Smith was not the ordinary nineteenth-century Democratic boss. President of a large Newark bank, the head of several leather manufacturing concerns, and the publisher of a morning and an evening newspaper, he was by nature an aristocrat. He was one of those Irish Catholics who had arrived early and had had no difficulty acquiring the style and mannerisms of the Protestant elite. He had sent three sons to Princeton and knew Wilson slightly. The suave, immaculately groomed Smith, six feet tall, with the face of an innocent child, and the intense, aloof college president met as equals. They shared a common friendship with ex-President Grover Cleveland, who was living in Princeton.

In 1910 Smith needed a winner. Since 1895, all his hand-picked Democratic candidates for governor had failed. Numerous young progressives in New Jersey were calling for his retirement. Not only did Wilson's views on utilities and railroads seem safe: in an article entitled, ''The States and Federal Government,'' the Princeton president had praised the American system, which left the selection of candidates to a few persons who made a business of it. ''They are the political bosses and managers,'' wrote Wilson, ''whom the people obey and affect to despise. It is unjust to despise them.''

Over fervent protests from progressives, Smith bludgeoned the state convention into accepting Wilson as the Democratic candidate for governor. There was a great deal of underground opposition. When the secretary of the convention described him as ''Woodrow Wilson of Mercer,'' that county's delegates roared in protest. ''Accredit him to Virginia,'' shouted someone in the balcony. ''He isn't a Jersey man.'' In his nominating speech, Smith candidly admitted that he was the only delegate in the hall who had any acquaintance with Wilson. In fact, Smith's son-in-law, James Nugent, a talented politician in his

2. James Kerney, *The Political Education of Woodrow Wilson* (New York: Century Co., 1926), p. 33.

own right, told James Kerney, editor of the *Trenton Evening Times,* that Smith was the only delegate from Essex County who favored Wilson. But in 1910, the "Big Fellow," as everyone called Smith, was a one-man landslide.

Smith and Hudson's boss, Bob Davis, did not realize they were dealing with another idealist who was also an astute political animal. Wilson soon became aware of the power of the New Idea philosophy among the voters, and he accepted the nomination with an impassioned speech declaring that he was unbossed and pledged to remain unbossed.

Nobody believed Wilson until George Record of Jersey City put him to the test. Wilson had said he was ready to debate the issues with any Republican in the state. Record accepted his challenge. The Democratic bosses were horrified. By this time, Record was acknowledged as a leading philosopher of the Progressive party. He was also a skilled public speaker. The bosses saw him demolishing the dignified Wilson on a public platform. They did everything in their power to keep Record at bay. The Republicans sniffed their panic and insisted on a debate.

Wilson finally decided on a shrewd compromise. He offered to debate Record by letter, claiming that the Democratic Committee had filled all his speaking dates. Record promptly sent Wilson nineteen questions designed to elicit Wilson's stand on nearly every progressive objective. Wilson replied on October 26, 1910. He declared himself in favor of a public utilities commission with the power to set just and reasonable rates, a comprehensive direct primary law, the direct election of U.S. senators, uniform ballots, the selection of primary and election officers by an impartial agency such as a court, a drastic corrupt practices act, and a strong workmen's compensation law.

Finally, Record asked: "Do you admit that the boss system exists as I have described it? If so, how do you propose to abolish it?"

Wilson replied:

> Of course I admit it. Its existence is notorious. I've made it my business for many years to observe and understand it. . . . I will join you, or anyone else in denouncing and fighting every and any one of either party who attempts any outrage against . . . public

> morality. . . . If elected, I shall not either in the matter of
> appointements to office or assent to legislation or in shaping any
> part of the policy of my administration, submit to the dictation of
> any person or persons, 'special interests,' or organizations.

When old-line Republicans read Wilson's response, they reportedly said, "Damn Record: the campaign's over." Record himself was reported as saying, "That letter will elect Wilson governor." Wilson, sensing he had been handed the winning issue in the campaign, repeatedly hit bossism in both parties in his remaining speeches. He ended his campaign on November 5 in the Krueger Auditorium in Newark. Practically repudiating the county machine that had nominated him, Wilson declared, "Politics in recent years has degenerated in New Jersey, as elsewhere, into a struggle for control, into an effort to preserve the integrity and power of an organization which held the people at arm's length, and all over the country there has been the starting of opinion, the starting and gathering of revolt against the processes of politics because they are the processes of selfishness and not the processes of patriotism." He called on the people of New Jersey "to set an example" and take control of their government.[3]

Wilson won a landslide victory. The railroads inadvertently helped him by betraying their Republican protectors and raising commuter fares 20 percent. They, too, were obviously convinced that there was little to worry about in a Wilson victory. If the professor was safe enough for James Smith and Bob Davis, he was surely safe enough for them. The railmen did not realize how badly the New Idea had disunited the Republican party. Wilson not only won big but carried a Democratic majority into the legislature.

The new governor immediately went to work on an ambitious reform program. He also made good on his pledge that he would be unbossed. James Smith passionately desired to return to the U.S. Senate—he had already spent a term there in the 1890s—as the capstone of his political career. Wilson refused to

3. David W. Hirst, *Woodrow Wilson, Reform Governor* (Princeton: D. Van Nostrand Co., 1965), pp. 103–105.

support him and declined to deal with Smith's son-in-law, James Nugent, the Democratic state chairman, on patronage. A young Jersey City Irish American, Joseph Tumulty, who had carved a reputation as a progressive, became Wilson's adviser and eventually his secretary. Tumulty was a conduit for New Idea men and programs, many of them brainchildren of the ubiquitous George Record. More than once, Record not only drafted the reform bill but also browbeat key senate Republicans into supporting it.

Before the bosses or the corporations knew what was happening, the Wilson-dominated legislature began producing the reforms that his Republican predecessor had promised in vain. An Election Law created bipartisan boards and a direct primary for all state offices. A Corrupt Practices Act promised stern justice for ballot box stuffing and other notorious voting violations. A Public Utilities Law gave a three-man board the power to regulate rates and limit franchises. A Workmen's Compensation Act gave laboring men and women financial protection if they were injured on the job.

This tidal wave of reform made Woodrow Wilson and New Jersey national bywords for a new era. People began calling Governor Wilson a presidential candidate. He acted like one, zooming around the nation to give speeches on progressivism in government. Nationally, the Republican party was coming apart. Millions of thoughtful, middle-class voters urged the party to adopt progressivism and reform as its platform. But President William Howard Taft found it impossible to shed the old-guard alliance with corporations and special interests. Theodore Roosevelt broke with Taft and announced himself as a third-party candidate on the Progressive party ticket.

This Republican split meant that the man who got the Democratic nomination was almost a guaranteed winner. The fight for this prize was fierce. Wilson, by now an avowed contender, was opposed by Congressman Champ Clark of Missouri. To stay in the race it was absolutely necessary for Wilson to win the support of the New Jersey delegation to the convention. This support had to be obtained in the teeth of ferocious opposition from the Smith-Nugent machine in Newark. The governor left his

New Jersey advisers, especially Joe Tumulty of Jersey City, in charge of distributing the patronage that would create a pro-Wilson delegation. To stabilize Hudson County, Tumulty persuaded Wilson to appoint as chancellor Edwin R. Walker, an able lawyer without corporate affiliations. This was the ranking judgeship in New Jersey's chancery court, the final court of appeals. The office of secretary of state went to the Democratic leader of Monmouth. Essex County politicians who risked the wrath of Smith and Nugent to support Wilson were rewarded with a wide variety of jobs. Mollifying the liquor interests was an even touchier problem. They had cooled on Wilson because he supported local option. Tumulty put a New Brunswick saloonkeeper who doubled as head of the liquor lobby on the state tax commission board. A prominent Paterson brewer was named candidate at large for the Democratic National Convention. All of these moves helped to create a Wilson organization in New Jersey that was able to beat Smith in every county but Essex. "Tumulty's master plan," as his biographer put it, prevailed. The majority of the New Jersey delegation went to the national convention pledged to Woodrow Wilson.

In later years, Wilson was fond of remarking that anyone who did not get a complete political education in a year or two of New Jersey politics would be advised to seek another line of work.

Wilson won the presidential nomination on the forty-sixth ballot, when William Jennings Bryan switched his support to him, convinced that the New Jersey governor was a sincere reformer. With "The New Freedom" as his campaign slogan, Wilson won the presidency as a minority candidate, running far behind the combined Taft-Roosevelt vote, even in New Jersey. The Democratic machines of Hudson and Essex counties no longer had any enthusiasm for the professor.

In the last months of his gubernatorial term Wilson persuaded the legislature to adopt another piece of dazzling reform, the Seven Sisters Acts, which effectively took New Jersey out of the corporation charter business. To onlookers it seemed a final flourish of a master politician. New Jersey had reached perfection and Wilson could now go to work on administering the same medicine to the rest of the country.

By 1920 a disgusted legislature, angry at seeing numerous corporations leave New Jersey for other states that were busy tailoring their laws to fit the owners' needs and greeds, had repealed all seven of these reforms. Many of Wilson's other reforms were equally illusory. This was particularly true of the direct primary. It was hailed by newspapers and pundits as the death knell of boss rule. Actually, it was an open invitation for a man with a concentrated supply of one-party votes to take over a county. This potential already existed in Jersey City with its preponderance of the population of Hudson County. The man who controlled Jersey City would in turn control Hudson's even more massive Democratic party and consequently would dominate the statewide nominations of the party. A minor Wilson reform substituted a nine-man board of chosen freeholders as the rulers of Hudson County, replacing the much larger and unwieldy board that had had representatives from all the county's municipalities. No one noticed, but this too was another step in the domination of the county government by Jersey City.

Although Wilson's Jersey City secretary, Joseph Tumulty, tried to keep him abreast of local politics around the state, the governor had very little interest in the subject. He was particularly cool to fellow progressives like H. Otto Wittpenn, and he made no attempt to support Wittpenn when the German American tried to become the Democratic leader of Hudson County. "Little Bob" Davis had died of cancer in 1911. E. F. C. Young had also died, creating a political vacuum that Wittpenn, having won re-election three times as mayor, was well qualified to fill. The ambitious Wittpenn was also hoping to win the party's nomination as Wilson's successor in the governor's chair. Wilson starved Wittpenn on patronage and gave short shrift to his gubernatorial ambitions. As a result, the leadership of the Democratic party in Hudson County passed to a tall, lean Irish American named Frank Hague.

14

Workers of New Jersey, Unite!

WHILE the New Idea men in both parties struggled to rally the average voter to challenge the political control of the industrial aristocrats, other Jerseyans were fighting the power of entrenched wealth in a more direct and dangerous way. They were trying to unionize the state's workers and win decent wages and working conditions for them.

The segregation of the immigrant working classes into a few counties and cities, and the perception of them as foreigners with different, unsettling social habits and an alien religion made it easy for Jerseyans to view with relative complacency the low wages they received and the horrendously unhealthy and dangerous factories in which they toiled. Add to this the irresponsibility of the industrial aristocrats, and we have the setting for the labor violence that shook New Jersey for decades.

Although there were strikes and unrest in Newark, Jersey City, and Trenton, Paterson was the city that attracted national attention. There the roots of the antagonism between the workers and the employers went deep. The S.U.M. tradition of total control was the guiding philosophy of Paterson's silk makers. In the 1870s and 1880s they worked their millhands, who were mostly women and children, thirteen and a half hours on an average day. When a do-gooder suggested establishing a night school, he was told by a writer who knew the city well that this

160

was a silly idea. The writer proceeded to describe the life of twelve-year-old millhands in Paterson. They had to

> rise ere dawn of day, consume their morning meal by candle light and trudge to the mill to commence their labor ere the rising of the sun: at noon a very short time was allowed them for dinner, and their labor terminates at what is called eight o'clock at night, but which is really (by the time they have their frames cleaned) much nearer nine o'clock. They then take supper and immediately retire to bed in order that they may arise early in the morning.

Meanwhile, Paterson's industrialists grew fantastically rich. Their supremacy was dramatized by Catholina Lambert, one of the city's leading silk manufacturers, who built a castle on Garret Mountain, the large hill which overlooks the city. It was an almost unbelievably naive proclamation of the reign of these ersatz aristocrats. Complete with turreted stone battlements, Lambert's Castle was a weapon, supplied out of sheer arrogance, which men filled with hatred and bitterness used to alienate further their fellow workers.

Elsewhere in New Jersey, skilled tradesmen were organizing into politically moderate craft unions that eventually affiliated on a state and national basis to become the American Federation of Labor. Camden's Peter J. McGuire, founder of the Brotherhood of Carpenters and Joiners Union, was the man who suggested the creation of Labor Day. He wanted to honor "the industrial spirit, the great vital force of the nation." But among the unskilled workers of Paterson the potent voices belonged to men like Joseph P. McDonnell, a Socialist and leader of the radical International Labor Union. McDonnell published his newspaper, the *Labor Standard,* in Paterson for many years. He popularized the term *scab* for strike breaker. For this bit of verbal defiance, he was hauled into court and fined $500 by a Paterson judge. The workers paid his fine out of their own pockets.

By discouraging naturalization and threatening to fire people, Paterson's bosses even managed to prevent most of the workers from voting. In the election of 1850, for example, only 536 people voted from a population of 11,300. The S.U.M. and the other factory owners controlled the government and the press, as well as the factories. When someone complained that S.U.M. paid no taxes, the local paper solemnly assured its readers that the corporation paid full taxes—a blatant lie.

But the workers, whether they were English, Irish, or later comers, Italians, Hungarians, and Jews, did not accept this treatment passively. That is the most amazing part of Paterson's story. In spite of so much power on the employers' side, the workers fought for more equal liberty as Americans. Between 1881 and 1900 137 strikes were recorded in Paterson. Every one failed, but their existence testified to a virtual state of war between the employers and the workers.

Inevitably, the hostility spilled over into politics in a symbolic election in 1902. One of Paterson's textile kings, Col. William B. Barbour, decided to run for Congress and easily brushed aside the incumbent Republican congressman. He was challenged by Irish-born William Hughes, who had worked as a reel boy in the Barbour Mills. Hughes had studied for the bar by "reading" in a local attorney's office. "Lawyer Billy" went straight for Barbour's jugular, denouncing him as an exploiter of "little boys, little girls, young women and old women." Hughes won the election—a stunning defeat for Republicans in a hitherto-safe district.

But symbolic victories were not enough to satisfy the embittered workers in the mills. They discharged their rage in other ways. Riots were a frequent feature of Paterson strikes. Machinery was wrecked and factories torched. Vandalism of public and private property was a constant problem. When one of the silk kings donated a park to the city, the workers smashed vases and urns, chipped noses and ears off the statuary, and even cut branches from the trees until the place was a denuded, polluted wreck.

Paterson became the headquarters of American anarchism. In 1900, the man who assassinated King Humbert I of Italy, Gaetano Bresci, got his assignment by drawing lots with a group of the city's anarchists. Thousands of anarchists held a meeting to applaud the assassin. A year later, when President William McKinley was assassinated, the anarchists celebrated the news with a ball. The following year, 1902, the anarchists led a strike that ended in a riotous attack on ten mills. One of the leaders, William MacQueen, was arrested and sentenced to five years in prison for inciting to riot and malicious mischief.

In 1905, a group known as the New Jersey Socialist and Unity Conference held a series of meetings in Paterson, Newark, and other cities. They passed a resolution commending the Industrial Workers of the World because "instead of running away from the class struggle [it] bases itself squarely on it." The IWW, or "Wobblies," as they were called, were the left wing of the labor movement. They proposed to fight the growing concentration of industrial power by organizing "one big union." Paterson was made to order for their rhetoric and tactics. They believed there was no hope of a compromise between the owners and the workers. "Between these two classes," said the preamble of the IWW Constitution, "the struggle must go on until the workers of the world organize as a class, take possession of the earth and the machinery of production and abolish the wage system."

The Wobblies arrived in Paterson in 1913, after leading a sensational strike in the textile mills of Lawrence, Massachusetts. Power looms had replaced the old hand looms in Paterson's mills, and workers were required to operate three and four looms instead of one or two. In February 1913, 8,000 weavers and dyers walked off their jobs, demanding the reestablishment of the two-loom system, an eight-hour day, and a minimum wage of $12 a week. The IWW took charge of the strike and brought a "who's who" of American radicalism to Paterson. At their head was William D. "Big Bill" Haywood, a huge one-eyed man with "a face like a scarred battlefield." At his side was the fiery "rebel girl," Elizabeth Gurley Flynn. The anarchist Carlo Tresca, the novelist Upton Sinclair, and the young Harvard-educated journalist John Reed were among the other big names. They mesmerized the workers with visions of a fantastic future. In every factory there would be "a wonderful dining room. . . . Your digestion will be aided by sweet music. . . . Your work chairs will be Morris chairs, so that . . . you may relax in comfort."

For five months Paterson was a city torn by insurrection. Gangs of workers and police roamed the streets attacking each other. The owners refused to negotiate with the IWW, calling them subversives who threatened American society. Drunk on their dreams of a socialist revolution, Haywood and his friends played into the owners' hands with such statements as, "We will have a new flag, an international flag . . . the red flag, the color of the working man's blood. Under that we will march." Another IWW leader, Patrick Quinlan, declared in a speech in New York's Union Square, "We are going to win this strike or Paterson will be wiped off the map. If the strike is not won, Paterson will be a howling wilderness."

After the assassination of President McKinley, New Jersey and many other states had passed a law outlawing the advocacy of "criminal anarchy." This law gave the Paterson police the authority they felt they needed to arrest most of the IWW leaders. Patrick Quinlan was arrested even before he spoke at one mass meeting. Hundreds of strikers were also arrested on charges of unlawful assembly and incitement to riot. In clashes between pickets and factory guards, two workers were killed. John Reed was also arrested. While he was in jail, he got an idea that made the Paterson strike one of the most famous of the twentieth century.

With the help of New York friends, particularly the many writers, artists, and actors Reed knew in Greenwich Village, Reed staged a tremendous pageant in the old Madison Square Garden to tell the story of the strike. More than a thousand strikers took part in the show. A vast choir sang a funeral march Reed had composed, and they piled huge red carnations onto the burial caskets of those two slain workers. The desolate atmosphere of the mills on a cold winter morning, the overwhelming noise of the factory whistles, the clattering looms, the battles with the police were captured, in the words of one newspaper reporter, with "a poignant realism that no one who saw them will ever forget." The pageant also dramatized another IWW technique that won widespread sympathy—the evacuation of the children of the workers as funds and food ran low. The show ended with a blazing speech by Haywood, and the workers on the stage and the audience rose to sing the "Internationale."

Unfortunately, the pageant, which was supposed to raise funds as well as make propaganda on behalf of the workers, lost money. Moreover, it created jealousy among the strikers between those who got a chance to enjoy the plaudits of the crowd and those who endured the endless picketing and semistarvation.

The owners remained intransigent. Catholina Lambert urged each of them to follow his example and mortgage every piece of property he owned to hold out. He was quoted as saying that he would never surrender the right to fire a man just because he did not like his face. The courts backed the bosses with harsh sentences for the arrested IWW leaders. Patrick Quinlan was sentenced to two to seven years. Alexander Scott, editor of a Socialist weekly, the *Passaic Issue,* was sentenced to one to fifteen years for calling the Paterson police chief and other city officials anarchists. By July, some 1,300 pickets had been jailed. More than a hundred received prison sentences. The Summit Mills, located near Paterson, offered to give its workers an eight-hour day and a 25- to 35-percent wage increase if they withdrew their insistence on recognition of the IWW. The battered, starving strikers accepted the offer, and the great strike collapsed. The workers split up into some 300 shop committees, most of whom accepted much smaller settlements than the one offered by the prosperous Summit Mills. The IWW leaders, who were more interested in international revolution than in getting a better deal for Paterson's workers, departed to hunt headlines elsewhere. The workers had lost $5 million in wages, the millowners $10 million in profits. The strike left Paterson a spiritual and economic wreck.

During the next decade, the textile tycoons remained intransigent, and strikes continued to agitate the mills. After World War I, a new source of turmoil entered the labor scene—the Communist party. For employers Communism was an even worse scare word than Wobbly. The Communists inherited many of the IWW's more violent activists, such as Haywood and Elizabeth Gurley Flynn, a lineage that did not improve their image among middle-class Americans. When strikes erupted in Paterson in 1924, they were quickly broken by an upsurge of hysterical patriotism. Groups ranging from the Ku Klux Klan to the Royal Riders of the Red Robes called upon the strikers to end their "brazen, open, arrogant and defiant slap at American- ism in this community." The mayor tried to deport the strike leaders, calling them foreign agitators. A court injunction against picketing was extended to a ban on addressing workers against their wills "with a view to persuading them to refrain from . . . employment." Turn Hall, where the strikers rallied, was closed to them by court order. The strike soon collapsed, but the newly formed American Civil Liberties Union chal- lenged the prohibition against public meetings. The ACLU founder, Roger Baldwin, led a crowd to City Hall Plaza, where the Paterson chief of police arrested him.

"The next time you come here," the chief told Baldwin, "I'm going to take you out in front of the City Hall and make you kiss the Constitution and the flag."

"You couldn't make me kiss my own mother if I didn't want to," Baldwin replied.

The New Jersey Supreme Court, in a decision that surprised everyone, struck down the injunction as unconstitutional and freed Baldwin. But the preceding dialogue—and a comment by one of the judges—underscored New Jersey's instinctive dislike of New Yorkers like Baldwin. "If they will only let us alone in this state and not bring in outsiders to tell us what to decide, it'll all come out all right," the judge said.

Two years later, Paterson's neighbor, Passaic, exploded from the same combination of outside agitators and inside injustice. Like Paterson, Passaic was a divided city. Geographically it was bisected by the main line of the Erie Railroad. On the west side it was a typical New Jersey suburban city. Merchants, business executives, managers, professional men, and New York com- muters lived in comfortable homes on generous lawns. One- tenth of Passaic's 70,000 people lived in this half of the city. On the east side of the Erie tracks, it was a different story. Lawns and trees were practically nonexistent. Backyards were described by one reporter as "frequently hideous." A quarter of these mostly foreign-born Passaicans could not read or write, one of the highest illiteracy rates of any city in the United States. "The whole section [of the city]," one reporter wrote, "is obviously devoted to just one purpose—that of affording shelter to a maximum number of human beings at a minimum cost."

Most of the people living in the slum section of Passaic were from eastern and central Europe. They spoke as many as twenty different languages and regarded each other with almost as much hostility as they viewed the millowners. The German and Irish immigrants of earlier decades, who gave the east side such picturesque nicknames as "Dundee," had moved upward on the social scale to better jobs and better housing elsewhere.

Throughout the twenties, Passaic's mills had been having serious economic difficulties. Many hands were on half time, or less. In spite of a protective tariff of 73 percent, textiles were still a sick industry, plagued by overproduction, antiquated plants, and a crazy-quilt pattern of ownership, ranging from huge companies like Passaic's Botany Mills to small cutthroat operations—"Cockroaches" that undersold the giants and kept prices and wages low. Passaic workers were averaging less than $1,100 a year when the mills began to cut wages 10 percent supposedly to meet competition from other states.

Walkouts began. On the scene was the Communist party. Their man in Passaic was Alfred Weisbord. He organized the United Front Committee, which demanded recognition as the representative of all the Botany workers. The company replied by firing the entire committee.

A brilliant organizer and a fiery orator, Weisbord soon spread the strike to other mills in Passaic and the nearby towns of Clifton, Garfield, and Lodi. Soon 10,000 workers walked out, and the battlelines were drawn. The workers called Weisbord "Jescusko," or Little Jesus. The Passaic police banned picketing and used clubs, firehoses, tear gas, and guns to enforce the edict. The strikers used mass picketing and threats of force to intimidate workers reluctant to join them.

Once more, big names in radical circles rushed from New

York to participate in the drama. Norman Thomas came and was arrested. The aging rebel girl, Elizabeth Gurley Flynn, was chosen as permanent secretary of a joint committee uniting the ACLU, the League of Industrial Democracy, and other left-wing groups. As in Paterson in 1913, the presence of Weisbord and these radicals enabled the owners to wrap themselves in the American flag and refuse to negotiate with subversives.

New York newspapers, particularly the tabloids, sent squadrons of photographers and reporters to cover the action, arousing much anger among Jerseyans, who considered them biased and interested only in the sensational aspects of the conflict. A number of photographers had their cameras smashed, and outsiders were again denounced for disturbing New Jersey's peace. But New York Rabbi Stephen S. Wise, whose daughter, Justine, had worked in the mills and helped to organize the strikers, replied: "The very fact that from 10,000 to 12,000 workers went out under the leadership of a man entirely unknown to them shows that the system must be to blame."

Rabbi Wise was undoubtedly right, but more realistic labor leaders called the struggle a "picture strike," a typical Communist tactic to get publicity for the party, with little interest in improving the lot of the workers. "Calling thousands of men and women out in mid winter when they had been working for months on half time and less, with no prospect of improvement meant defeat from the beginning," said Henry H. Hilfers, secretary of the New Jersey Federation of Labor.

Nevertheless the strike lasted twelve bitter, chaotic months. The reason for this unparalleled demonstration of labor strength was the terrible conditions under which Passaic workers toiled. At hearings before the Senate Committee on Education and Labor, W. Jett Lauck, former secretary of the National War Labor Board, an economist who worked for several unions during the 1920s, described the workers' lives.

> In order that families may exist at all, wives and children must go to work in the mills in order to supplement the earnings of the husband and father. . . . The usual custom in Passaic is for the husband to work in the daytime, while the wife works during the night. Because of the economic pressure upon the mother, she can

secure no relief even during the period of pregnancy, because it is then that family expenses increase. There are many instances of babies being born in mills. Frequently the time taken from work by mothers amounts to no more than a few days before and after the birth of the child.

Lauck spelled out with grisly statistics the impact of this practice. "Passaic has 43 percent greater mortality than has the entire state of New Jersey among children under one year of age, 52 percent greater for children under five years of age, and 52 percent greater among children from five to nine years of age."

One of the strikers, Gustaf Deak, a Hungarian immigrant, told the Senate committee how he went to work in the Botany Mills at the age of fourteen, starting at ten cents an hour. At the time he testified, he worked from 7:20 to 5 o'clock daily and averaged $19 or $20 a week.

"What kind of machine do you work on?" asked one of the senators.

"The drying machine," Deak replied. "You are supposed to work eight hours a day at a hundred and ten degrees, drying the stuff that is wet as it goes through."

"You are in a room where the temperature is one hundred and ten degrees?"

"One hundred and ten degrees without change right straight through."

Even more shocking was a report on the health of the Passaic workers done by the New York Workers Health Bureau with the co-operation of Dr. Alice Hamilton of Harvard, a physician who had won national fame for her pioneering studies of industrial health hazards. Four hundred and four Passaic textile workers were selected at random and examined by a team of doctors. The study began by pointing out the major health hazards in textile mills. Respiratory infections were caused by the presence of a fine wool or cotton lint in the air, together with a moist, overheated atmosphere; high blood pressure, heart disease, and other stress illnesses, could be traced to constant standing and the continual loud noise and vibration of the machines. In dyeing and finishing the textiles, the workers came in contact with a number of chemicals that were irritants and poisons. The doctors found the workers' tuberculosis rate was twelve times higher than that found among Metropolitan Life policyholders in 1921. Seventy-seven dye workers in the group had a wide variety of illnesses. All were in poor physical condition. Fourteen and six-tenths percent had heart disease, compared with 1 percent for Metropolitan policyholders; 23.3 percent had high blood pressure, compared to 7.2 percent for the Metropolitan policyholders. Overall the Passaic workers had a disease rate six times higher than the rate for garment workers in New York, five times greater than for printers, and three times the rate among furriers.

Clearly, Passaic workers were people with nothing to lose. Edward F. McGrady, a congressional lobbyist for the labor movement, told the Senate investigating committee, "We hear a great deal about Communism in this country and about Bolshevism. I want to say to you as an American citizen that the people who are controlling the mills of Passaic . . . are doing more to create Bolshevism and Communism in this country than all the other influences combined."

The Communist control of the Passaic strike short-circuited support it might have received from the American Federation of Labor. The established unions were dominated by largely Catholic German and Irish immigrants of the nineteenth century, and they loathed the arrogant atheism of the Communist party as much as they distrusted their "picture strike" approach to union organization. Albert Weisbord wrote letters to William Green, president of the AFL, addressed "Dear Sir and Brothers," begging the unions for help. Green coldly replied that a charter had been issued by the AFL to the United Textile Workers of America, giving it sole authority to organize all those employed in the textile industry. "We know nothing of the United Front Committee of Textile Workers Organization, which you explain you represent," Green wrote. This was an astonishing statement, since the committee had been making headlines across the nation. A few months later, Green told AFL members to stop contributing funds to the strikers' relief organization. Watching from the sidelines, the *Christian Cen-*

tury commented, "It is within the truth to say that, if the strike is broken, the AFL will have played a conspicuous part in breaking it."

At the end of July, Weisbord faced the inevitable and agreed to withdraw from the strike in return for a promise from the AFL that they would commit their union, the United Textile Workers, to a major effort to maintain the 15,000-man and woman organization that the United Front Committee had created. One of the biggest mills, Botany Consolidated, dropped the 10 percent cut in wages, and the UTW announced that it had signed an agreement with Botany to represent the company's 6,000 workers. But this soon proved to be a paper victory. Forstmann & Huffmann, another major company, refused to have anything to do with the union, and their workers finally called off the strike. There and at Botany, the most active strikers were soon fired or demoted. The UTW made no attempt to keep up the militant spirit of the workers. Their membership dwindled to the vanishing point in the next two or three years. As for the Communists, in 1929 they lamented that their party unit in Passaic had only fifteen members.

Although it failed, the Passaic strike became another landmark in the history of the American labor movement. It proved that unskilled workers could be galvanized into a determined bloc for months—more than enough time to intimidate the average employer. The great mass of unskilled workers in New Jersey and other states came a step closer to achieving a more equal liberty in this epic struggle. Justine Wise contributed a poignant footnote to this process in Passaic.

> Many workers, in America twenty years, learned to speak
> English for the first time at the daily strike meetings. Only since the
> beginning of the strike have workers of different nationalities met
> together day after day and learned that they had much in common,
> that they were all American workers, and that to achieve anything
> for themselves or their children, they must look upon one another as
> comrades, not potential enemies.

But the alienation and resentment revealed by these words could not wait for that distant nirvana, the dictatorship of the proletariat. The immigrants of New Jersey, both the unskilled factory hands of Paterson and Passaic at the bottom of the working class and those who had risen to a modest affluence in craft unions, were looking for a man who would show them how to settle a half-century of scores with the native Protestants who had abused and oppressed them. They wanted a leader who would march them into political battle. They found him in Jersey City.

15

The Boss of Bosses

*F*RANK HAGUE came out of the Horseshoe, that slum-ridden slice of downtown Jersey City christened by the Republican gerrymander of 1871. Perhaps the least-known and most remarkable part of his astonishing rise to ruler of New Jersey is his early image as a reformer. He came to local power thundering his support of Woodrow Wilson–style government. One of Wilson's many reforms, the Walsh Act, provided Jersey City with the machinery to change from a mayor-council form of government to the suddenly popular commission plan. Commission government had won national acclaim from the superb job a commission of citizens had done resuscitating hurricane-wrecked Galveston, Texas, in 1900. It was supposedly superior to the mayor-council form because each commissioner was directly responsible to the people for the operation of his department. It was the crystallization, so it seemed in the last of those optimistic good years, 1913, of the progressive Republican idea that the best government could and would be created by moral, efficient businessmen working under the voters' aroused scrutiny.

Hague went all out for this reform measure, calling it an ideal way to get rid of an "incompetent" mayor—his chief opponent in Hudson County, H. Otto Wittpenn. The voters approved the change in government and candidates blossomed by the dozen for the first commission election. Wittpen entered a slate of fol-

173

lowers but did not run himself because he was campaigning to succeed Wilson as governor. Hague turned his campaign for a seat on the commission into a crusade against the so-called Wittpenn "machine." On June 9, 1913, the *Jersey City Evening Journal* ran a cartoon showing the city awakening from a long slumber. Beside it was an editorial urging the voters to "kill machine rule forever." The voters responded by choosing Frank Hague as police commissioner.

Proof that the reform spirit was still strong was the re-emergence of Mark Fagan, who ran ahead of Hague and all the other candidates and was named mayor. From Hague's point of view, Fagan's election was practically irrelevant. Fagan was still a Republican. Control of the Democratic party in Hudson County was far more important, and Hague demonstrated that this now belonged to him by rescinding the Hudson County Democratic Committee's endorsement of Wittpenn for governor. Hague threw his support to Hudson's James Fielder, who as president pro tem of the state senate had become governor for the rest of Wilson's term when he departed for Washington. Out of touch with Hudson's realities, Wilson asked Wittpenn to withdraw from the contest because he had lost the support of his home county.

The scent of total power inspired Hague to tackle his public duties as police commissioner with ferocity. He launched an all-out assault on police laxity. His motive was twofold. First, it was vital for him to protect his reform image in the shadow of Mayor Mark Fagan. Second was the opportunity to open an unparalleled number of jobs to his dispensation. As many as 125 patrolmen were put on trial in just one day for violating department regulations. Hundreds of police officers were ruthlessly demoted or dismissed. Into the opened ranks Hague poured his tough young Horseshoe followers, from whom he culled an elite squad of plainclothesmen, called "Zeppelins," who wove a web of secret surveillance around the entire force.

The transformation Hague wrought in the police seemed a marvellous thing to most citizens of Jersey City, including the Republican editors of the *Jersey City Evening Journal*. The police had been a municipal disgrace for decades. Former Boss

Bob Davis had run Jersey City as a wide-open town. Redlight districts flourished, saloons served liquor into the dawn, and gambling was uninhibited. Hague's cops began enforcing for the first time city laws against prostitution and after-hours drinking. Women were barred from the thousand saloons of Jersey City, and any saloonkeeper who violated this ordinance was punished by fines, loss of his license, and less legal kinds of mayhem. The results, to the average voter in Jersey City, seemed almost miraculous. Police Commissioner Hague had literally cleaned up the city.

Next came a more crucial test of Hague's power—the gubernatorial election of 1916. Nobody knew it, but it was the last gasp of progressivism in New Jersey. Wittpenn won the party nomination for governor, but he got no help from President Wilson, who was fighting for his own political life. Both in the state and nation the Republicans were formidable once more. The old guard and the progressives had negotiated a truce. But the progressive Wittpenn could have beaten them in New Jersey—except for Frank Hague. Hague reversed the engine of the Hudson County democracy and wrecked his enemy's bid for statewide power by giving Wittpenn the smallest majority a Democratic gubernatorial candidate had received from Hudson County in decades—a puny 7,430 votes. In 1913, the Hudson Democrats had given Fielder a majority of 25,959.

Time was running out for the anti-Hague men in Jersey City, and they knew it. The mayoral election of 1917 found them in a frantic mood. Wittpenn and Mayor Fagan both begged President Wilson for help, but they could not agree on a united front. Wilson was too absorbed with saving the world to pay any more attention to New Jersey. By the time the election took place on May 8, America had declared war on Germany .Hague and his four candidates, with a prominent Protestant ex-Wittpenn man, A. Harry Moore, among them, ran as "the unbossed" Democratic slate. All five romped to victory. In a tumultuous scene in the city hall council chamber, packed with howling Horseshoe supporters, Hague was unanimously chosen mayor of Jersey City by the new commissioners. More than three decades would pass before another man stood there to receive similar acclaim.

Having purportedly banished boss rule, Hague now went to work on other progressive targets—the utilities and the railroads. Progressives like Fagan had raised corporate tax assessments to levels they thought were reasonable and yet would not produce violent counterattack by the companies. Hague abandoned such restraints. In 1917 and 1918, he increased the tax assessments on the Standard Oil Company from $1 million to $14 million; on the Public Service Corporation from $3 million to $30 million; and on the railroads from $67 million to $160 million. The corporations rushed to the state board of taxes and assessments in Trenton. The board cancelled all Hague's escalations.

The Republican-dominated board did not realize until it was much too late that they were part of a scenario Hague was to create more than once to make him the most powerful politician in New Jersey. Hague furiously denounced the board members as tools of the interests and summoned his Hudson legions to elect a Democratic governor who would appoint a new tax board. For his candidate he chose Edward I. Edwards, protégé of E. F. C. Young and his successor as president of the First National Bank of Jersey City. Edwards's campaign was aimed straight at the Republican philosophy of law and order and a dry antiliquor lifestyle. Prohibition, legalized by the Eighteenth Amendment, became the symbol of the difference between the two parties. Edwards said that he was against the amendment and would make New Jersey "as wet as the Atlantic Ocean," no matter what the federal government said. He won by 31,073 votes.

The 1919 campaign polarized new and old Americans in New Jersey as never before and added another even more important weapon to Frank Hague's arsenal. With rare skill he combined his reformer's war against the industrial aristocrats and the decades of Catholic immigrant resentment of nativist attacks on their Americanism. The interests, the millionaires who were stealing the state blind, Hague thundered, were the same people who supported the American Protective Association and other organizations that slandered Catholic Americans, and were now depriving the workingman of his God-given right to have a

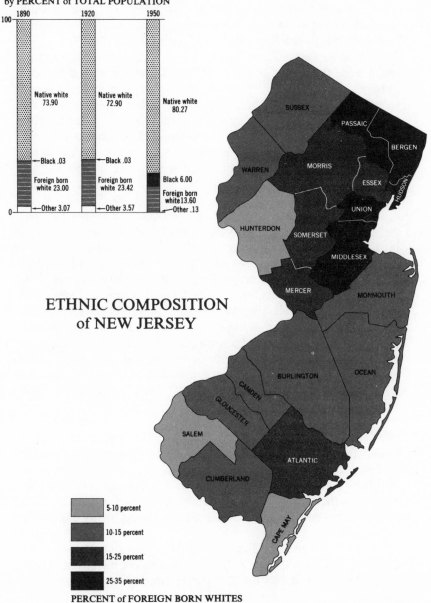

ETHNIC COMPOSITION of NEW JERSEY
by PERCENT of TOTAL POPULATION

ETHNIC COMPOSITION
of NEW JERSEY

PERCENT of FOREIGN BORN WHITES
in TOTAL POPULATION by COUNTIES, 1920

Harold Faye

drink. Seldom have ideological chickens come home to roost in more horrendous shapes or dangerous sizes. The two appeals enabled Hague to create an awesome political machine despite a national shift to the Republicans.

Hudson replaced Essex as the dominant Democratic county and Hague proceeded to consolidate his position with two more gubernatorial victories. In 1922 George Silzer of Middlesex County succeeded Edwards, who won a U.S. Senate seat the same year. A. Harry Moore of Hudson County succeeded Silzer, booming into Trenton in 1925 atop a Hudson County avalanche of 103,000 votes. In eight years, Hague had quadrupled the standard Hudson majority. Even subtracting the extra votes he gathered from woman suffrage, it was still a remarkable achievement.

During this nine-year period, Hague exultantly concentrated on appointing Democrats to the state board of taxes and to a breathtaking number of other jobs that the New Jersey governor had in his power. The surge of progressive thought in New Jersey between the emergence of Fagan and the departure of Wilson had included the reform idea of the short ballot. Scores of jobs that had been elective were placed under the governor's appointive power. There were more than eighty different boards and commissions plus judgeships in fourteen court systems at Hague's disposal. Most important were the judgeships. His greatest coup in this area was the installation of his former corporation counsel, Thomas Brogan, as chief justice of the New Jersey Supreme Court.

Like Democrats before him, Hague never won control of the New Jersey legislature. His governors seldom carried more than five of the state's twenty-one counties. But Hague was as astute at doing business with Republicans as he was with everyone else. He traded jobs by the dozen to Republican politicians in return for their votes and got the appointment for Brogan. The new chief justice promptly designated Hudson County as his circuit.

Hague penetrated the Republican party, not only by job trading, but also by helping the Republicans select their candidates. He first performed this bit of legerdemain in the 1928 gubernatorial primary. The man favored to get the Republican nomination was Robert Carey, a former Jersey City judge and a fierce critic of Hague and his organization. On primary day some 20,000 "instant Republicans" flowered in Hudson County and not one voted for Carey. All their enthusiasm—and the nomination—went to a colorless state senator from Middlesex County named Morgan Larsen.

Worse, the galled Republicans discovered the ploy was perfectly legal. Hague's lawyers had spotted a loophole in the election law that permitted a man who had not voted in the previous year's primary to switch his party affiliation without penalty. Like a shrewd general, Hague had simply ordered 20,000 loyalists to skip a primary and stand by, on reserve status, to name the Republican of his choice.

In the beginning, New Jersey Republicans could not believe what was happening in Hudson County. The only answer they could produce to match Hague's maneuvers was a gimmick to pin the state closer to the coattails of the national Republican ticket, which still looked like a winner. They called for a referendum to lengthen the governor's term to four years and to elect him in presidential years. In a special election in September 1925, the proposal was defeated 200,716 to 135,288. Of the *no* votes, 100,002 were from Hudson County. As one politician to another, New Jersey Republican Senator Walter Edge congratulated Hague for his performance.

Contrary to the myth, Hague did not roll up this killer vote by annotating every available graveyard and stuffing boxes with paper ballots. Whenever they could get away with it, Hagueites voted a tombstone or the name of someone who had long since moved out of the county. The state's permanent registration law offered an irresistible opportunity for fraud, especially when the local election bureau was lackadaisical about keeping track of the dead and departed. Newark and other cities had been caught voting dead or nonexistent souls, and repeaters were shipped from Philadelphia in railroad-car lots to vote in Republican-dominated Atlantic City on election day. But fraudulent votes were only the crest of Hague's 100,000-ballot avalanche. Most of the machine's power was the result of Hague's executive ability.

With the same driving energy he had exhibited in cleaning up

the Jersey City Police Department, Hague overhauled the structure of the Democratic organization in Hudson County. In every
election, every district in every ward was canvassed—which
meant that every voter was personally asked to come to the
polls. Lists of the aged and infirm were carefully compiled, and
fleets of cars were at the disposal of every ward leader to transport even the dying to the polls. Names were carefully checked
off as people entered the polling booths, and the final hours of
each election day were devoted to telephoning and even visiting
those who had not yet voted to ask them why. Ward and district
leaders were rewarded—or punished—on the basis of their turn-
outs, just as corporations monitored plant managers for produc-
tivity. One journalist of the era, Clinton W. Gilbert, summed up
Hague's methods: "If the reform side of him is twice as efficient as reform itself ever was, the Tammany side is twice as
efficient as Tammany ever was."

There was another ingredient in the Hague saga: money. Few
political organizations spent it as freely on election day. Previous political bosses had relied on the corporations for their
personal cash as well as their public disbursements. Hague decided this made a boss too sensitive to corporate pressure—and
an easy target for reformers. He decided to rely completely on
the money he could raise as a politician. With that same combination of efficiency and ferocity he displayed in everything else,
Hague was soon pumping cash out of city hall as skillfully as
the old hydraulic engineers had sent the waters of the Passaic
River rushing through the raceways of Paterson's industrial district. Each year every officeholder in Hudson County had to
contribute 3 percent of his or her salary to city hall. A third or
half of every raise a civil servant received went to city hall the
first year. So did perhaps half of the annual salary of a someone
who was paid for nominal work on a state board or commission.
No accounting was made of this flood of cash—which swelled
to at least five hundred thousand and probably a million dollars
a year.

Then there were the real estate deals. Dummy corporations
headed by shadowy figures in New York bought land shortly
before Jersey City or Hudson County condemned it. The
faceless owners resold it to the government at fabulous prices.

One of these operations cleared a profit of $628,145 between 1919 and 1924. Most lucrative of all was the gambling take. Among the sports columnists and betting fraternity, Hague's Jersey City was known as the "Horse Bourse." In the downtown tenements, major bookmakers set up a system of telephone and telegraph connections that handled enormous quantities of off-track betting on races all over America and Canada. Beside this golden stream flowed the by-no-means inconsiderable payoffs of the numbers racketeers. These, too, were controlled by the organization. Finally, each ward was given the okay for a carefully regulated number of card and dice games, each of which paid a monthly slice of its "handle."

All of this money Hague regarded as his personal possession. He was prepared to spend it freely on election day, but a hefty portion of it enabled the boss to live like a millionaire. In seven years he laid out $392,910.50 for real estate, a remarkable performance for a man supposedly living on a salary of $7,500. Additional hundreds of thousands of dollars were invested in the stock market in Hague's name. For several months in the mid-twenties, a clerk in the city tax department was given an old suitcase and told to make a series of stops at brokerage houses and banks in New York. The suitcase was taken into back rooms and then politely returned to him, considerably lightened.

"What the hell is in that thing?" he asked Hague one day.

"Money, you stupid bastard," he was told.

Hague's ostentatious display of wealth became his Achilles' heel. The owners of the *Jersey City Evening Journal* and other supporters found it harder and harder to explain his winter sojourns in Florida, where he displayed an almost childish fondness for flashing thousand-dollar bills at racetracks. The flaw destroyed the most creative political idea Hague produced—his proposal to merge the numerous municipalities of Hudson County into Greater Jersey City. In 1929 a committee from the New Jersey legislature, convened to investigate election irregularities in Hudson County, asked Hague a number of questions about his personal finances. He declined to answer. He defied not only the committee but both houses of the New Jersey legislature, assembled in righteous panoply.

The legislators charged him with contempt. Hague remained

defiant. The court of errors and appeals decided in his favor, ruling that the legislature did not have the judicial power to probe for felonies. But it was a barren, legalistic victory. It ruined Hague's image as a reformer. The *Newark Evening News* summed up the sentiment of the state. "If Mr. Hague himself would come clean; if he would tell the truth and shame his enemies with the truth, what a triumph would be his! A man who has nothing to conceal, a man whose life is an open book, does not fall back on right of privacy or other technical safeguards when his reputation is at stake."

Hague won re-election as mayor in 1929 by a sharply reduced majority. He seemed to be tottering. One of his favorite candidates, Edward I. Edwards, had lost his bid for re-election to the U.S. Senate in the Hoover landslide of 1928. Morgan Larsen, the state senator whom Hague had helped nominate, won the governor's chair that same year and took office in 1929. A Republican governor meant that the all-important office of county prosecutor was no longer an appointment under Hague's control. Then an event occurred across the river in New York that transformed the politics of the nation. The bottom dropped out of Republican prosperity on Wall Street, and the gray dismal years of the depression settled on the United States. It not only rescued Frank Hague from political oblivion. It signalled the rise of a new class in New Jersey: the politician with access to unparalleled amounts of money and power flowing from Washington, D.C.

16

Power to the Politicians

$\mathcal{A}$S the private sector of the economy shrank under the impact of Wall Street's collapse, Frank Hague was transformed from a politician on the run to a titan with steadily swelling power. The loss of local tax revenue forced him to trim his city and county payrolls, but the jobs and money that flowed from Washington, D.C., more than made up this deficit in the patronage on which the machine depended.

Far from fighting the Hudson colossus, Franklin D. Roosevelt and his New Deal reformers gave Hague access to thousands of federally created jobs and millions of dollars of federal money. At first, relations between Roosevelt and Hague were prickly. Hague had vociferously backed Al Smith at the 1932 Democratic convention. As Smith's floor manager, Hague had predicted that Roosevelt would not carry a single state east of the Mississippi. But one of Hague's lesser-known gifts was his ability to yield to an opponent at the right moment. He telephoned Roosevelt's campaign manager, Jim Farley, who was vacationing in Atlantic City, and said, according to Farley's recollection, "There was no soreness on his part over what had happened, he was whipped in a fair fight, and that if Governor Roosevelt would come to New Jersey to open his campaign, he would provide the largest political rally ever held in the United States." [1]

1. Quoted in Lyle W. Dorsett, "Frank Hague, Franklin Roosevelt and the Politics of the New Deal," *New Jersey History* 94 (Spring 1976): 26.

Roosevelt and Farley accepted Hague's invitation. Hague delivered on his promise. Special trains carried tens of thousands of the Hudson County faithful to Gov. A. Harry Moore's summer residence in Sea Girt. Farley and Roosevelt goggled at the immense crowd, which was considerably more than a hundred thousand people. Riding the crest of Hague's Hudson majority, Roosevelt swept New Jersey in the 1932 election. When New Deal–created jobs began pouring into New Jersey, Frank Hague decided who got them. Governor Moore explained the situation in 1933, when he wrote to one jobseeker: "I do not have the power to appoint to these federal positions. They are made upon recommendation of the local organizations to Mayor Hague, who, in turn, sends them in. . . . I would suggest that you also get in direct touch with the Mayor."

A contented Frank Hague wrote Roosevelt a few months later, "Your recognition of our state organization has been substantially manifested and in return I feel we owe you this pledge of loyalty. Should the occasion ever arise when New Jersey need be counted, I am yours to command."

Not only the Irish-American New Yorker, Farley, who handled most of Roosevelt's patronage in the 1930s, co-operated with Hague. Harry Hopkins appointed a Hague man, William Ely, as the first director of the Works Progress Administration in New Jersey and gave Hague absolute control over some 97,000 jobs. Hopkins ignored stacks of testimony and sworn affidavits from men and women who said that they were forced to vote for Hague's candidates and pay 3 percent of their salaries to the machine in return for their jobs. At one point, Hopkins stretched the letter of the law well beyond the breaking point and used WPA funds earmarked for labor costs to buy seats and plumbing for Jersey City's new baseball park, which was by no accident named Roosevelt Stadium. Even more impressive was the immense Medical Center, built with WPA funds. A pioneering venture in socialized medicine, it offered free care to everyone in Jersey City, regardless of ability to pay. The organization of course defined "ability" with a heavy bias toward regular Democrats.

This symbiotic relationship between local politics and big government in Washington, D.C., was significant both for New

Jersey and the nation. For the first time politicians had access to huge amounts of *legal* money and jobs. No longer did they have to rely on padded loyal payrolls and money from illegal gambling and phony real estate deals. Although Hague continued to farm both these sources of power in Hudson County, the federal aid enabled him to roll up stupendous majorities in succeeding elections. The man who had been fighting for his political life in 1929 won re-election as mayor in 1937 by 110,743 to 6,798.

In this new phase of his reign, Hague tolerated no rivals and abandoned all pretensions of social reform. Theodore "Teddy" Brandle, president of the New Jersey Building Trades Council, had delivered the state labor vote to Hague throughout the twenties. In 1931, when the Pulaski Skyway connecting Newark Airport and the Holland Tunnel was built, contractors were suddenly permitted to hire nonunion labor and to retain guards to protect them from Brandle's organizers. When Brandle fought back, Hague denounced him as a labor racketeer, and Brandle was soon powerless and bankrupt. Hague proceeded to take over almost every union in Jersey City. He then proclaimed the city free of labor troubles and invited industry to enjoy the enforced tranquility.

In 1938 Hague's rule was challenged by the Congress of Industrial Organizations, which was attempting to unionize the unskilled workers of the nation. Hague called them Communists and refused to let them organize in Jersey City. He won the backing of the AFL and practically every citizen of Hudson County, who demonstrated their support in massive rallies that were both tributes to the organization's power and Hague's ability to manipulate people with appeals to patriotism and religion. CIO workers were arrested for distributing literature on corners. "We're enforcing a Jersey City ordinance, not the Constitution," a police captain explained as he escorted one organizer to jail. The U.S. Supreme Court, in a landmark free speech decision, struck down the ordinance, and William J. Carney, president of the state CIO, declared that "the Hague machine is cracking." Carney said the CIO in Hudson County would fight Hague until he is "either in jail or political oblivion." Two months later the local CIO leaders and the boss negotiated a truce that left Hague's power intact.

Roosevelt and Hague remained political allies in spite of the negative treatment of Hague in the national press. Norman Thomas, Morris Ernst, and other radicals and liberals rushed into the CIO fray. They were pelted with rocks and rotten vegetables while the local police smiled in benign approval. Hague loyalists in the post office opened letters addressed to Ernst and were caught at it. Ernst and his friends howled for Hague's scalp. Roosevelt ignored them. "We had a hell of a time getting Hague out of that one," James Farley later admitted.

Hague in this phase was not in the least averse to doing business with the heirs of the state's old industrial aristocrats. In 1933, a former Paterson city attorney tried to rid that city of the S.U.M. by suing to prove that the society had violated its charter. The corporation had long since been acquired by New Yorkers, who formed a water supply branch that sold 75 million gallons a day of Passaic River water to the citizens of north Jersey for a nice profit. The 1791 charter of S.U.M. had forbidden it to deal or trade "except in such articles as itself shall manufacture." It surely did not manufacture the Passaic water, and the Paterson attorney thought any jury would agree that the society had violated its charter. But a Hague judge blocked the jury trial, and when the attorney finally procured a hearing before the New Jersey Supreme Court, Hague's chief justice, Thomas Brogan, gave the attorney thirty minutes to present his case. S.U.M. lawyers got an hour. The outcome was predictable.

Hague continued to penetrate the Republican party. He occasionally combined this penetration with statesmanship. As his plan for a Greater Jersey City demonstrated, he was not without political vision. By the mid-1930s the state's finances were in terrible shape. The railroads and other corporations that had once paid the expenses of the Trenton government had slid into bankruptcy with the rest of the country. The Republican governor, Harold Hoffman, decided that it was time for Jerseyans to pay the first statewide tax since 1776, and proposed a sales tax of 2 percent and a state income tax at one-half the rate of the federal income tax. He could not persuade his fellow Republicans to support the measure, and Hoffman turned to Hague for help. In exchange for hundreds of patronage jobs, the governor got his sales tax through the legislature with twenty Hague Democrats and only eleven Republicans voting for it. Angry Republicans led a voter revolt that repealed the tax before the end of the year. The forces of righteousness nominated a Protestant minister, Lester Clee, to run for governor and purge the GOP of "Hague-Hoffmanism." Clee succeeded in purging the GOP but Hague beat him with his favorite Protestant Democrat, A. Harry Moore.

It is ironic but undoubtedly true that by 1940, Frank Hague's power had made New Jersey more influential on the national scene than she had been since William Paterson rose to cry, "Never!" in the Constitutional Convention. Working closely with the boss of Chicago, Ed Kelly, who was a personal friend, Hague provided much of the power for the Roosevelt 1940 steamroller. After the president was nominated practically by acclamation for his controversial third term, a prominent anti-Roosevelt Democrat ruefully declared, "Mayor Hague has more stuff on the ball than anyone else here in Chicago."

Personally, Roosevelt disliked Hague. The Jerseyan was never invited to Hyde Park or Warm Springs like Edward Flynn, the suave boss of the Bronx. But the president never unleashed the T-men on Hague, as he had done with Missouri's boss, Tom Pendergast. Instead, Roosevelt decided to try another ploy. He persuaded Hague to accept Charles Edison, a son of Thomas Edison, the inventor, as the Democratic nominee for governor in 1940. Edison was an independent Democrat who had plainly spent some time in the library reading Woodrow Wilson biographies. With Hague sitting at his right hand and 150,000 Democratic faithful in the audience at Hague's by-then traditional Sea Girt rally, Edison declared, "It is my happy privilege to stand here today and tell you that if you'll elect me, you'll have elected a governor who has made no promises of preferment to any man or group . . . I'll never be a yes man except to my conscience."

Hague listened to this with comparative complacency. He thought it was the kind of eyewash a candidate had to administer to the voters. He was astonished when Edison began practicing the independence he had preached during the campaign.

This gubernatorial integrity soon produced violent hostilities. Governor Edison recalled one classic exchange when he differed with Hague over a judicial appointment. Edison insisted that his preference was a man of integrity. "The hell with his integrity," Hague roared, "what I want to know is, can you depend on the S.O.B. in a pinch?"

Edison was no match for Hague. An idealist, his rhetoric was reminiscent of early twentieth-century progressives. He had no organization and made no attempt to build one. Worse, the governor, trying to solve the financial collapse of the state's railroads, forgave them some $81,000,000 in back taxes. Almost half of this money belonged to Jersey City.

It was like old home week for Frank Hague. He began belaboring Edison for selling out to the interests. The Edison script, which called for a Wilson-style confrontation ending in the boss's rout, followed by a leap to the presidency, ended in political disaster. When Edison left Trenton, Hague was still state chairman of the Democratic party and vice-chairman of the Democratic National Committee, and as invulnerable as ever in Hudson County. Throughout the brawl, Roosevelt said not a word on Edison's behalf. He knew that he needed Hague to carry New Jersey for his fourth term.

Edison did create some significant breaches in Hague's support outside Hudson County. The Republicans elected two governors in a row for the first time since Hague had come to power. This was a serious blow to Hague's position. From 1941 to 1949, counting Edison's term, the boss was voiceless in Trenton. Dozens of key appointments to the state's boards and commissions fell into Republican hands as the terms of Hague Democrats expired. Deaths and resignations accounted for still more. Furthermore, a new state constitution, with a provision that would force public officials to answer embarrassing questions, was being proposed.

Hague still had claws. When Walter Van Riper became attorney general of New Jersey in 1944, he launched a series of raids on Hague's sacrosanct Horse Bourse. Within months, Van Riper was indicted by a federal grand jury for kiting checks and for selling black-market gasoline at a service station he partially owned. He was acquitted on both counts, and there is strong evidence that some of the witnesses for the prosecution committed perjury. But Van Riper, once considered a shoo-in as the next governor, was politically dead.

The new constitution seemed certain of approval by the voters. Hague and his machine were strangely quiescent until a week before the election. The complacent Republicans thought the boss was accepting the inevitable. They were wrong. With no prior warning, the archbishop of Newark, Thomas Walsh, denounced the constitution because, he claimed, it would force a priest to reveal the secrets of the confessional. The archbishop's reading of one obscure clause was tortured at best. But it was the signal for a tremendous barrage from Hudson County deploring the constitution as a tool of the Protestant Republicans and the railroad interests. Stupidly, the Republicans had added a clause enabling the legislature to set special tax rates for the ailing railroads. When the votes were counted, the constitution was a dead duck.

The next Republican governor, Alfred E. Driscoll, learned from this hard lesson and worked out a constitution that was acceptable to Frank Hague, as well as to the Republican party. Special treatment for the railroads was labelled unconstitutional. Pro-Hague Democrats were appointed to various posts in Hudson County. Governor Driscoll maintained that his soft line was good for the Republican party as well as the state of New Jersey: "As an integral part of the vital New Jersey industrial area, I have never agreed that Hudson County could be ignored or discriminated against in any important affair of state. I've always believed that if the Republican Party treated all of the state's political subdivisions alike, it would remove one of the major issues on which Hague has flourished—that he was Hudson's only savior." [2]

This may have been shrewd policy. But it did not destroy Frank Hague. He destroyed himself. After thirty years of power, the intricacies of an organization like the one Hague had constructed became Byzantine. Contrary to the standard image,

2. Quoted in Richard J. Conners, *A Cycle of Power* (Metuchen, N.J.: Scarecrow Press, 1971), p. 155.

the machine was not a static entity. It was composed of quarrelsome, power-hungry human beings, and a strong consistent hand was needed to keep them working together. "It's like that fellow in the circus standing on a team of running horses," wrote one Hudson County reporter. Hague grew weary of providing that strong consistent hand. He spent more and more of his time in Florida and New York.

Even more important was the steady erosion of Hague's image as a man of the people. His mansion on the Jersey shore, his even more lavish Florida estate, his trips to Europe, his sojourns at the Plaza Hotel in New York, his constant association with the rich and famous, his long absences from Jersey City, made more than one Democratic loyalist wonder about the idealism of the organization. Not even the achievement Hague considered proof of his altruism, the Medical Center, could obscure the fact that Frank Hague had become a political aristocrat as remote if not quite as indifferent to the average man as the industrial aristocrats he had replaced.

Revolts—really quarrels over graft and patronage—exploded in Bayonne and Hoboken. Finally, Hague was challenged in Jersey City when he resigned as mayor in 1947 and tried to hand on his power to his nephew, Frank Hague Eggers. The challenger was John V. Kenny, who was the political leader of the Second Ward, the heart of the old Horseshoe from which Frank Hague had risen. Running on a "Freedom Ticket" that pilloried Hague for living like a millionaire, Kenny beat the boss on his home turf in 1949 and broke his power forever. The weapons the early Hague had used so well, denunciations of the rich and powerful in the name of Hudson's poor, were turned against him.

It is hard to look back on Frank Hague's thirty-two-year reign with a historian's perspective. It is easier to dismiss him as a monster, an aberration. But the dialectic that this book has been attempting to trace in New Jersey is visible in Hague's tumultuous career. Hague won elections because he voiced the resentments, the deprivations of Jerseyans who had been denied a full participation in America's opportunities because of their religion or ethnic origin. He continued to win elections even after it became obvious he was corrupt, because he brought these people into the mainstream of New Jersey's political and economic life. Everywhere Hague's power extended—into the state's banks, its judiciary and legal system—he and his organization gave Catholics, usually but not always Irish Americans, positions of power and influence. Ultimately this was good for New Jersey and the nation. A people committed to a more equal liberty cannot impose second-class citizenship on any part of the body politic without breeding alienation and violence.

The heritage of corruption that Hague carried with him from Jersey City's Horseshoe stained and deformed this victory, and often caused deep moral and spiritual anguish in the lives of those who supported him or fought him. Worse, the boldness with which the boss of bosses combined corruption and power became a legacy that continues to haunt New Jersey.

17

When Will the People Rule?

*W*HEN the rush to the suburbs began after World War II, New Jersey's open acres were a logical target for millions of New Yorkers and Pennsylvanians. Tens of thousands of Jerseyans from Newark, Jersey City, Paterson, Trenton, and other cities also headed for the lower taxes and putative serenity of the countryside. The state population leaped an astounding 1,200,000 in ten years—an influx that was preceded by a jump of 700,000 in the decade between 1940 and 1950. Farmers by the thousands yielded to the profits offered by developers and sold out for three or four times the value of their acreage as farm land. The biggest growth came in the counties of Bergen, which added 140,000 people between 1950 and 1960; Middlesex, with a leap of 169,000; and Monmouth, with 109,000 new residents.

By no means were all these people bedroom commuters. New industry flooded into New Jersey during World War II. Among the more interesting changes was the development of the state as a research center. Nearly one-fifth of all the research scientists in America now live in New Jersey and work in some 700 research laboratories. The wealth of the affluent sections of the state has become awesome. Bergen, the richest county, accounts for $5.5 billion in effective buying income. It is ahead of New York's posh Westchester County in all sales categories, from clothes to automobiles.

192

These remarkable developments transformed New Jersey into a giant, the sixth-most populous state in the union. But the new arrivals only accentuated New Jersey's paramount problem: her lack of a sense of identity, of community. Her history of bitter political and religious divisions, of sectional conflict, the tendency to be distracted by the politics and economics of Philadelphia and New York City, made it difficult to focus the people's attention on the state government in Trenton. As early as 1945 a state tax commission declared: "No industrial state has done so little in the past fifty years to bring its tax structure into line with its social, economic and political development as has New Jersey." In particular, the Trenton government lacked a statewide tax to give it the funds and personnel to deal with New Jersey as an entity. Most of New Jersey's tax dollars were raised and spent by towns, cities, and counties from the old-fashioned property tax. Inevitably this practice reinforced New Jersey's already-intense localism.

At the same time, changes were occurring in New Jersey that would make this failure of community a new source of division and upheaval. Not all New Jersey newcomers moved to the suburbs. In Jersey City and the other industrial towns of Hudson County, in Newark and in Paterson, hundreds of thousands of newcomers repeated the immigrant experience of the Irish, the Poles, the Italians, the Slovaks, and Jews of earlier decades. Many of these newcomers were Puerto Rican or Cuban. Most were black.

No fewer than 130,000 blacks moved to Newark between 1950 and 1970, while at least that many white Newarkers fled the city for the suburbs. The black influx was the culmination of a migration from the South that began during World War I. In that era the newcomers found little to justify Newark's self-description as the city of opportunity. They were forced to live in the slums of Newark's Third Ward where, according to the Negro Welfare League, "most of the dwellings were poorly heated and of considerable age, and a substantial proportion of them lacked lighting facilities, inside toilets, and running water." One woman described the arrival of a black family from Alabama in 1919. The man, his wife, and seven children were paying $14 a month for three rooms, "the central room perfectly dark." A white family who had preceded them paid $9. "The landlady downstairs said quite explicitly that she charged these people $14 because they were colored."

In 1930, a study by the Urban League reported that blacks were 5½ percent of the population of New Jersey, but 3½ percent of the gainfully employed and 25 percent of the relief load. "White folks were yelling their heads off because there were so many blacks on relief," commented Harold Lett, the executive secretary of the league.[1] Between the wars, real estate agents and property owners continued to force Negroes into Newark's ghetto, where they endured substandard housing and other forms of economic deprivation. Union membership, particularly in the skilled trades, was closed to them. Simultaneously, numerous industries began leaving Newark for the lower-taxed suburbs, further reducing economic opportunity. One Newarker recalled a dramatic instance of what this meant for the city. "When I was head of the Unity Community Fund, in 1953, I looked around a board meeting. There were fifty-odd people there, and all of a sudden it dawned on me that I was the only resident of Newark there."[2]

Between the two world wars, segregation was the order of the day for blacks in Newark. They were not accepted in white restaurants, they sat in separate sections of the city's movie houses, and they were barred from the swimming facilities of the public bathhouses. Newark was by no means the only New Jersey city that followed such a pattern. E. Frederick Morrow, who was born and grew up in Hackensack in the twenties, wrote in a memoir of his youth,

> The only difference between the slave era and then was the fact that physical slavery had been abolished, but all the mental and spiritual

1. Clement A. Price, "The Beleaguered City as Promised Land: Blacks in Newark, 1917–47," essay in *Urban New Jersey Since 1870,* ed. William C. Wright (Trenton: New Jersey Historical Commission, 1975), p. 41.
2. Kenneth T. and Barbara B. Jackson, "The Black Experience in Newark: The Growth of the Ghetto, 1870–1970," essay in *New Jersey Since 1860, New Findings and Interpretations,* ed. William C. Wright (Trenton: New Jersey Historical Commission, 1972), p. 41.

and philosophical attitudes developed in slavery toward the Blacks remained. The whites were adamant in fostering and retaining the status quo, which meant inequality in every facet of community life. On the other hand, the Negroes had been so brainwashed, and had become so weary from the burdens and toils of life, that most accepted the inevitability of second-class citizenship."[3]

Morrow, who rose to become executive assistant to Dwight Eisenhower in the White House, tells in bitter detail the uproar his sister caused in Hackensack when she applied for a job as a teacher in the public school system. Almost every white organization in town, from Daughters of the American Revolution to the Knights of Columbus, rose in protest. The Ku Klux Klan marched through Hackensack in a fiery night parade.

The saddest part of the story was the reaction of the Hackensack Negro community. They were as vociferously opposed to Nelly Morrow's appointment as the whites, claiming they did not want their children taught by an "inferior" teacher. Nevertheless, she got her job and served for more than forty years in the local school system, eventually becoming its most admired teacher. The Negro community was expressing its dislike of her and the Morrow family in general for trying to be "white."

With such a legacy, the massive post–World War II influx of blacks to Newark virtually guaranteed tragedy. Fewer than half the newcomers found employment in Newark's declining industries. Some 40 percent of them had to travel to work outside the city every morning while 300,000 suburban workers poured into the central district to work in giant insurance company offices or in the remaining industrial jobs. A wisecrack became locally familiar: "The people who work in Newark don't live there, and the people who live in Newark don't work there." The unemployment rate among black males soared over 30 percent. The rate of narcotics addiction was among the highest in the United States.

Between 1960 and 1970, Newark "tipped"—the number of blacks passed 50 percent and they became the predominant

---

3. E. Frederic Morrow, *Way Down South Up North* (Philadelphia: United Church Press, 1973), p. 20.

group in the city. But they were still largely powerless. The city remained in the grip of white politicians, who ran it with the co-operation of power brokers in Trenton and Washington along the lines developed by Frank Hague. Government had become a business that made money by winning elections and vice versa. It no longer had much to do with the aspirations of the people it purported to represent. By 1967, in the words of a close student of the city, "a large part of Newark had become a racial and economic ghetto." Municipal services had broken down and the Governor's Select Committee on Civil Disorder reported "There was a pervasive feeling of corruption."

In July 1967, Newark's black community exploded. Four days of rioting and burning left the central city devastated. Ten million dollars worth of property had been looted or destroyed. Twenty-three people were dead and hundreds injured. The riots hastened the exodus of manufacturers and merchants. Hundreds of boarded-up storefronts defaced the streets. The city lost 23,000 private jobs between 1967 and 1972. It was labelled a dying city.

A similar statement could have been made about Jersey City at the same time. There the problem that underlay Newark's racial upheaval was more brutally visible: a government of political operators whose only interest was the profits of power. For twenty years Frank Hague's successors looted the city and county in the unlovely tradition the boss had created.

The new boss, John V. Kenny, did not try to rule the state. This power was beyond his grasp in postwar New Jersey. The enormous growth and redistribution of the population created a new political pattern. No longer could the vote of one crowded country dominate the state. There were too many populous counties now.

On the other hand, this situation made it easier for a shrewd politician—and Kenny was very shrewd—to operate as a boss. With too many games to watch, the forces of the law were distracted. The strategy of the day was to maintain a low profile. Kenny did not try to dominate all aspects of Hudson County life, in Hague's style. Only on crucial issues and appointments did he exercise his power. One reporter of the county's politics described the way the system worked:

"The rules of the game are simple. If you are told to do something and the person telling you prefaces his orders with 'Kenny says,' you do it. . . . . The problem of the game is that too many people are using the magic words and the players occasionally become confused. When this happens, Hudson County's political leader, John V. Kenny, after whom the game is named, has to step in and referee."

Like bosses before him, Kenny was careful to protect himself from local attacks. Candidates for sheriff, controlling the all-important grand juries, were exclusively chosen by Kenny. The county prosecutor was an appointment he insisted on getting from governors if they wanted his co-operation in the legislature. When James A. Tumulty, Jr., was sworn in as prosecutor in 1963, he stated his political philosophy quite simply: "I'm Kenny. . . . Lest there be any misunderstanding, for the record, make that John V. Kenny."

In spite of several local revolts that at one point forced him to announce his retirement, Kenny survived because Democratic presidents, particularly John F. Kennedy, did political business with him and so did Democratic governors, beginning with Robert Meyner and continuing through Richard Hughes. For Jersey City the Kenny regime meant accelerated decline. Hague's populist beginnings and innate executive ability created a high level of municipal services and an aura of concern for the average man and woman. Under Kenny, all pretenses to a government by the people and for the people vanished. Public services practically collapsed. Uncollected garbage lay in festering heaps. An investigation revealed that the county mental hospital had 1,070 patients and no psychiatrist.

The motivation and techniques of this new class were uncovered in the investigation of Kenny's attempt to hijack the city's incinerator plant. Kenny and his gang spoke of it as the deal that would finance their retirement. First they concocted a corporation, North Jersey Incineration, run by a corrupt crew that included Joseph Bozzo, the Republican leader of Passaic

County. (In the new class of politic'ans for profit, party labels mean little. They are all in the same business.) Next, Kenny and the mayor of Jersey City gave the favored corporation all the information they needed to make a low bid to take over the operation of the incinerator plant. They claimed there was a national trend in favor of such "contracting out" of municipal services to private companies. Actually, no such handing-over of a completely equipped and operating city facility had ever occurred in the United States. Kenny and his "boys" then negotiated a seventeen-year contract with North Jersey Incineration to operate the plant at a cost of $1.25 million a year—three times the actual cost. The extra money was to be divided between the civic looters.

Similar maneuvers were the order of the day in Republican Atlantic City. Under its commission form of government, each elected lawmaker administered a city department. Whether the commission members were all Republican or part of a coalition, the techniques of rigged bids and favored corporations, followed or preceded by payoffs, were routine. During the tenure of Arthur Ponzio as public works director, for instance, twenty-four out of twenty-six contracts for vehicles drew only one bid. Everyone knew that the arrangements were made before the bidding, and there was no point in competing once "the fix was in."

In 1960, Kevin Lynch, member of the Center for Urban and Regional Studies of the Massachusetts Institute of Technology, selected Jersey City as a case study in how average citizens saw their city. He compared their reaction to the citizens of Boston and Los Angeles. In the other two cities there was a wide variety of comments, ranging from favorable to hostile. In Jersey City, the dominant reaction was blankness, no image at all. The question, "What first comes to mind with the words Jersey City?" proved to be a baffling one for practically every resident. Again and again the subjects repeated, "nothing special."

These were the remarks of a beaten, weary people, who had mustered the courage to oust Frank Hague, only to find him replaced by agents of an even greasier corruption. Their attitude resembled the response of a Moscow resident in the 1920s, asked by tourists how things were under the Communist regime. "The same as under the Tsar," the Muscovite replied, "only shabbier."

In 1969 this era came to a startling close. The Republican victory in Washington put a dynamic new prosecutor in the federal attorney's office in Newark. Frederick Lacey zeroed in on Jersey City as his number one target. The entire top leadership of the Kenny organization, including "the Little Leader," John V. himself; the mayor of Jersey City, Thomas Whelan; the city council president; and a half-dozen other officials were found guilty of extortion and similar crimes and sentenced to long jail terms.

Frederick Lacey and his successors, Herbert Stern and Jonathan Goldstein, have used the federal attorney's office to create a veritable reign of terror among Jersey politicans. After demolishing Kenny and his ring, they did a similar wrecking job on Mayor Hugh Addonizio of Newark and his gang of thieves. Next they put the Republican mayor of Atlantic City in jail. Between 1969 and mid-1975, the federal attorneys indicted 148 public officials and convicted 72 of them.

Although this record returned a measure of honesty to New Jersey politics, it had an unfortunate backlash effect, deepening the already substantial cynicism of most Jerseyans for politics and politicians. This backlash may be one explanation for the incredible volatility of New Jersey voters in recent years. Republican William Cahill was elected governor in a landslide in 1969. Democrat Brendan Byrne was beneficiary of a counter-landslide in 1973. In recent gubernatorial elections, the swings in the vote have averaged 14.1 percent—equivalent to one of every seven voters changing his mind in four years.

This voter independence may mean that party loyalty is practically dead in New Jersey, as it is in many other parts of the nation. But there is another explanation, which has a message of hope for New Jersey. For the first time Republicans and Democrats are distributed throughout the state's twenty-one counties in almost equal numbers. Now there is political competition in every county, from Cape May, with an average 42 percent of the vote going Democratic, to Mercer, with 62 percent. On the other hand, many residents of Hudson County have learned to vote Republican despite fears that their immigrant fathers and grandfathers are spinning in their graves. Moreover, recent analyses reveal that there is now little difference between New Jersey Republicans and Democrats in social class, religion, age, or place of residence, outside the central cities.

There is a growing awareness that the new entrenched class in New Jersey is the political operator. Polls revealed that in the 1973 gubernatorial election, there was widespread confusion among the voters about where the two candidates stood on the issue that got the biggest play in the papers, the state income tax. But a remarkable number of those who voted for the winner, Brendan Byrne, said that they had done so because they thought his record as a county prosecutor and judge made him the best man to fight corruption in government. This is heartening evidence that the people have not given up on the system, that they still want honest, representative government and believe it is possible, in spite of repeated frustrations.

Perhaps most remarkable has been the demonstration of this faith among the voters of the supposedly dying cities. In the late sixties and early seventies, both Paterson and Jersey City elected young vigorous reform mayors who radically altered the boss-style politics of both cities. Around the same time, Newark elected a gifted young engineer, Kenneth A. Gibson, as the city's first black mayor. It has developed a group of young, knowledgeable administrators who have made perceptible progress in improving public safety and cleaning up the city's physical environment. Experts like James Mahon, a former senior partner of Coopers and Lybrand, one of New York's "Big Eight" accounting firms, have written studies pointing up Newark's economic strengths. It is still the hub of one of the largest industrial concentrations in the East. "Hundreds of America's major companies and countless smaller ones are located within twenty miles," Mahon says. "The city is the undoubted financial and service center for this remarkable concentration."

Newark's business leaders are not quitting the city. On the

contrary, they are driving hard to maintain its vitality as a community. Sentiment and loyalty are not the only reasons. As Mahon points out, "Newark is far and away the leading city in New Jersey—the standard-bearer. New Jersey's future prestige among states may depend to a great extent on Newark's ability to adapt successfully to the traumatic social changes that have invaded it."

Several recent developments have bolstered hopes for Newark's early revival. The completion of the $300 million sports complex in the nearby Jersey meadows in the face of vicious opposition from New York was proof that the Newark financial community had faith in the region. They absorbed much of the massive bond issue when New York banks boycotted the sports complex bonds. The continued growth of the port of Newark and the expansion of Newark Airport accentuates Newark's best hope for revival—its location. With a sixty-berth deepwater seaport ready to handle freight in the most modern manner, Port Newark is the containerization capital of the world, with an annual volume of nine million tons. Already there is a vast transportation warehousing and distribution complex operating out of the Newark area carrying goods as far north as Montreal, as far south as Richmond, and as far west as Pittsburgh. If this complex continues to grow, it could create an additional 25,000 jobs in the 1980s.

Perhaps the best thing that is emerging in Newark is local pride on the part of the black community. With a mayor of their own race and three blacks on the municipal council, blacks are able to think about Newark as their city for the first time. This new spirit was especially visible at the Bicentennial Founders' Day Meeting at Old First Church on Broad Street in Newark. This was the church whose members had founded Newark. One of its early pastors, Alexander MacWhorter, was with Washington when he crossed the Delaware. The elite of Newark have worshipped there during the 300 years of the city's history. At this bicentennial service, an eloquent black clergyman, Dr. Edler C. Hawkins, joined the white pastor, Dr. Lloyd George Schell, on the altar. Half of the congregation was black. Mayor Gibson led the list of speakers at the luncheon that followed the service. Here was proof that black Americans were ready to put aside the bitter memories of the past and share with white Americans a common heritage without self-consciousness or apology.

The fact that another speaker at the luncheon was the son of an Irish-Catholic politician from Jersey City is also worthy of mention. New Jersey's old antagonisms, seemingly so insoluble fifty years ago, have faded. Many of the old injustices or their perpetrators have also vanished. Paterson's Society for Useful Manufactures went out of business in 1946. Jersey City has finally wrestled its waterfront from railroad control and is beginning to develop it. Labor unions have made vast strides, in spite of a nasty feud between the AFL and CIO in the state. But new divisions and new injustices have replaced the old wounds in the body politic. There are new barriers to the achievement of "a more equal liberty" for a dismaying number of New Jersey's citizens. They are rooted not only in race but in the state's (and the nation's) hostility to cities. Perhaps by using the hard lessons of the past, New Jersey can devise ways to solve these problems without the pain endured by previous generations.

In this history, we have watched generations struggle toward a more equal liberty, only to be distracted by lesser issues, or upheavals like the Civil War, or to be frustrated by the machinations of those who held great wealth or great political power. But the defeats of one generation have often been the victories of the next generation. The focus of the struggle has shifted from a more equal share of the land to a more equal share of the fruits of great industrial enterprises to its present stage—a more equal share of the tax dollars of a rich nation and a wealthy state.

This focus on equity is why it is essential to destroy the grip of the dishonest political operator on state and local government. Only by programs that really reach the urban poor, programs that are not cynical boondoggles, can we break the cycle of poverty in which many city dwellers in New Jersey are trapped. It is encouraging to see that New Jersey's voters are at least aware of the minimum necessity for this achievement—a corruption-free government. But the brawl over the state income tax made it clear that most voters and most legislators were not ready to accept the corollary to this new struggle for a more equal liberty—the more equitable distribution of tax dollars.

The struggle for a statewide tax to reduce (not eliminate) the inequalities of New Jersey's localism has been as important in post–World War II New Jersey as the more publicized and sensational struggle against political corruption. In 1965, 1969, and 1973, the people of New Jersey elected three distinguished governors, Richard Hughes, William Cahill, and Brendan Byrne, each with a hefty majority of his own party in the legislature. But neither Republican Cahill nor Democrats Hughes and Byrne could convince a majority of the legislators to vote for the most equitable statewide tax, an income tax. Hughes settled for a sales tax in 1966—a victory of sorts, because it at least established the principle of statewide taxation, and gave the Trenton government some of the funds it needed to deal with New Jersey as a community.

But a sales tax, like the property tax, is a regressive tax, which takes a higher percentage of income out of the pockets of the poor. New Jersey legislators exempted a wide range of items such as food, medicine, and clothing from the 1966 sales tax, which limited its regressive impact. But it had almost no impact on the use of property tax dollars to support the area where the struggle for more equal liberty begins—education.

In 1973 the state supreme court ruled that New Jersey could no longer depend on property taxes to fund its public schools, because such taxes were barriers to equal educational opportunity. A growing state deficit, the need for drastic expansion of the state's higher educational institutions, made a state income tax the only sensible answer to the crisis. But Gov. Brendan Byrne's proposal of this measure at a special session of the legislature met with violent resistance from Democratic leaders in the senate and the house. The governor's bill died in committee in the senate.

The following year, the New Jersey Supreme Court issued an ultimatum which would have required the state to close the public schools if alternative methods of funding were not passed by the legislature. Even in the face of this Armageddon, it took months of furious infighting and feuding to get an income tax bill through the legislature. Whether Democrats or Republicans, Whigs or Tories were in charge, Jerseyans still hated to pay taxes.

The legislature finally staggered to a minimal income tax in a brawling frenzy that was redolent of the past. It was clear that without the court ultimatum, the measure would never have passed. Yet the tax may have far-reaching impact on the future of the state—particularly on that slippery, perhaps indefinable something called New Jersey's identity. As we have seen, many of the old divisions—geographic, ethnic, religious—have dwindled, if not disappeared. Simultaneously, nearly bankrupt New York City and a fading Philadelphia have declined drastically as centers of prestige and influence.

New Jersey is finally in a position to reap a dividend from her long vassalage to New York and Philadelphia. Because of their dominance, the state never oriented itself around a major city. Newark, Jersey City, and Paterson have remained small enough to be revitalized without enormous investment. With political imagination and courage, they can be integrated into the surrounding suburbs to create a metropolitan society that is neither brutally urban nor pastorally suburban, but which partakes of the best aspects of both lifestyles. Most important, with a decisive shift in financial power from local communities to Trenton, there is a chance for politicians to build a new sense of New Jersey as a distinct community. A metropolitan New Jersey is in no danger of covering the state with concrete and gasoline stations. No less than 42 percent of New Jersey is still forest and non-farm woodland, and another 21 percent is still in fruits and vegetables.

For the present New Jersey remains disparate. It remains divided into Jersey City, where sociologist Kevin Lynch can all too accurately say, "The drabness, dirt and smell of the town are at first overpowering"; and Newark's infamous Third Ward, which black novelist Curtis Lucas described in one blunt word: "hell." Forty minutes away are the winding roads of the Short Hills, with their expensive homes nestled in idyllic hollows and on shaded slopes. Another forty minutes and we are in Jugtown

Mountain in Hunterdon County, where voters still decide at town meetings whether the police chief should have a radio in his secondhand patrol car and summer people are accused of "not wearing enough clothes to pad a crutch."

Contemporary New Jersey is still what Governor Belcher called it in 1745—"the best country for midling fortunes, and for people who have to live by the sweat of their brows." Most Jerseyans have sweated and achieved that more equal liberty the Founding Fathers defined as the goal of America. But the struggle to extend that equality, to deepen its meaning without sacrificing its essential link to liberty, continues.

Perhaps it would be wise to admit that it probably will never end. There will always be losers and winners in every social arrangement. But as New Jersey history repeatedly teaches, trouble begins when the winners display an arrogance and greed that push the losers to rage and desperation.

At this point, New Jersey might well heed two voices from her past. One belongs to a recognized hero, William Livingston. In accepting the governorship of the independent state of New Jersey in September 1776, he called upon all Jerseyans to join him in "setting our faces . . . like a flint, against that dissoluteness of manners and political corruption which will ever be the reproach of any people."

The other voice belongs to one of New Jersey's unrecognized great men, George Record. "It seems to me," he said, in a speech in Essex County in 1909, "that there is a great national battle going on, and the issue that takes precedence is, are the people going to rule? . . . Let the first gun be fired . . . right here."

An old idea and a New Idea that are both very much alive for the citizens of New Jersey—and the United States of America.

Suggestions for Further Reading

Those who want to read more about New Jersey will find a wealth of interesting, well-written books. For the early years, *Colonial New Jersey—A History,* by John E. Pomfret (New York: Charles Scribner's Sons, 1973), is a well-organized, judicious study. *Path to Freedom: The Struggle for Self-government in Colonial New Jersey,* by Donald L. Kemmerer (Princeton: Princeton University Press, 1940) focusses more exclusively on the political aspect of the prerevolutionary years. For the revolutionary years, Leonard Lundin's *Cockpit of the Revolution: The War for Independence in New Jersey* (Princeton: Princeton University Press, 1940) is still a valuable book. For vivid details on one corner of the struggle, few have surpassed *The Revolutionary War in the Hackensack Valley,* by Adrian C. Leiby (New Brunswick, N.J.: Rutgers University Press, 1962). The author has used a similar approach to recover the importance of the battle of Springfield in *The Forgotten Victory* (New York: Reader's Digest Press, 1973). Two other illuminating books are *New Jersey in the American Revolution, 1763–1783—A Documentary History,* ed. by Larry R. Gerlach (Trenton: New Jersey Historical Commission, 1975) and *Prologue to Independence: New Jersey and the Coming of the American Revolution,* by Larry R. Gerlach (New Brunswick, N.J.: Rutgers University Press, 1976). Also worthy of attention is an excellent series of pamphlets issued by the New Jersey Historical Commission, "New Jersey's Revolutionary Experience," under Gerlach's general editorship. Twenty-eight in number, including study guides for secondary and elementary teachers, they cover almost every aspect of New Jersey in the eighteenth century from music to medicine.

The best book on the Lenni-Lenape is by Dorothy Cross, *The Indians of New Jersey* (Trenton: Archaeological Society of New Jersey, 1958). Another good book is Adrian C. Leiby, *The Early Dutch and Swedish Settlers of New Jersey* (Princeton: D. Van Nostrand Co., 1964). Adequate biographical treatment of the prominent New Jerseyans of the colonial and revolutionary eras is scarce. There is an 1883 biography of Governor Livingston, *Memoir of the Life of William Livingston,* written by Theodore Sedgwick, a descendant, but it is inadequate. The forthcoming edition of the papers of William Livingston, under the editorship of Carl Prince, will possibly remedy this defect and perhaps speed a formal biography. Also lacking is a decent biography of William Alexander, Lord Stirling, who rose to the rank of major general in the Revolution.

For New Jersey in the postrevolutionary era, an excellent book is *Experiment in Independence,* by Richard P. McCormick (New Brunswick, N.J.: Rutgers University Press, 1950). Dr. McCormick has also written a superb book on a topic extremely germane to New Jersey's struggle for political maturity, *The History of Voting in New Jersey* (New Brunswick, N.J.: Rutgers University Press, 1953). Another important topic, transportation in New Jersey, is well covered in the book, *From Indian Trail to Iron Horse,* by Wheaton J. Lane (Princeton: Princeton University Press, 1939). John T. Cunningham's *Railroading in New Jersey* (New York: Associated Railroads, 1952), brings the story to modern times. Equally valuable as a special study is Hubert G. Schmidt's *Agriculture in New Jersey* (New Brunswick, N.J.: Rutgers University Press, 1973). Another good book on a special topic of growing interest is *The Geology and Geography of New Jersey,* by Kemble Widmer (Princeton: D. Van Nostrand Co., 1964). Mr. Cunningham has also written a good history of New Jersey's industry, *Made in New Jersey* (New Brunswick, N.J.: Rutgers University Press, 1954). There is a wide range of other special studies in the New Jersey Historical Series, published by D. Van Nostrand in the 1960s. These include *The Story of the Jersey Shore,* by Harold F. Wilson; *Radicals and Visionaries: A History of Dissent in New Jersey,* by Morris Schonbach; *The Research State: A History of Science in New Jersey,* by John R. Pierce and Arthur G. Tressler; *The People of New Jersey,* by Rudolph Vecoli; and *Organized Labor in New Jersey,* by Leo Troy.

Entertaining, if not always accurate in its recounting of New Jersey politics in the late-nineteenth century, is William E. Sackett's *Modern Battles of Trenton* (Trenton: John Murphy, 1895; New York: Neal, 1914). For those who want to read more about George Record, Mark Fagan, and New Jersey progressives, Ranson E. Noble's *New Jersey*

Progressivism Before Wilson (Princeton: Princeton University Press, 1946) is a good book. For Woodrow Wilson as a Jerseyan, the most authoritative book is Arthur F. Link's *Wilson: The Road to the White House* (Princeton: Princeton University Press, 1947). An older book that I found delightful for its vivid pen portraits of New Jersey politicians is *The Political Education of Woodrow Wilson*, by James Kerney (New York: The Century Co., 1926). Another superb study of this period from a special vantage is *Joe Tumulty and the Wilson Era*, by John M. Blum (Boston: Houghton Mifflin Co., 1951).

For a look at urban history and class warfare in New Jersey, a good place to start is *About Paterson*, by Christopher Norwood (New York: Saturday Review Press, 1974). For more background on the IWW and the 1913 strike, *The Wobblies*, by Patrick Renshaw (New York: Doubleday & Co., 1967) is readable and objective. The 1926 Passaic strike is given an excellent documentary treatment in *The Passaic Textile Strike of 1926*, ed. Paul L. Murphy (Belmont, Calif.: Wadsworth Publishing Co., 1974). There is no adequate biography of the man who dominated New Jersey's politics for the first half of the twentieth century, Frank Hague. Two brief treatments of him are, "I Am the Law," by Thomas Fleming, *American Heritage Magazine* (June 1969) and Richard J. Conners's *A Cycle of Power* (Metuchen, N.J.: Scarecrow Press, 1971). For those wanting a good look at post–World War II New Jersey politics, Alan Rosenthal and John Blydenburgh have edited an excellent series of essays, *Politics in New Jersey* (New Brunswick, N.J.: Rutgers University Press, 1975). Another book with some juicy tales about Garden State corruption is *The American Way of Graft*, by George Amick (Princeton: The Center for Analysis of Public Issues, 1976).

For those who enjoy a ramble through New Jersey combining folklore and history, Henry C. Beck's books are highly recommended. They include *The Jersey Midlands, Forgotten Towns of Southern New Jersey*, and *Tales and Towns of Northern New Jersey*, published by Rutgers University Press. Another good book for those who want to ramble while they read is John C. Cunningham's *This Is New Jersey, From High Point to Cape May* (New Brunswick, N.J.: Rutgers University Press, 1953). Equally entertaining, though dated now, is the book compiled by WPA workers during the depression years, *New Jersey: A Guide to Its Present and Past* (Newark: New Jersey Guild

Associates, 1939). It has recently been updated and reissued by Hastings House. Another good book that pulls together all sorts of fascinating bits and pieces of information about New Jersey is *The New Jersey Almanac* (Upper Montclair, N.J.: New Jersey Almanac, 1963).

Finally, for those who want to do some really scholarly digging into the history of the state, the best guide is Nelson R. Burr, *A Narrative and Descriptive Bibliography of New Jersey* (Princeton: D. Van Nostrand Co., 1964), which reports on hundreds of books and magazine articles.

Index